EMPOWERING MIGRANT WOMEN

Gender in a Global/Local World

Series Editors: Jane Parpart, Pauline Gardiner Barber and Marianne H. Marchand

Gender in a Global/Local World critically explores the uneven and often contradictory ways in which global processes and local identities come together. Much has been and is being written about globalization and responses to it but rarely from a critical, historical, gendered perspective. Yet, these processes are profoundly gendered albeit in different ways in particular contexts and times. The changes in social, cultural, economic and political institutions and practices alter the conditions under which women and men make and remake their lives. New spaces have been created – economic, political, social – and previously silent voices are being heard. North-South dichotomies are being undermined as increasing numbers of people and communities are exposed to international processes through migration, travel, and communication, even as marginalization and poverty intensify for many in all parts of the world. The series features monographs and collections which explore the tensions in a 'global/local world', and includes contributions from all disciplines in recognition that no single approach can capture these complex processes.

Also in the series

Gendered Struggles against Globalisation in Mexico
Teresa Healy
ISBN 978-0-7546-3701-1

Encountering the Transnational
Women, Islam and the Politics of Interpretation
Meena Sharify-Funk
ISBN 978-0-7546-7123-7

The Price of Gender Equality
Member States and Governance in the European Union
Anna van der Vleuten
ISBN 978-0-7546-4636-5

(En)Gendering the War on Terror
War Stories and Camouflaged Politics
Edited by Krista Hunt and Kim Rygiel
ISBN 978-0-7546-4481-1 (Hbk)
ISBN 978-0-7546-7323-1 (Pbk)

Series titles continued at the back of the book

Empowering Migrant Women

Why Agency and Rights are not Enough

LEAH BRIONES

Routledge
Taylor & Francis Group
LONDON AND NEW YORK

First published 2009 by Ashgate Publishing

2 Park Square, Milton Park, Abingdon, Oxfordshire OX14 4RN
52 Vanderbilt Avenue, New York, NY 10017

Routledge is an imprint of the Taylor & Francis Group, an informa business

First issued in paperback 2020

British Library Cataloguing in Publication Data
Briones, Leah
Empowering migrant women : why agency and rights are not enough. - (Gender in a global/local world)
1. Women migrant labor - France - Paris 2. Women migrant labor - China - Hong Kong 3. Women domestics - France - Paris 4. Women domestics - China - Hong Kong 5. Migrant labor - Legal status, laws, etc. - France 6. Migrant labor - Legal status, laws, etc. - China - Hong Kong
I. Title
331.4'08624

Library of Congress Cataloging-in-Publication Data
Briones, Leah.
Empowering migrant women : why agency and rights are not enough / by Leah Briones.
p. cm. -- (Gender in a global/local world)
Includes bibliographical references and index.
ISBN 978-0-7546-7532-7
1. Women migrant labor--Philippines. 2. Alien labor, Philippine. I. Title.

HD6195.B75 2009
331.4089'9921--dc22

2008045427

ISBN 978-0-7546-7532-7 (hbk)
ISBN 978-0-367-60561-2 (pbk)

Contents

List of Figures and Tables *vii*
List of Abbreviations *ix*
Series Editors' Preface *xi*
Acknowledgments *xv*
Glossary *xvii*

PART I: VICTIMS OR VICTORS? FILIPINA DOMESTIC WORKERS IN PARIS AND HONG KONG

1 Capability and International Labor Migration for Domestic Work 3
2 Development: The Structural Context of Global Domestic Work Migration 29

PART II: AGENCY AND FILIPINA OVERSEAS DOMESTIC WORK

3 Empty Agency: The Oppressed Third World Woman 51
4 Beyond Rights: Embodying and Empowering Agency 71

PART III: AGENCY, CAPABILITY AND FILIPINA OVERSEAS DOMESTIC WORKERS

5 The FODW Institution 85
6 A Capability Approach to Agency 111
7 Agency, Capability and the Migrant Domestic Worker 137

PART IV: CONCLUSION

8 A Capable Agency Approach: Livelihood, Resources and Human Rights 165

Appendices
1 Respondents' Profiles 183
2 Profiles of NGOs and Associations Contacted during Fieldwork 189
3 Typical Migration Cycle of a Migrant Worker 193

4 RESPECT—Migrant Domestic Workers Charter of Rights: Rights, Equality, Solidarity, Power, Europe, Cooperation, Today 195
5 Interview Schedule (English Version) 197

Bibliography *205*
Index *229*

List of Figures and Tables

Figures

5.1	Structural properties of institutions	88
5.2	Structural properties of the FODW institution	93
7.1	"Structure of structure"	145
7.2	The process of agency	147
7.3	Agency in the FODW Context	149

Tables

5.1	Characteristics of individual participation in overseas domestic work using FODWs' experiences in Paris and Hong Kong	96
6.1	FODWs' own classifications of their work situations in Paris and Hong Kong	119
7.1	Agentic functions of respondents	153

List of Abbreviations

AMC	Asian Migrant Centre
AMCB	Asian Migrant Coordinating Body
APWLD	Asia Pacific Forum on Women, Law and Development
APMM	Asia Pacific Mission for Migrants
CA	Capability approach
CAA	Capable agency approach
CCEM	Comité Contre L'Esclavage Modern
EU	European Union
FDH	Foreign domestic helper
FDW	Foreign domestic worker
FMWU	Filipino Migrant Workers Union
FODW	Filipina overseas domestic worker
HK	Hong Kong
HKLD	Hong Kong Labor Department
HKSAR	Hong Kong Special Administrative Region
ICMR	United Nations International Convention on the Protection of the Rights of All Migrant Workers and Members of their Families
MDW	Migrant domestic worker
MFMW	Mission for (Filipino) Migrant Workers in Hong Kong
NCS	New condition of stay or Two Week Rule
NGO	Non-government organization
NIC	Newly industrializing country
POEA	Philippine Overseas Employment Administration
PWC	Philippine Women Centre
RESPECT	Rights, Equality, Solidarity, Power, Europe, Cooperation, Today (migrant domestic workers' network in Western Europe)
SAPs	Structural Adjustment Programs
TNCs	Transnational corporations
UNDP	United Nations Development Programme
UNIFIL	United Filipinos in Hong Kong

Series Editors' Preface

Leah Briones' innovative interdisciplinary volume, the sixteenth in our series, offers much to the literature on gendered migration. It updates our knowledge of gender and migration at a time when international migration is increasingly polarized in terms of inequalities between sending and receiving countries. Migrants are also stratified by class, racialization, and gendered employment scenarios. Overall, global flows are feminized with women comprising around 50 percent of global migrants. Presenting a strong example of all of these trends, Philippine labour export constitutes a prototypical global migration flow which has been relatively well documented in terms of the political and economic circumstances shaping the nation's history of migration, and the shifting gender composition of the migration flow. But, as Briones argues, there have also been some blind spots in the characterization of women migrants relative to questions of structure (historical political economy) and agency (individual women's decision-making and potential for empowerment). *Empowering Migrant Women: Why Agency and Rights are not Enough* thus advances the debate over how best to conceptualize and represent the exploitative conditions of women who work in global labour markets as domestic workers. Given the constraints upon women's agency, how, she asks, can we move beyond victimizing discourses of exploitation and the limitations of a rights-based approach to better protect the rights of these workers?

Hence, the volume builds upon and advances the significant literature analyzing the gendered consequences of Philippine reliance on women's participation in service sector work abroad. Briones first evaluates existing feminist analyses of the experiences of women migrants, read against adaptations in migration policies that must always address contradictory goals; to address migrants' rights while maintaining labour export as both necessary for migrants' livelihoods and a core component of the nation's political and economic agendas. Her synthesis of the interdisciplinary and international literatures on Philippine gendered migration represents a significant contribution to the literature in and of itself. However, the project is even more ambitious in providing a novel theoretical and policy formulation. The analysis also draws upon Briones'own ethnographic research from two global sites where Filipina labour in "domestic work," Paris and Hong Kong. In a careful review of the limitations in both agency and rights-based approaches, sometimes conflated in current debates, she proposes a model of agency conceptualized through a synthesis of structuration theory and a capabilities approach. Her goal is to provide a sound platform for policy action and for further research. We believe she achieves this end. The ethnographic, theoretical, and analytical framework, linked as it is to policy formulation, make this book a "must read" for migration researchers and advocates, or anyone interested in worker empowerment in gendered global labour markets. It provides a comparative perspective to other volumes in our series which address global workers as migrants and as citizens; for example, Elias, Davids and van Driel, Healy, and Tastsoglou and Dobrowolsky.

Pauline Gardiner Barber
Jane Parpart
Marianne Marchand

For Alili, Amity, Ana, Bernie, Delia, Ellen, Felise, Gemini, Gudilia, Helena, Indiana, JB, Jinky, Lani, Lilia, Loveley, Melanie, Michelle, Mila, Minda, Nene, Red, Sally, Virgo.

And for Mum, Rosario Raagas, especially for your courage to leave home.

Acknowledgments

Jane Haggis and Susanne Schech, your work at the Centre for Development Studies, Flinders University, meant that I could find answers to my long-held questions: *why weren't I and my family home? Why were so many Filipinos away from home?* Your concerted support and direction throughout my research has produced the central concepts of this book—Jane, thank you for your sociological direction on agency, and Susanne, thank you for your feminist geographer's guidance on the capability approach.

Thank you to Ben, family, friends and colleagues for your love, support and encouragement. Special thanks to Dr Michele Ford and Dr Nicola Piper. Thank you Nina Tuazon and Maya Jezewski for your friendship and research support in Paris. And thank you everyone in the Mission for Migrant Workers in Hong Kong, especially Norman Uy Carnay and Ate Cynthia Tellez .

Glossary

Agent:	An individual who exerts power.
Agency:	The act of exerting power.
Capability:	Transformative power; the power to do and be for intended, valued ends.
Capable agent:	An individual who exerts transformative power.
Capable agency:	Exertion of transformative power.
Resistance:	Exertion of counter-power.
Resources:	Media for transformative power; for conversion of power into capabilities.

PART I
Victims or Victors? Filipina Domestic Workers in Paris and Hong Kong

Chapter 1

Capability and International Labor Migration for Domestic Work

It is no less heartbreaking to look back now at my first Sunday in Hong Kong. I was enraged and in tears when I saw congregations of overseas domestic workers in the streets of Central, which was so crowded that many had to sit on newspapers and flattened cardboard boxes on the ground. *Why aren't they home? They should be home*, I remember thinking over and over again. At that stage, I had already experienced one month with the Filipino domestic worker community in Paris. I had already been informed that they came to, and remain in, France to escape the conditions of poverty in the Philippines: *dahil sa hirap ng buhay saatin* [the hard life back in our homeland], they had all said.

More and more women from poor areas of the world are migrating to rich countries for domestic work. Women from the Philippines form one of the more widely-known groups of migrant domestic workers whose livelihoods have become intrinsically tied to international labor migration.[1] Faced with high unemployment and insufficient wages within their own national economic settings, they resort to participating—both through documented and undocumented means—in the global market for domestic work. While participation allows many to access wages sufficient to sustain livelihood expenses, which can range from raising families to raising capital for micro-enterprises, it is often at the expense of their human rights.

The large volume of published research on their exploitation and "slavery" has been influential in orienting policy action towards their protection as victims. It has become increasingly obvious, however, that far from protecting livelihood needs, the "victim" approach legitimizes the protection of rich countries' borders, allowing migrants' rights to be undermined by receiving states' claim to the rights of sovereignty. An emerging perspective underscoring migrant women's agency is producing a counter-approach that fights for migrants' rights, not as victims but as workers. Yet despite this important development in research and policy agendas, increasing inequality in the global economy along with stringent immigration policies, which can constrain migrants' agency to the point

1 Of an estimated 86 million international labor migrants, almost 50 percent are women (ILO 2004b). The International Organization for Migration 2005 Report (IOM 2005) concludes that international female migration to developed countries have been consistently high since the 1970s while low and declining to developing countries. In the Philippines, women's share of international labor emigration in the unskilled service sector has reached as high as 92 percent (Shuto 2006, 206).

of paralysis, leave both the applicability and efficacy of a rights-based approach questionable. How is it possible then, to protect the rights of these workers? The short answer is to shift approaches from the paradigm of protection to that of empowerment. Just what empowerment means, how it can be achieved, and what theoretical and practical factors must be involved, questioned and challenged in this notion of empowerment is the overarching concern of this book. I argue that it is on a consolidated appreciation of migrant workers' agency *as existing in the context of victimization* that a paradigm of empowerment must rest. I propose that the starting point for this holistic appreciation of agency is the evaluation of its efficacy in overcoming victimization using Martha Nussbaum's capabilities approach. Before evaluation is possible, however, it is necessary to reconcile the polarized theories underlying the victim and rights-based perspectives—feminist structural theory and migration agency theory, respectively. For this task, I draw on Anthony Giddens' structuration theory to explain how analysis can shift from the identity categories of "victim/slave" and "agent/worker" to a "field of action" (see here also, Hesford 2005). It is then that it becomes possible to evaluate the capability of agency in (inter/trans) action. In synthesizing structuration theory with the capabilities approach, the study is able to refine the conceptualization of agency from a highly ambiguous and contestable rights-based framework to a more theoretically sound and feasible approach—that which I term, the "capable agency approach (CAA)." The main hypothesis is that agency requires capability to successfully mediate victimization; agency in itself is insufficient. In practical terms, this means that while protecting rights doesn't guarantee livelihoods, protecting livelihoods creates the opportunity or capability for securing rights. But while I claim this approach, it is by no means solely self-produced. The CAA is a product of learning from the experiences of Filipina overseas domestic workers in Paris and Hong Kong. It is they who enabled me to understand why agency and rights are not enough, and to discover how it is "capability" that can turn the "slave" into "the worker" and empower "the worker" from turning into a "slave."

Research Significance

The Question of Slavery or Work?: Migrants' Rights Violations, and Limitations

Most studies on overseas domestic workers[2] analyse their labor market participation through a feminist lens that underscores structural gendered inequalities in the global political economy. This feminist-structural lens focuses on the feminization of migration, drawing a direct link between the increase

2 Used interchangeably in the literature with foreign domestic helpers (FDHs), foreign domestic workers (FDWs), migrant domestic helpers, and migrant domestic workers.

in poor women's migration for work and the expansion of a patriarchal global political economy. Neoliberal trade policies and the development policies of the International Monetary Fund (IMF) and the World Bank are viewed as responsible for the concurrent rise of paid female domestic service in advanced capitalist economies with the number of women domestic workers migrating from the developing world (see especially Ehrenreich and Hochschild 2002; Sassen 1988, 1998, 2002a, 2002b). Underlying this has been, on the one hand, the contraction of welfare provisions and privatization of basic family services such as health, housing and education, and on the other, the increase in income inequality between nations (see here especially, Misra et al. 2005). The result, they argue, has been the particular exclusion of poor women in, and from, the Third World from the economic benefits of globalization (see especially, Aguilar and Lacsamana 2004; Sassen 1998). Moreover, the gender bias in global political economy processes extends to the immigration and domestic labor employment policies of receiving countries, which devalue migrant women workers and render them invisible. Feminist structural studies thus describe migrant domestic workers as export-import traded commodities whose labor is reduced and confined to slave-like servitude within the precarious employment sector of domestic work in the host countries (Altink 1995; Anderson 2000; Bals 1999; Chang, K. 2000; Cheng 1996; Chin 1998; Constable 1997; Heyzer et al. 1994; Li et al. 1998; Lindio-McGovern 2003; Parreñas 2000, 2001; Pratt 1997). These observations have been supported by human rights-based non-governmental organizations (NGOs) whose findings have revealed high rates of abuse and violence experienced by overseas domestic workers, worldwide. These findings include a combination of withholding of wages and passports, overwork, near or total confinement in employers' homes, rape and other sexual abuse, physical beatings, burning, psychological and verbal abuse as well as constant threats of violence (see for example, Human Rights Watch 2006; Social Alert 2000).

My initial thoughts on the situation of Filipina overseas domestic workers (hereafter FODWs) were also rather structuralist (Briones 2001). I was thoroughly convinced by feminist-structuralist explanations that FODWs, as "poor Third World women," were clearly victims. In the course of further research, however, two major issues complicated these assumptions. The first was my growing awareness of emerging feminist works which used the concept of "agency" to highlight the positive aspect of migrant workers' experiences. In contrast to the structural-based studies, agency-centred studies underscore the individual migrant's decisions to pursue livelihood opportunities in the global labor market and foreground the migrant's social and financial gains from international labor migration (Barber 2000; Ebron 2002; Ford 2001; Gibson et al. 2001; Mozère 2001; Tacoli 1999). These studies draw on the increasing acknowledgment in migration studies that labor migration can empower poor migrant women. Migration enables the formation of transnational households in which these women become significant or main income earners, thus altering gender power-relations by enabling their decisions to become more influential back in their own households (Hondagneu-Sotelo 1994; Morokvasic 1984). In addition, international labor migration can politically empower migrant women to participate in collective resistance through migrant networks (Yamanaka and Piper 2003, 1–2). Agency-based works thus represent the "victorious" side of what Momsen (1999) has aptly identified as the "victim or victor?" debate in the current literature on migrant domestic workers.

The second issue that complicates my "structuralist" assumptions fortifies these agency-based arguments. Since the Flor Contemplacion and Sara Balabagan cases in 1995,[3] the Philippine media, as well as many women and migrants' rights-based NGOs, have regularly reported the rampant abuse and enslavement inherent in overseas domestic work. Yet significant numbers of women continue to leave their families in the Philippines for overseas domestic work. My tentative research question then, was: is the FODW a "slave" or "worker?" That is, although the FODW's highly precarious situation put her in a position of (ready) enslavement, her migration for work does entail a voluntary choice, whose rationale is supported by a significant number of recorded narratives on "success stories" in which the health, education and daily needs of families left behind were paid for by remittances, and also by which homes, small businesses and community centres were built.

This question, as well as its policy implications, shares much in common with the feminist debate over prostitution in less-developed countries, and more recently, over trafficking in sex from less-developed countries. Kempadoo (1999) and Agustìn (2005; 2006), for instance, note the tensions between advocates of "the victim" who emphasize aspects of violence and sexual slavery in prostitution, and advocates of "the agent" who propose prostitution as "work" for women who have limited livelihood options. Both Kempadoo and Agustìn subscribe to the agent/worker framework. Similarly, Doezema (2002) shows how the debate over prostitution in developing countries is dichotomously framed around the victim's "coercion" and the agent's "consent" in international anti-human trafficking policies. She traces the debate back to western feminist

3 In 1995, Flor Contemplacion was hanged in Singapore for a crime which many migrant rights-based NGOs considered unproven. Flor had been accused by her employers of murdering another FODW and her Singaporean charge. Angered by what they alleged as the Singaporean government's unquestioning stance on the employers' claims, the NGOs lobbied the Philippine Government to respond. Despite a period of animosity between the two countries, the extent of the Philippine Government's response was confined to improving its own policies on migrant workers' rights protection as the sending country. The case of Sarah Balabagan occurred later in that year, in the United Arab Emirates. She was sentenced to death for stabbing her employer. However, Sarah had pleaded that her actions were in self-defence since her employer had tried to rape her. After protests from Filipino migrant NGOs around the world, and the Philippine government, Sarah's sentence was reduced to flogging plus a year in prison, after which she returned to the Philippines.

abolitionists in the early twentieth century who, under the banner of human rights, called for the protection of the female victim from trafficking and other forms of slavery. Doezema (1998, 2000, 2002) argues, however, that such policies result in justifying repressive measures that deny prostitutes their autonomy and agency, while restricting their mobility to cross international borders in search of work.

The inclusion of domestic work as a type of labor vulnerable to trafficking in the United Nations Trafficking Protocol in November 2000 has raised similar divisions and similar issues for those working with migrant domestic workers.[4] At one end of the debate are those who subscribe to the victim-centred approach. The feminist-structuralist works and human rights NGOs findings on domestic slavery, for example, have resulted in a "modern slavery" discourse which has enabled some NGOs to lobby for the "protection" of victims under anti-trafficking laws (see for example, the NGOs mentioned in the policy reports by the Council of Europe on domestic slavery, 2001, 2004). There is increasing evidence, however, that policymakers' idea of protection are failing to respond to migrants' needs for empowerment, with current protective measures focused more on the receiving-country concerns of border control than on the issue of sustainable livelihoods for migrant workers (Agustìn 2005; Anderson and O'Connell Davidson 2003, 55; Limanowska 2004; Pécoud and de Guchteneire 2005, 3; Piper 2005; van den Anker 2004, 3–4). At the other end of the debate are those who are calling for a paradigm shift in policy approaches from the protection of human rights, to the assertion of human rights. Schwenken (2003, 2005), for instance, uses the case of RESPECT, a Europe-wide network of overseas domestic workers and their supporters, to demonstrate that viewing migrant domestic workers as women with voice and agency, rather than as passive victims, allows their rights to be heard and upheld by the receiving state. RESPECT has drawn up a Migrant Domestic Workers Charter of Rights which calls for rights to mobility both within the states of the European Union (EU) and the EU itself. It also calls for migrant workers' right to earn their livelihoods by being recognized as valuable workers doing "proper work" (see Appendix 4). Schwenken argues that recognizing the domestic worker as bearer of political rights provides the platform from which a political imperative for foregrounding her agency can be achieved.

4 The full name of this international protocol is the "Protocol to Prevent, Suppress and Punish Trafficking in Persons, especially Women and Children, Supplementing the United Nations Convention Against Transnational Organized Crime." The definition of trafficking was traditionally considered as trafficking in prostitutes/sex workers. It was not until November 2000 that other highly exploitative situations, such as those of domestic workers, were included in the UN Trafficking Protocol. See Article 3, paragraph A of the Protocol (United Nations Trafficking Protocol 2000).

The Concept of Agency

However, much like the state of the debate on "prostitution," the growing case for overseas domestic workers' agency and rights rarely go beyond paying lip service to the root cause of migrants' needs for sustainable livelihoods (Agustìn 2006). At the conceptual level, agency seems to be conflated with rights. It is not clear how having agency directly, or certainly, leads to having rights. Nor is it clear what type of agency is being conflated with what type of rights. In the particular issue of FODW livelihoods, for example, can a FODW earn a livelihood by being a slave? Is she therefore practising a type of agency without rights? Or is she using her agency to practise her right to earn a livelihood over her right to non-enslavement?

These difficulties with the concept of agency are put into context when considering the feasibility of the rights-based approach in the political arena. Firstly, much talk on rights is concerned with the domestic labor laws and related immigration rules *within* the borders of the receiving states. This ignores those who undertake circular migration, or who are yet to enter or cross these borders to work in a non-EU destination, or to return to their country of origin. Indeed, Cox (1997) and Sim (2002) have identified that the vulnerability of overseas domestic workers extends beyond the workplace destination, and occurs as a process that begins from preparation and recruitment for going abroad, to working abroad (where this might entail several host destinations), but also to returning home (see Appendix 3 for the typical migration cycle). In this regard, it is unclear how the rights-based approach improves on the anti-trafficking approaches that reduce migrant livelihoods to border control concerns. Secondly, because the focus on rights is based on the receiving or demand side of overseas domestic work, the supply side, as bound in underdevelopment and lack of livelihood access in countries of origin, does not receive appropriate attention. Nor is the supply-demand relationship, which structural studies have convincingly highlighted, sufficiently accounted for. This leads to the third problem in agency-based analysis, of failing to incorporate the role of broader structural contexts that push and facilitate the movements of migrant workers through multiple borders, on multiple occasions.

The fourth problem pertains to the applicability of rights in host settings as well as in the international political arena. In host settings, the issue of rights is in itself precarious and is received differently. Thus, for example, while migrant workers' rights in western European receiving countries may be attached to the right to citizenship, their rights in receiving countries in Asia can be limited to short-term contracts (Battistella 2002; Bell and Piper 2005). Moreover, Bell and Piper (2005, 215–22) observe that the western liberal democratic notion of rights is in itself flawed and not entirely applicable to the East Asian context. They argue, for instance, that domestic workers are incorporated into the receiving Asian society not in terms of citizenship rights but through the traditional notion of extended families as underscored by a Confucian cultural heritage that is mutually shared, and perhaps even preferred, by migrant domestic workers who come from Asian backgrounds themselves. Internationally, the fight for migrant workers' rights seems futile in the face of a lack of political will by receiving states. The 1990 United Nations Convention on the Rights of All Migrants and their Families (ICMR) remains unratified by receiving countries. Where it has been ratified by the sending country, implementation problems have included the limited technical and financial capacity of state administrations to enforce the rules of the Convention (Pécoud and de Guchteneire 2004, 12–17). Ultimately, however, the current state of the ICMR, as Piper (2004, 81) puts it,

> underscores the age-long conflict between the international norms of human rights and state sovereignty—a particularly thorny issue in the context of cross-border migration. Ultimately, the "rights of states" clearly prevail over the "rights of migrants" with states retaining the right to set the conditions under which foreigners may enter and reside in their territory.

Fifth, a rights-based approach fails to consider the impact of increased rights on the sustainability of livelihoods even within borders. More rights could lead to demands for better wages and working conditions, and probably citizenship. This in turn could lead to receiving states closing off the migrant domestic labor market since pressure on state resources would make it preferable to encourage citizens to undertake the work. After all, the reason why migrant domestic workers are "imported" (and tolerated, if undocumented) is that they are cheap, flexible and expendable. Conversely, increased rights can speed up the process of saturation of the overseas domestic work labor market at the same time as supply from the poor and populous countries rapidly expands. In both cases, the issue of sustainable livelihoods for migrant workers could become even more precarious as employment opportunities contract. Lastly, and underlying these concerns, is the very notion of the appropriation of rights by neoliberal ideologies in which empowerment through rights can really be enjoyed only by individuals who already have a powerful political economic standing (Close and Askew 2004, 25; Hesford and Kozol 2005, 15–21)—a standing which FODWs clearly lack.

This book is concerned with the under-theorization of agency and its relationship with the limits of a rights-based approach in migrant domestic work. While the concept of agency has received acknowledgment within structural analyses (Constable 1997; Anderson 2000; Parreñas 2001), it remains largely unexamined (Moors 2003; Parker 2005a). Inquiries into migrant domestic worker agency have rarely gone beyond employing Foucaultian notions of everyday and collective forms of resistance which, based on a fluid concept of power, enable the identification of spaces in which migrant workers exercise power but do not explain how they can take, keep, or indeed, be entitled to power. Thus, as Aguilar (2002, 7) observes, although such works intend to "valorize domestic workers as empowered agents," they end up confirming the migrant worker's oppression and can thus resonate "with the conservative tactic of blaming the victim."

This observation remains true for Abdul Rahman's study on Indonesian overseas domestic workers (2003, 2005), which to date (2006) is the only one to provide a systemic account of overseas domestic worker agency. Abdul Rahman reveals how resistances come about through agency-structure relations (or structuration). In considering the power of Indonesian overseas domestic workers, she uses Foucault's notion of power to complement Giddens' notion of power as existing in action; as both enabling and constraining. However, it is Foucaultian resistance and not Giddens' transformative concept of agency which Abdul Rahman identifies as the "essential insight to power" (Abdul Rahman 2003, 26–32). Parker (2005c, 6) observes that examining agency and resistance in Foucaultian terms does not escape the hold of dominant powers; that these powers, "be they of nation-states, of institutions of global capital and development ... or of the discourses of human rights ..., [or] of feminism[,] ... allow the expression of agency as a safety valve that will enable the main project [of structural oppression] to continue." Thus, while Abdul Rahman's use of Giddens is an important point of departure, she begins from, but also stops at a structural or constrained view of agency. Unsurprisingly therefore, she concludes that both the agentic power of the individual Indonesian domestic worker and their collective resistance ultimately remain powerless to alter structural conditions. Her study goes no further than to confirm the subordinate status of the migrant domestic worker, and correspondingly, the peripheral place of her agency amidst oppressive societal, national and global structures.

I argue that when examining agency, it is important to retain Giddens' notion of the agent in his structuration theory as the basic unit of structures, and that this agent is capable of transforming these structures (Giddens 1984a, 1–28). Within the context of the current state of inquiries into migrant domestic worker agency, an understanding of how agency negotiates structures needs to advance to how it negotiates *with* them (for an important beginning see Ogaya 2004a). In the particular case of FODWs, the present study seeks to go beyond discussions of their agency per se, to *how they can continue to practise agency despite structural constraints.* Conceptually, this requires reconciling the "victim" with the "agent" by theorizing agency within the context of, rather than being the analytical nemesis of, victimization. To do so will involve shifting the analytical focus from looking at agency within a structural context to that of agency within its own agentic context—in Lyn Parker's (2005d, 85–6) words, from "subject effects" to "subjects." This allows the focus of inquiry to move beyond altering structural conditions to altering agentic conditions—to make them more capable, for instance—since, if we are to follow the logic of structuration theory, it is on agency that the process of structural (trans)formation depends. As the current challenges faced by both the victim and agency-based approaches show, unless migrant domestic worker agency is conceptualized and evaluated in terms of its capability to be practised, it will continue to provide little impact on the progress of polarized policy actions on who to protect—the migrant domestic *slave* or the migrant domestic *worker*; and what to protect—rights or livelihoods.

The Question of "Capability:" Development, Migration, and Agency

The Analytical Framework: Global/Locale and Structuration

The main objective of this book is to conceptualize and evaluate the capability of FODW agency by examining their circumstances in the locales of Paris and Hong Kong. To meet this objective, I revise and build upon the current frameworks or structural complex used to analyse the situation of FODWs.

I identify the structural complex of Filipina overseas domestic work using an analytical paradigm which I term a "structural-structurationist approach." The structuralist component refers to the neo-Marxist theory of migration. This theory sees migration as an outcome of social and spatial structures which create conditions that produce migrants rather than as constituted by the aggregate actions of self-determining individuals. The feminist adoption of structuralist migration theories (discussed earlier and in detail in Chapter 2) underlies the structuralist approach in particular reference to overseas domestic work. The structurationist component refers to Goss and Lindquist's holistic approach to understanding migration. Employing Giddens' "duality of structure," it coherently articulates structure and agency and thereby reconciles micro and macro elements in migration processes. The "duality of structure" is a dialectical process that explains structures as both medium and outcome of agents' recursive use of rules and resources in everyday social (inter) action, which in the longer term, evolves into institutions. From a structuration perspective, migration is therefore the product of a complex articulation of social action between agents across time and space, transcending not only state borders but also *locales* (Goss and Lindquist 1995, 319, 335).

The transcendental characteristic of its social constitution makes the concept of locales an important marker for the study's "physical" (that is, in terms of state borders and state-based relations) as well as conceptual framework (the acknowledgment of the multi-dimensional and temporally fluid experiences of FODWs). Giddens (1984a, 118) argues that individuals' knowledge and social contacts are limited in the sense that social interaction occurs in specific locales—the physically or symbolically bounded space or "place" setting for agents' actions and interactions. However, although they may act as physically constraining structures, locales are also characterized by "presence-availability." That is, locales denote a physical location where agents of various social positions, but also from various contexts of time-space, "are able to 'come together'" (ibid., 118–23). Locales are thus where co-presence in time and space occurs between individuals and their social systems; where they "literally face ... the institution, where the particularistic interactions of everyday life are engaged by the social system, and where ultimately agency connects with social structures" (Goss and Lindquist 1995, 333). In this sense, the concept of locales is very much a structuration or sociologically-based expression of the geographer's "politics of scale" in examining "transnational spaces and everyday lives" through the intrinsic connection of the global with the local (Ley in Nolin 2006, 5–6). Only here, the transnational is conceived as the *translocale*, wherein a connecting dimension is added into the global/local formulation—that of the dimension of the institutional.

Within this global/local/institutional matrix, my analytical approach identifies the FODW structural complex as contoured not only by immigration policy and labor law constraints in host countries, but also by two other structural elements. The first addresses the need for a more complete structural context of Filipina overseas domestic work, as including processes of development that equally take into account constraints associated with the country of origin. I use Hong Kong and Paris to account for both documented and undocumented locale settings with which the Philippines, as a country of origin, actively engages. As discussed in Chapter 8, this more complete structural context is particularly important for responding to the disjunction between the main research and policy areas of "migration" and "development," where migration-based work tend to remain concentrated on host-country concerns while development research and policies are largely confined to countries of origin.

The second is a structural element with which FODWs most immediately engage, and which the study identifies as the "FODW institution." The "FODW institution" serves as the structural context of FODW agency within the broader structural context of overseas domestic work. The conceptualization and evaluation of capability in FODW agency is as much about constraints as it is about possibilities or enabling resources for overcoming constraints. Discussed in detail in Chapter 5, it is within the FODW institution that we can see these dynamics more clearly. Importantly also, the evaluation of capability is integral to correcting underlying assumptions in current migration-development nexus policies that base migrants' motives and actions on a concept of functional (i.e. cost-benefit analysis) rather than capable (i.e. the cost of no benefit analysis) agency.[5] This receives more discussion in Chapters 2 and 8. In the meantime,

5 For example, discussion on migration and development in the World Migration Report 2005 (IOM 2005) , focuses only on how migrants, through their remittances, can aid development in their home countries and not on how development can protect the migrants themselves. The Report gives due consideration to grass-roots return migrants initiatives such as the AMC's integration program, discussed in Chapter 4. In currently dominant debates, remittances are therefore seen as financial/capital resources separate from the migrant's sacrifices and suffering. I argue that the issue of remittances must be discussed using the migrant as both the starting and end points. Remittances are migrants' hard-earned money. They are not for officials in sending-country governments or in the development industry to use or manipulate in the name of "assistance" (see here

the discussion must turn to livelihood, resources and human rights as integral elements for a concept of capability that ensures the agent or migrant can overcome constraints in her structural contexts.

Livelihood, Resources and Human Rights

When considering the livelihood of FODWs, it is important to recognize that their earning power is not only tied to work in the wealthier countries, but also to sustaining life for families back home, including their own upon return. In other words, they make their living in the world within a context of unequal globalization; a practice that Olwig and Sørensen (2002) call "mobile livelihoods." In particular, this involves means and strategies for sustaining life transnationally.

> "Means" refers to assets and resources in cash and kind that people can access. "Strategies" are connected to social institutions, such as kin, family, village and other social networks facilitating and sustaining diversified livelihoods. Pursuing mobile livelihoods can thus be seen as a poverty-reducing strategy involving refashioning resources dispersed in space into family livelihoods. (Sørensen et al. 2002a, 53)

Mobile livelihoods is an important concept that allows an appreciation of resources in the FODW context as constituting both means and strategies used to access, as well as remain in, paid overseas domestic work. It further allows identification of the resources specific to FODWs' basic needs; that is as cash in the form of wages from domestic work (means), and as networks in the form of the migrant institution and social and political migrant networks (strategies). These resources are in turn used to reduce poverty, or the occurrence of poverty, by being refashioned in terms of savings, capital accumulation and investments and/or for daily livelihood expenditures such as food, shelter, medicine and education for themselves and their families.

Of central importance to issues of livelihoods and resources for the FODW, is the recognition that they are pursued. This means that they simply do not exist for the taking. Rather, they exist in a highly political environment of restrictive immigration controls that constrain FODW use of domestic work migration as a livelihood strategy, but also of oppressive development policies that obliterate livelihood access in countries of origin for them. As discussed earlier, the role of rights-based migrant NGOs has been crucial as both a means and strategy to provide continued access to overseas domestic work by opposing inadequate immigration and labor policies. However, their inefficacy was also highlighted, pointing in particular to a poor articulation of what rights actually constitute

also, Luan 2005). Having said this, debates on the migration-development nexus have also produced arguments for a strong partnership between migration and development policies towards poverty reduction in the sending country (see here especially, Sørensen 2004; Sørensen et al. 2002a, 2002b). This is certainly a welcome beginning.

in the case of FODWs, and how they can best be articulated in development policies.

Empowerment and the Capability Approach

Martha Nussbaum's adaptations of Amartya Sen's capability approach (CA) is useful in explaining how issues of human rights, and their interrelation with FODW livelihoods and resources, can be more fully grasped as an issue of capability. The CA is a broad and multidimensional framework for evaluating individual well-being and the intrinsic experience of development and justice this entails. It argues for a concept of human development to challenge the economic growth-centred orthodox model of measuring development within a country, and thus articulates resources qualitatively rather than quantitatively. Development is seen in "human" terms; in terms of a quality of life and what people are able to do and be, rather than as a measure of how many resources people have or are given by the state. This departure from treating people as factors of production to seeing them instead as agents of production, foregrounds the immediacy of capability over functionality. As Nussbaum (2002) puts it: "… about a variety of functionings … of central importance to a human life, we ask, is the person capable of this or not?" Since, in this way, capability is seen as a pre-requisite to what a person can actually do and be, the CA finds both theoretical and practical resonance with human rights.

Theoretically, Nussbaum (see especially 2005) explains the relationship of capability with human rights through what she terms the "basic," the "internal" and the "combined" aspects of capabilities. Basic capabilities refer to capabilities that are innate to the human condition such as that of practical reason and imagination. Internal capabilities refer to "states of the person herself that are, so far as the person herself is concerned, sufficient conditions for the exercise of the requisite functions." Combined capabilities are "internal capabilities combined with suitable external conditions for the exercise of the function" (Nussbaum 2002, 132). Through these dimensions of capability, Nussbaum shows how human rights can be understood in two distinct yet integral ways. First, rights can be understood in terms of basic capabilities as "prior to and a ground for the securing of a capability" (ibid., 136). Thus to take, for example, a FODWs' call for a right to a livelihood even when her circumstances obviously do not secure such a right to her, Nussbaum (ibid., 135) here would argue that, "just in virtue of being human, a [FODW] has a justified claim to have the capability secured to her." Second, rights can be understood as equivalent to combined capabilities. In this regard, "to secure a right to a [person] is to put them in a position of capability to go ahead with choosing that function if they should so desire" (ibid.). Because people cannot function without basic capabilities, and cannot function freely as they see fit for their own circumstances without combined capabilities, Nussbaum (ibid., 131) argues that "capability, not functioning, is the political goal." Nussbaum's

CA thus defines what it means to secure a person's rights while it also ensures the explicit inclusion of the larger structural context involved in securing a person's rights or "combined capabilities." As Nussbaum (2005, 175) asserts, the CA "makes it clear that securing a right to someone requires making the person really capable of choosing that function…[and also] makes it clear that all human rights have an economic and material aspect." Here, the distinction between having rights and being empowered becomes particularly clear, where the latter necessarily involves an acknowledgment of the inherent role of greater structural processes to facilitate, but also to correct, inequalities and deprivation (see here also, Blackmore 2005, 260).

In practical terms, Nussbaum has captured the intrinsic relationship between capability and rights by creating a working list of capabilities to ensure that certain capabilities essential to a quality of life are constitutionally secured to the individual. Nussbaum argues for a capabilities constitution[6] because the rights approach with particular regard to individuals (in the developing world) vulnerable to unemployment, hunger, and other resource-challenged situations has proven futile in theoretical, epistemological and practical/enforceable terms. The existing provisions for livelihood, development, economic and social security in various international human rights declarations and conventions are exclusively state-oriented. The very methodology of setting up such conventions is also state-dependent. In contrast, understanding rights as a person's capability transcends traditional distinctions within human rights approaches; between the private realm of the family and the public sphere as well as between state action and state inaction in implementing rights, since securing capability in a person will necessarily require state action to provide the economic and material resources necessary to secure that capability (Nussbaum, 2000; 2005).

The articulation of rights in terms of capabilities also serves a fundamental role in providing a basis from which to understand the relationship of agency and capability in the FODW context. Approaching rights from a capability perspective enables a richer appreciation of rights and capabilities as issues of empowerment through human security[7] ("making the person really capable of choosing that function") rather than as issues of rights protection based on human agency. A human security paradigm centralizes the problems of unequal human development as FODWs experience and respond to it; as a problem rooted, but also structured transnationally, by their lives in the host country as well as back in their homeland. In this way, capabilities can be seen to provide an informational base that allows tangible and achievable outcomes for the highly abstract and highly contentious notion of human rights.

---

6 A working list of "capabilities" to act as basic constitutional principles that can articulate the protection of human rights through a more tangible understanding of an individual's potentials, skills and opportunities.

7 For a full treatment of this non-militaristic/state-based concept of security, see Gasper and Truong (2004), Shaw et al. (2006) and Thomas (2000).

As we will see in Chapters 6 and 7, it is a valuable characteristic of the CA that by exposing the limitations of both "rights" and "agency," it fortifies—or empowers—them with capabilities and capability, respectively. As such, it is able to provide the basis from which a theoretical framework for correcting the conflation of rights with agency is achieved. In both theoretical and practical terms, it illuminates FODW agency in the more accurate context of FODW capability as *the right to access resources in overseas domestic work for the function of sustaining a livelihood.* Shifting thus, the FODWs' orientation of their agency from its right to its capability to be practised, it becomes possible to grasp a more appropriate understanding of FODW agency that questions how far notions of their agency, which differ to the type of policy being promoted, can be imposed on them.

Study Parameters

Given the vast and porous analytical framework presented above, it is perhaps instructive here to highlight the parameters of the study.

Firstly, the study focuses on FODW agency. That is, agency within the particular setting of overseas domestic work, and as undertaken by the particular group of Filipina overseas domestic workers. Second, it employs the notion of slave-like conditions within this setting, and as propagated by NGOs that have dealt with cases of this type of "slavery." The FODWs I interviewed themselves shared this definition. However, this does not mean that they do not build upon, or have additional definitions of what constitutes their slavery (see Chapters 6 and 7). Third, because this book examines the case of FODWs, further studies are required to determine the degree to which the processes described here also fit other groups of workers in terms of nationality/ethnicity, gender, and also the national context of the work itself, where domestic work as undertaken "overseas" necessarily differs to that undertaken internally in the countries of origin.[8] Similarly, it does not examine domestic workers in the destination states who are not migrants and therefore are not subject to immigration policies. Fourth, the study's analyses emphasize the international context of domestic work. It thus places the analytical framework of the book in the "overseas" aspect rather than on the "domestic work" aspect of overseas domestic work, which has already been comprehensively examined by Bridget Anderson (1993, 2000) and others.

Fifth, although the literature stress the importance of gender-based constraints in subjecting women to (overseas) domestic work, this study does not foreground the issue of gender in its analytical framework. This is not to say that gender-based oppression is not a main facet of the current study. The issue of gender is fundamentally incorporated into the analytical framework

8 For instance, overseas domestic workers earn so much more than domestic workers in the home country that the former is able to employ the latter.

in terms of its *(feminist-)structural-structurationist* framework. Moreover, the CA in itself, and as particularly developed by Nussbaum, is based on gender justice. Indeed, *Empowering Migrant Women* is first and foremost a feminist critique of "how to avoid reproducing the spectacle of [Third World women's] victimization while not erasing the materiality of violence and trauma, and recognizing the interdependence of material and discursive realms" (Hesford and Kozol 2005, 13). I mean merely to caution here, that male experiences of overseas domestic work have yet to receive attention in the currently biased approach towards women migrant workers (Agustìn 2005, 97; 2006, 23–6; Piper 2003, 26). In particular, the historical accounts of paid domestic work as once a male-dominated sector (Momsen 1999b, 2–5) has yet to be incorporated into current analyses. Similarly, more studies need to be undertaken on the experiences of Filipino male low-skilled workers in being treated like "dogs" and "slaves" within their own context of international labor migration (Marigold 1995). Future studies also need to examine the fuller structural context of overseas domestic work which creates employment for women in the sending countries while men remain unemployed.[9] In addition, studies that look into the nature of the working relationship between female overseas domestic workers and their female employers have found that the issue of citizenship rather than the issue of gender, underlies the domestic worker's oppression within the employer-employee relationship (e.g. Lan 2000; Mattingly 2001). I thus contend, that until what Pratt (2004, 67) has called the "disciplining effects of feminism" in current research agendas are challenged to incorporate male experiences of overseas domestic work, it is difficult to see how women's overseas domestic work experiences are different from those of their male counterparts.

Finally, the study only examines the situation of FODWs in Paris and Hong Kong. Global cities, by virtue of their "developed" economic status in the global political economy, share the same political-economic setting. However, immigration and immigrant policies are also largely influenced by the culture of the receiving society and the politics of the state. Thus, other labor-receiving settings should also be the concern of future inquiries.

As the Researcher and Author: Working Feminism

Caught thus in a binary, I needed to reconcile my thoughts on the FODW situation if I was to understand the nature of her *capability* to become and remain a "victorious agent." The global/locale or dynamic multi-dimensional analytical framework forces analysis to appreciate as well as synthesize seemingly opposing concepts. The structural-structurationist approach I propose in this

9 Philippine international labor migration has been male-dominated since 1909. The trend reversed when the demand for male migrant workers declined and increased for female unskilled service sector work (Chapter 2).

book is therefore an important framework within which I could work towards a reconciliatory approach. The framework allows not only reconciling agency with structure, but also more specifically, reconciling a particular type of agency (FODW agency) with its particular set of structural constraints. In effect, it is the intrinsic relationship between victim-slave/agent-worker that defines the situation of the FODW. It is a relationship of being "forced to choose" (Doezema 1998)—forced by structural factors and practising choice through agentic maneuvers within structural constraints. The following discussion elaborates on the paradigmatic context of my reconciliatory approach, and explains the qualitative and interview methods used to collect and understand primary data on the research questions. Fieldwork was conducted over a period of two months, from September 8 to November 9, 2003; one month in Paris and one month in Hong Kong. The following discussion also underscores the problems inherent in data analysis when, as apparent in the works of Anderson (1993, 2000; 2001a, 2001c, 2002, 2004c, 2004a; with O'Connell, 2003) and Pratt (2004) (further discussed in Chapter 3), there is the equally immediate need to reconcile theory with practice if the research is to have any useful impact on the daily lives of its subject matter.

Paradigm and Strategies of Inquiry

My methodological approach stems largely from the perspective of my academic discipline which takes a cultural studies approach to contemporary development studies (Schech and Haggis 2000, 2002). By foregrounding the role of power and discourse in constructing otherness, the approach challenges basic binaries in theoretical and methodological practices such as structure/agency, development/underdevelopment (especially Bhabha 1994; Pries 2002; Wilks 1995). While binaries rampantly infiltrate the book, I hope to unsettle them in order to take analysis beyond a black and white photographic shot of the FODW, so to speak, to that of a colored cinematic account that captures the contrasts of her spatial context, as well as the dynamics of her temporal experience.

It is within such an approach that it becomes possible to examine both the actor and her actions. In this respect, Giddens' concept of agency in structuration theory is particularly useful as it allows understanding to go beyond structure/agency to "structuration." This perspective, as discussed earlier, enables a dynamic and transformative conceptualization of how the agent relates to her structure. This in turn, is important to gain insight into the ways in which this relationship impacts on the well-being of the agent, which is the central concern of current works, whether directly, as in agency-based inquiries or indirectly, as in the structuralist works. A particular way in which this insight may be gained, is to draw from other fields of research that deal with the imbalances of power, knowledge and resources in a certain structural order. For this study, the field of development studies has been the most appropriate both in terms of providing a more complete knowledge of the structural context of overseas domestic work, and of providing readily useable theoretical frameworks for issues of agency. Giddens' sociological concept of agency can thus be easily fused with agency as used in the capability approach (Chapter 5). It has also been useful in providing the basis for an agent or actor perspective, used as a methodological tool for tackling "the interlocking of theory and practice" within development research (Long and Long 1992).

The study employs similar qualitative methods of primary data collection and analysis as used in extant inquiries, which are based on ethnographic, anthropological and interview data. The study builds on issues raised by current works. It therefore seeks to test a continuity of the main findings on "slaves and victims/workers and agents" in the narratives of FODWs. Importantly, qualitative methods are complementary to the study's adoption of a structuration viewpoint of agency. Giddens (1984a, 284–310) notes how a qualitative approach based on ethnographic method is useful for examining the actors' views and experiences of structural constraints. Ethnographic research provides detailed insights into the agent's reasonings and motivations for their participation in structures, including dealing with its constraints. In this way, it is particularly informative of the extent of an agent's "knowledgeability;" that is, her ability to know how to go on in daily life, within a given structural complex. Therefore, in order to get to know the actors, and what they "already know and have to know to "go on" in their daily lives" (ibid., 284) as overseas domestic workers, the study adopted the ethnographic methods of interviewing and participant observation in fieldwork (Spradley 1979, 1980).

A "Feminist Ethnographic Interview" Method

Although anthropologists (e.g. Clifford and Marcus 1986) and feminists (e.g. Behar and Gordon 1995; Visweswaran 1994) have provided substantial critique on the ability of an ethnographic approach to adequately represent the orientalized and oppressed "other," I retain Visweswaran's and others'[10] rethinking of culture and power in ethnographic research within the critical study of colonial discourse and feminist scholarship. According to Visweswaran (1988, 1994), while ethnographic methods can never be entirely representative of its subjects, they are nevertheless sufficient if considered as a set of tools and resources for considering cross-cultural representations among women in different positions of economic and historical power. This feminist ethnography allows the woman in the relative position of economic and historical privilege to place her "self in the experience of oppression in order to liberate it" (Visweswaran 1988, 29). This location of the self, however, must be acknowledged as "experimental." It is thus "marked by disaffections, ruptures and incomprehensions" (ibid., 30), which must be embraced as a given reality that replaces any ethnographic goal of total understanding and representation. It is within this experimental

10 See *Inscription Journal* (1988) 3:4.

feminist reading of ethnography that I adopt the use of ethnography as a tool for locating myself in the experience of the FODWs in this study.

The Field: Paris and Hong Kong

The locations of Paris[11] and Hong Kong were chosen for comparative purposes to reflect the international context of Filipina overseas domestic work. Building on Parreñas' (2001, 8–11) justifications and findings for her comparative study of Rome and Los Angeles, I wanted to discover the extent of FODWs' "parallel lives" across national settings that receive their labor officially (Hong Kong) and unofficially (France). The Sino-British Joint Declaration on the Question of Hong Kong and the Basic Law provide the Hong Kong Special Administrative Region with full authority on its own matters of immigration control. It is in this respect that I refer to Hong Kong as a national setting or "state" in this study. Parreñas uses the term "parallel lives" to describe similar dislocations experienced by FODWs across Rome and Los Angeles. She locates FODW dislocations within several aspects of migration, such as migration's relation to the nation-state, the family, the labor market and the migrant community in host settings. However, she ultimately concludes that it is the FODWs' parallel socio-economic and political dislocations in the global economy that confine them to the shared position of "servants of globalization." Within the particular comparative context of documented-undocumented settings, I wanted to find out how, and to what degree, FODWs remained "servants" or oppressed by current processes of the global economy. In particular, to what degree, if any, did the FODW's inclusion as either documented worker or undocumented worker entitle her to greater citizenship and other rights-based claims? As there are the parallel lives and dislocations of FODWs as "servants of globalization," could there also be the parallel lives or productive *re*locations of FODWs as "victorious agents in globalization?" To pose this counterpoint is important for the study, if it is to be able to determine the nature of a FODW's capability to become and remain a "victorious agent."

Participant Observation/Observer Participation

Bernard (1994) distinguishes between participant observation and observer participation by suggesting that a participant observer does not have to tell the informants what she is researching, whereas an observer participant usually tells the informants what is being examined and researched. However, as de Laine (2000, 119) has observed, "fieldwork roles are varied" and are not fixed entities. Indeed in my fieldwork, the roles of participant observer and observer

11 Interviews were conducted in urban Paris (l'agglomération Paris). However, some respondents worked in the *banlieue* or suburban regions which are geographically outside of the city-proper but socio-economically considered to be part of the *région parisienne* or Parisian region.

participant proved inseparable. While those who agreed to interviews and other key informants interested in the research were informed of the details of the research, others with whom I spoke in social and political gatherings, or on the streets of Paris and Hong, were not informed, or were not necessarily interested, in the research.

On the whole, participation was undertaken to maximize association, and therefore learning, from the FODW communities in Paris and Hong Kong. This required attending and participating in social, political and church gatherings, but also participating in some of the "street life" of Paris and Hong Kong as experienced by Filipino migrants. This includes waiting at bus-stops and hanging out at shops selling Filipino products. Activities such as these provided the opportunity not only to meet potential participants but for countless conversations with FODWs who had a few minutes to give instead of a few hours. They proved a useful supplement to the interviews. I also spoke with community leaders including priests, embassy staff and migrants' rights activists, and was able to meet and converse with male Filipino overseas domestic workers both in Paris and Hong Kong. I also maintained email and SMS text correspondence with some of the respondents and some members of the organizations I visited.

The Interviews—Design and Sample

A main aim of the study is to provide a holistic picture of agency, where this necessarily involves constraints in Filipina experiences of overseas domestic work in Paris and Hong Kong. To reflect this, the main areas of investigation explored as many avenues of constraints and opportunities as possible. Thus aside from seeking to learn from the experiences of FODWs in documented and undocumented settings at the level of the state, the study also seeks to learn from individual migrants' experiences and explores the ways experiences of enslavement and other forms of abuse, but also those of gainful and abuse-free employment, impact on migrants' decision to stay in overseas domestic work.

Because abuse and enslavement in FODW experiences are very sensitive issues, and their immigrant status controversial, special care was taken to have a methodologically and ethically well-controlled design. The interviews were conversational in style, with the most sensitive issues discussed later in the conversations. Due to time, financial as well as participant access constraints, the interviews were small in number. The topics covered, however, were comprehensive (see Appendix 5). Analytically, the small sample enabled a more intimate and focused analysis of the individual FODW, while at the same time, placed within the wider context of amply available ethnographic studies and interviews with FODWs. This enabled insight into the extent of how the experiences of the FODWs interviewed for the present study reflected, as well as consolidated with, extant findings. Technically, however, given both the small sample and the few ethnographic studies available on FODWs in France, the experiences presented in this study are illustrative rather than representative.

An equal number (12 per setting) of FODWs from the two settings of Paris and Hong Kong were interviewed, using the same sets of themes and questions. In order to fully account for insights into the issues of capability, the sample in each country consisted one third who could be said to be/was in an enslaved situation; another third, who could be said to be oppressed and/or abused (in ways that the respondents' considered different from enslavement), and the last third, of those who enjoyed better working and living conditions and who saw their situations as similar to other wageworkers in gainful employment. The criteria for determining who is enslaved, oppressed/abused or contentedly employed rested on how the FODW herself classified her situation. Thus variations to the three given categories were discovered (see discussions in Chapter 6). It is important to note here also that FODWs who experienced the worst forms of by slavery were those who I could not access due to house imprisonment. However, contact with those recovering in a shelter enabled insights into these conditions. For example, when I met Lani who was living in such a shelter in Paris, it was only two weeks after she had been rescued from such slavery. Notably, Lani and the other respondents who "reclassified" their situations from slave to wageworker (Chapter 6) provide insight into possibilities and solutions to deal with cases of slavery while ensuring the retention of their employment. As such, these experiences make this study more progressive in its theorization of FODW agency and capability than would otherwise have been possible.

Planning of Interviews

Introductory access to potential participants was made possible by NGOs in Paris, namely the Comité Contre L'Esclavage Modern (CCEM), the Euro-Pinoy Association and Maya Jezewski of Babaylan, and in Hong Kong, the Mission for Migrant Workers (see Appendix 2 for information on these organizations). The Mission was particularly helpful in providing half of the total participants for Hong Kong. In order to obtain more participants and to fulfill the categories required for the sample, a snowball method was used along with a random method of approaching FODWs individually. Access to potential participants was highly problematic within such short amount of time because of the nature of their work. In Paris, most are undocumented and are therefore unwilling to "expose" themselves. In Hong Kong, FODWs receive only one day off a week. However, I was able to obtain the desired amount and quality of interviews since our shared language, gender, cultural and class background enabled me to quickly blend in, and gain trust, among FODW communities.[12] This meant,

12 Rekha Narula, for instance, has commented on how it was "nigh impossible" for her to access FODWs during her fieldwork in Paris and London (personal email correspondence, June 7, 2004). While I was also accorded ready-access privilege in Hong

for instance, that I could be invited to employers' homes for an interview in the employers' absence while the respondents proceeded with the required domestic work for the day.

Structure, Content and Style of the Interview

The semi-structured interview schedule covered the main structural issues of ethnicity, immigration status, domestic worker status and motivations for migration. It also covered those issues that pertained to questions of agency such as their migration experience, including their experiences and/or views on abuse and slavery in their work situation; their political views on their experiences; and their views and experiences on their choices amidst the constraints of their work.

Interview conversations were informal and familiar. Only one interview was fully conducted in English. The rest were conducted in Taglish (a mixture of Tagalog and English), or in Paris, French-Taglish.[13] There was regular reference to my inclusion as a "Filipina" in our conversations, for example, *alam mo naman tayo/saatin* [as you know with us/in our homeland]. This was particularly insightful since although Filipinos are well versed in English, with the language commonly used in the public/wider society, Tagalog remains the language used to communicate personal life (Mulder 1997, 13).[14] The interviews were conducted mostly without the presence of others in the employers' homes, in their own apartments,[15] in parks, or in a private room in the particular case of those in the shelter in Hong Kong. Where the interviews were not conducted in private, they were always conducted among friends and a familiar environment to the respondent.

Kong, the documented status of FODWs means that they have less fear of deportation and are more willing to engage with "outsiders," albeit it seems, with certain conditions such as that outsiders are not of the domestic worker employing class within their own host locale, and that they must be able to communicate, if not in Tagalog, in English (see here also Lan's fieldwork experience, 2006, 22–7).

13 Having Tagalog as my mother-tongue and having formally studied French for a few years, I could readily participate in this language.

14 With Tagalog as the national language of the Philippines, it is also important to note that dialects from the different regions of the Philippines are perhaps the strongest means of communicating personal life. But for the purposes of the present study, which is not anthropological, communication via versions of Tagalog suffices.

15 In Paris only: where the bourgeois domestic architecture is long-established, with maids' living spaces placed within, or close to, bourgeois homes. These very modest quarters are called *chambre de bonnes*; commonly termed "apartments" by the FODWs.

Data Analysis and Presentation: Theory-Praxis

So why was it that I reacted in such a way once in Hong Kong? Certainly, the pure visibility of so many of "my kind"[16] and of those who I've thought about so often, literally all over the streets of Central, was a major factor.[17] But I want to consider here the value of this reaction to explain the necessity of a "working theory" in analyzing and presenting my ethnographic data on FODWs.

Why aren't they home?—Having been reminded by FODWs in Hong Kong of what the FODWs in Paris had already explained to me, what a silly question this seems now. However, it was a useful pointer towards a revision of my theoretical roots. As mentioned earlier, my theoretical discipline is rooted in a school of development studies that foregrounds "culture and discourse" in analysis. Although I knew of these women and their struggles, I knew of them and their situation from a discourse-analysis viewpoint, and not from their laboring, material bodies. My thinking had not been trained to be so palpably confronted with her "body." Notwithstanding the importance of culture and discourse as an analytical tool, Bynum's (1995, 1) critique of the approach nevertheless seems to find relevance here: "[t]he body that eats, that works, that dies, that is afraid—that body just isn't there."

How did my theoretical premise so grossly miss the point of the FODWs' practical lives and daily struggles? Indeed Agustìn's (2006) recent book, albeit focusing on sex workers, is a response against such a lack of practical accountability in the "Rescue Industry." But much of the answer to this question has already been answered by Pratt in *Working Feminism* (2004). She, too, had been confronted with gaps in the practical applicability of her theoretical premises as a feminist geographer. Pratt (2004, 8) tells, for instance, of how a FODW had "confessed that [a] theoretical discussion on the body ... had no meaning for her; it was irrelevant to her experience and struggles in Vancouver." It is, however, Pratt's (ibid., 169) account of her first workshop with FODWs at the Philippine Women's Center in 1995 that finds direct complementarity with the concerns of the present study:

16 It is not only my shared, migrant, ethnic, and gender, background with FODWs, but also my mother's shared class positioning in post-colonial Philippine society that compelled me to embark on a study of their situations in the first place. I would have most likely inherited the precarious situation of either a poor or middle-class Filipina if my mother had not migrated to, and brought me up in, Australia. The chance that I could have ended up resorting to the FODW life remains vivid in my daily consciousness. Indeed, my mother had come to, and remained in, Australia for the very same reasons given by the FODWs in this study.

17 I have, in fact, been to Hong Kong 12 years ago—a trip which first introduced me to the situation of FODWs—but not on a Sunday, when it is the day off for the great majority of overseas domestic workers.

> The first items … on the agenda for discussion was the [FODWs'] frustrations with nepotism in the labour market in the Philippines …, elaborate processes of moving through various institutional structures in the Philippines, the medical test, taxes and levies that they endured to come [to Canada]. It seemed that they most wanted to talk about their lives in the Philippines, and I wanted to hear about their lives in Canada. I have only begun to understand that their stories about life in the Philippines are stories about life in Canada.

Thus while for me the question was, "why aren't they home?," for Pratt, it was "why are they in Canada?" Minus the different geographical focus, these are the same question, albeit asked in a different context. Due to our theoretical and discursive premises as embedded in our secure socio-economic and political status as funded researchers and citizens of our respective "western" states relative to the status of FODWs, Pratt and I, in effect, prevented the "subaltern to speak" (Spivak 1988). In this way, both Pratt's and my initial approach to understanding the FODW reflect the ambivalent efficacy of migrant domestic workers' resistance—whether in the form of hidden transcripts or public protests—as no more than "the story of continuous subaltern insurgency, always failing, but continuous to this day" (Spivak in Landry and MacLean 1996, 291). Intrinsically consequential to this critique is not only Pratt's and Spivak's (especially, Spivak 1993, 1996), but also other postcolonial feminists critique (e.g. Ferguson 1998; Minh-ha 1989), of a western feminism that "doesn't work." For Pratt (op. cit., 4) in particular, to work on the situation of FODWs requires working *with* FODWs to "form a closer interaction between [feminist] theory and empirical analysis of [FODWs] … into a … more lasting association, from which there is no immediate release."

In line with Pratt and others, the present study closely, and in a long term manner, engages with "an empirical situation from which [FODWs] can not readily walk away" (ibid.). Hence, the book's core question of *how FODWs can continue to practise agency despite structural constraints*. Methodologically, this requires an approach based on a "theoretical reflexive ethnography" (de Vries 1992, 80–84) or a recognition of my own agentic role in the research process as having the responsibility of constructing the final text on "my FODWs subjects," who at the same time, have shaped my understanding of their "subjection" (Long 1992). In this study, and from this process, I attempt to fill in the meaning of agency with the embodied and materialist meanings it holds for the FODWs. So far, FODW agency has largely been understood as disembodied in a functionalist way, or in terms of an embodied identity in a feminist way that renders agency an "empty word" (Spivak in Landry and MacLean 1996, 294). These viewpoints have produced the hegemonic discourse on the situation of FODWs. I thus analyse and use the words of the FODWs in the "responding" chapters (5-7) to inform current discourses on the meaning of their agency. I have structured the book to balance the hegemonic discourses (Chapters 1–4) with FODW responses because, like Pratt (2004, 68, citing

Spivak), "I do not want to be read as implying that the words of [FODWs] are somehow more authentic or true than those of other speakers." As will become apparent, especially in Chapters 5–7, FODW agency and capability are intrinsically connected to those of researchers, journalists, policy-makers and activists associated with the hegemonic discourse.

In line also with the need to apply theoretical interpretations to their daily lives in overseas domestic work, the study, as discussed earlier, draws on the CA. This approach is holistically relevant in providing a more accurate theorization of FODW agency on the one hand, and in addressing the practical problems with the continued practice of FODW agency, on the other. Theoretically, it puts the context of agency within the context of capability and human development or well-being; what the actor is actually able to do and be for the purposes of a quality of life (Chapter 6). In this way, the approach is useful in demonstrating FODW agency as embodied by issues of underdevelopment that limit her livelihood options, and as therefore an issue of capability. With this identification, the kind of practical intervention becomes a task of ensuring capability in FODW agency (Chapter 8). For the particular case of FODWs then, a CA enables a more accurate understanding of, and response to, their struggles, as ongoing, and as their own. That is, struggles in terms of the problems of unequal development as they experience and respond to it; as a problem rooted, but also structured transnationally, by their lives not just in "Canada" or the host country, but also in the Philippines.

In constructing the final text then, I hope to use the FODW's given meanings of her agency in the context of capability. In line with a self-reflexive, experimental feminist ethnographic approach, the outcome of the final text will necessarily reflect my voice—"my discourse," on the topic over that of the respondents' narratives. However, my structuration approach embeds myself with their situation, making me part of them and their struggles (as I show in Chapter 5). My practical motive behind the use of the "capability approach" is thus also long term; I use it as a strategic analytical tool for direct policy intervention not just on the FODWs' immediate, but also future, concerns. As part of the established international Human Development program, employing the CA of course does not incite critique of the existing structures of protection, or as Agustin (2006) has termed it, the "Rescue Industry." The present study must therefore be read as part of the universalist discourse on, and instrumental applications of, rights, justice, human development and empowerment. In this, I make no apologies in the same way as Nussbaum has defended the need for the use of universal values if, in the current "protection industry" structure, we are to achieve material and gender justice for every individual (see here also footnote 68). Further, of absolute importance, and as the following chapters show, it is in the improvements within the Industry on which the survival of the FODW depends. Although in these ways, the study can only ever be an "experimental" undertaking, they nevertheless incite thinking and action towards some form of justice in the upholding of the FODW's human dignity.

Chapters to Follow

This introductory chapter has provided the basis from which the objectives and key questions of the study have been raised and placed in the context of current debates on the experiences and protection of FODWs. The next chapter contextualizes the study by providing the structural context of global domestic work migration as well as the analytical context of agency and capability within this structural context. It shows how the structural context of global domestic work migration is constituted not only by the interconnections of unskilled labor immigration control policies with societal stigma against domestic work and inadequate labor regulations of the domestic work sphere in the receiving locale, but also how these are directly connected to migrants' locales of origin by processes of unequal global development. This supra-structure importantly provides the framework within which we can enrich current theories on structure-agency in international labor migration by enabling analysis to link issues of agency and capability with FODWs' claim to a livelihood, and to human rights, earlier discussed in this chapter. Chapter 3 reviews the current literature on women overseas domestic workers, organized around the main theories of migration: functionalist, structuralist and structurationist, to highlight the gaps in current understandings of FODW agency and capability. Using insights from migrants' rights NGOs, Chapter 4 shows how a synthesis of the structuralist and structurationist perspectives can fill the gaps by providing a framework that incorporates issues of capability to issues of agency in overseas domestic work. The next three chapters allows engagement with FODW discourses, as mostly drawn from the interview data. Chapter 5 sets out the concept of a "FODW institution" in order to focus discussions on agency, but also structure, in the particular context of Filipina overseas domestic work. Chapter 6 outlines a theoretical framework that highlights the linkages between FODW agency and issues of capability. Chapter 7 builds on this framework by examining the role of capability in the agentic practices of FODWs. By bringing together respondents' insights with the main findings of the study, Chapter 8 takes the analysis further by discussing the role of livelihoods and human rights in determining FODW capability, and explores how the concept of "capable agency" could be used to better understand, as well as intervene against migrant domestic workers' oppression. In this way, the chapter is able to identify key directions for future research and policies.

Chapter 2
Development: The Structural Context of Global Domestic Work Migration

While we know much about the structural dimensions of overseas domestic workers within the host locale (Chapter 1, and see also next chapter), we know less about the structural conditions within the locale of origin, although studies (e.g. Gamburd 2000; Parreñas 2005) on transnational domestic worker families have given us some important indication of the central role that neoliberal economic development policies adopted by the countries of origin play in women's decision to migrate for domestic work. While we know much also about the structural continuities between the host and origin locales through works on globalization and its impact on women's (re)productive lives (Chapter 1), these works use the global political economy as a static metanarrative under which host-origin connections are made. In this chapter, I build on this metanarrative by conceptualizing it in action and interaction; from a static structure to a structural process. I draw on the concept of "Development" to give specific description to this metanarrative as it applies to global domestic work migration but also to link in change and process apparent in local narratives and meanings of "development." I propose here to see the metanarrative context as a structural complex, constituted by the intersection of receiving country immigration and domestic labor employment policies with processes of unequal global capitalist development. I illustrate this intersection using the relations between the Philippines as a developing and domestic labor-exporting economy, Hong Kong as a relatively recently developed and officially labor-importing economy, and Paris as an advanced economy that receives Filipina domestic work labor unofficially. In this way, it becomes possible to show how the massive international migration of Filipinas for domestic work has come about, and also why it is likely to continue. Concurrently, I propose that we understand the embeddedness of the "local narrative" in this structural complex by centralizing the role of FODW agency in both her migration and (human) development. This will involve reviewing the main theories of international migration to understand the role of agency and how it raises issues of development specific and immediate to the individual FODW, such as her access to rights and a livelihood. This chapter, in short, links back the migrant workers to their country of origin within the specific analytical context of global development.

Development and International Migration for Domestic Work

In the immediate years after World War II, the transition of the global political economy from an imperialist regime to a postcolonial setting produced two significant developments that shaped the characteristics of international labor migration today. The first was the increase in the number of nation-states as a result of decolonization. International migration, as Castles and Miller observe (2003, 53), "would be meaningless in a world not organized by nation-states." The ideas of popular sovereignty and of people belonging to a state that underlie the universally accepted concept of the nation-state, also underlie the universally accepted authority of a state to regulate movement into and out of its territory.

The second change involved the rise of the hegemonic ideology of development based on the Euro-centric notions of capitalist progress and modernization. The dissolution of the colonial empires saw the division of the world into three geographically, economically and culturally separate parts, giving meaning to the notion of a/the "Third World" (see e.g. Powers 1998, 592–4). This "Third World" constituted an increasing number of emerging postcolonial nation-states deemed "underdeveloped" by those in the First or Western World.[1] The "Third World" subsequently became a subject (in need) of development (Escobar 1995). This led to the establishment of a Development industry composed of the World Bank and other global institutions such as the IMF and World Trade Organization (WTO) to facilitate economic progress in developing countries. Hart (2001) distinguishes this big "D" development from little "d" development. She points out that "D"evelopment refers to an intended project of capital expansion while little "d" development refers to the "development of capitalism as a geographically uneven, profoundly contradictory set of historical processes" (Hart 2001, 650). In this sense, development is an imminent process that brings about economic, social and cultural change through the localization of capitalism (see here also, Cowen and Shenton 1996).

In the particular context of international labor migration, the "geographically uneven" effect of capitalist development is most evident in the greater volume of migration flow from developing economies to developed ones (IOM 2005, 380). As an imminent process, capitalist development underpins both the causes and consequences of migration from less developed areas of the world. Studies on the linkages of migration and capital penetration in developing

1 The "second world" is not relevant to the present study, but it referred to the then Eastern bloc of the Communist-Socialist states. The First World consisted of the democratic industrial countries of Western Europe, North America, Japan, Australia and New Zealand. More recently, the First and Third World divide has been expressed in terms of the "West and the rest," "North and South" or "the minority world and the majority world," respectively.

countries through foreign direct investment (Sassen 1988), as well as studies on migration and development in general (Massey 1988; Massey et al. 1993; Massey and Espinosa 1997; Massey et al. 1994; Widgren and Martin 2002), have found that it is development rather than underdevelopment that determines labor migration. In their work on Mexican emigration to the United States, Massey and Espinosa (1997) note, for example, that capital penetration through economic development transforms local economic life in Mexico by raising wages and consumer demand. "These transformations usher in a period of uncertainty and change ... that creates a need for capital," which, for many households in Mexico, can be gained only through international labor migration (Massey and Espinosa 1997, 969).

What Massey, Espinosa, and others leave implicit in such analysis, however, is the "contradictory processes" of development; that underdevelopment is integral to development. In the particular case of the relationship between migration and development, these processes are most evident in the restructuring of the global economy in the 1970s and 1980s when women and other disadvantaged groups in the developing world came to bear the brunt of global changes.

The Development Divide

Global restructuring was led by the developed countries and administered by the World Bank, IMF and WTO, which by the 1980s effectively became "the institutions of international economic governance" (Faux 2002). In the 1970s, the USA and other developed countries were faced with a combination of internal and external threats to capitalist expansion. Domestically, the period of stable economic growth from the early postwar years had produced high levels of government expenditure on social programs and enabled the establishment of powerful unions. As Ong et al. (1994, 8) note of those times, "[t]he welfare state had shifted the balance of power from capital to labour." One way of counteracting this shift was to relocate manufacturing industries to developing regions where wages were low and non-unionized labor was abundant. Thus became the growing significance of transnational corporations (TNCs), which, through continued technological developments in communications and transportations, were able not only to retain high-profit earnings for the advanced economies but also helped to produce, in some cases, capitalist growth in the host developing country (Kiely 1998, 46–8). At a global level, this considerable capital injection led to competition for manufactured goods from newly industrializing countries (NICs). At the same time, US fiscal policies that abandoned fixed exchange rates produced high commodity prices which were compounded by the steep rise in oil prices from the Organization of Petroleum Exporting Countries (OPEC) (Ravenhill 2005, 16).[2]

2 The rise in oil prices was brought about by the Arab-Israeli war (1973) in which Arab members of the OPEC significantly dropped production in its petroleum trade with the West since the West had supported Israel in its conflict with Egypt at the time.

Restructuring therefore had to counteract the rapidly declining manufacturing sector in the West. This entailed curbing the massive semi-skilled migrant labor, once used to expand the manufacturing sector, through strict immigration control policies (e.g. Castles and Miller 2003, 78; Salt 1992, 1105). Advanced economies then turned their interests towards a service economy, creating a demand for more flexible and temporary types of labor, which included highly-skilled workers as well as un/low-skilled ones to service the former (Castells 1996, 266; Ong et al. 1994, 23–31; Reich 1993, 95).

By the 1980s, it had become clear to the governments of the developed economies that state-centered development had failed them. High commodity and oil prices had greatly weakened the economies of many developing countries, leading to a deepening debt crisis. Restructuring thus began to take on a market-centered or neoliberal approach to development. Western powers, through the Washington Consensus on neoliberal development policies, tasked the World Bank and the IMF to manage the debt crisis and eradicate poverty in the indebted countries (Thomas 2005, 328). The World Bank and the IMF imposed structural adjustment programs (SAPs) to induce economic growth in these countries but which instead resulted in greater debt and impoverishment (Thomas 2005, 329–34). Overall, the changes brought about by neoliberal restructuring maintained the prosperity of the industrialized nations and led to industrialization in some countries such as in the NICs and in oil-rich OPEC countries. The majority of countries, however, became impoverished (see here especially, Stalker 2000). The income gap between the richer and poorer countries has more than tripled since the 1960s, with most of the world's 188 million unemployed people found in the developing countries (ILO 2004a, 37, 40-5).[3] While the Development industry has had to respond to its failures by more emphatically incorporating the social dimension of economic progress as set out in the Post Washington Consensus (1999), there remains much concern about how the change in language will actually translate to a change in practice (Hart 2001, 2002; Thomas 2005, 334–7).

The persisting divide between rich and poor countries continues to have a major impact on the nature of the demand and supply of un/low-skilled women migrant workers. Structural adjustment within the developed countries resulted in the erosion of welfare provisions which, for women, has meant greater pressure on their ability to meet family care needs (Chang, G. 2000a, 2004; Misra et al. 2005, 9). In addition, relative prosperity resulted in greater availability but not quality of employment for women in the industrialized countries. A segmentation of the labor market by gender, age and ethnicity placed many along with the youth and minority groups in the most insecure work in the casual and informal sector (Castles and Miller 2003, 78). Notwithstanding these high levels of insecurity in employment, overall greater participation by women in the public workforce has

3 This is the official record for 2003, but the ILO report also points out that figures would be much higher if the underemployed and the working poor were included.

led many to manage dwindling welfare support by employing "other" women, namely those from developing countries desperate for employment (Kofman 2004; Parreñas 2003; 2005, 12–29).[4] Consequently and conversely, it is in this way that overseas domestic workers shoulder the costs of SAPs both in their home countries and in the destination countries (Chang 2004).

Underlying this supply-demand nexus has been a sexual and racial division of labor in the international labor market that places unskilled migrant women's work at the lowest end of production and for the lowest pay, in the feminized jobs of domestic and sex work (De Dios 1992; Glenn 1992; Lee 1996; Mies 1998; Sassen 1984). This has produced what Sassen (2002b) has termed "global cities and survival circuits;" overseas domestic workers go to work for high-paid workers in global cities, and survival circuits are composed of migrant networks that facilitate recruitment, which sometimes involve precarious dealings with traffickers and smugglers, to ensure employment. For many low-income women in the developing countries, entering such a labor market, in such a way, has been preferable to enduring poverty in their country of origin (further discussed in Chapter 6).

At the political level, the concurrence of these global changes with the massive migration of refugees and asylum seekers caused by a combination of other factors[5] heavily impacted on the immigration policies of the developed countries (Appleyard 2001; UC-CIIP 2004; Zlotnik 1999). Border control of the rich countries has come to overshadow issues of development in immigration policies. The significance of development in causing, determining, but also in gaining from, migration has become highly politicized and obvious as an issue only for source countries (Hammar 2001; Hatton and Williamson 2005; Ramamurthy 2003; Skeldon 1997, 23; Sørensen et al. 2002a).[6] Where issues of

4 It is important to acknowledge here that only those women who belong to the (upper) middle class or who are in dual income households can, in reality, afford to employ a domestic worker. However, wage differential levels between country of origin and country of destination, combined with the degree to which migrant domestic work is saturated in a given host country's labor market, do complicate class-based explanations on which women can afford to hire a domestic worker. Lower-middle class families in Hong Kong, for example, are employing Indonesian domestic workers who, in contrast to the more established FODWs, are more likely to acquiesce with receiving pay below the legal minimum wage. In addition, the undocumented status of some overseas domestic workers can exacerbate their already highly vulnerable bargaining power in the labor market.

5 These included wars and natural disasters in some parts of the world, the end of communism in Eastern Europe and the disintegration of the Soviet Union in the 1990s, as well as the terrorist attack on the United States in September 2001.

6 Prior to World War I, most of global migration occurred between developed countries (North-North) and developing countries (South-South), was unregulated, and significantly contributed to poverty reduction in the source country (Hatton and Williamson 2005, 3; Ramamurthy 2003, 7). For a current revival of this view on policies see IOM 2005, 253–98.

development have been tackled by receiving states, it has either been reduced to an ad hoc role in immigration control policies that seek to raise incomes in the source countries on the unfounded basis that they will curb outward flows (for a critique on these current policies see e.g. Castles 1999, 15), or on remittances and their potential for development in the source country (see e.g. OECD 2006, 140–59).[7]

Recent Migration Trends and Control

To shed more light on the current environment in which immigration control policies are growing in relevance, but in which they are also being contested, it is useful to look at the main trends in contemporary migration. Castles and Miller (2003, 7–9) have identified five general trends. First, is the *globalization of migration,* where migration has become so embedded in the global political economy that it affects multiple countries at the same time. The second is its *acceleration* or rapid growth in volume in all major regions of the world. The third is its *differentiation* so that immigration countries receive many types of migrants, ranging from high-skilled migrants, temporary labor migrants to refugees, and where they merge into and out of types. The fourth is the *feminization of migration.* Finally, they identify a growing *politicization of migration*, where the nation-state has become the central player in the management, and in particular, in the securitization, of migration flows within their domestic and national security policies. The first and last trends are particularly characterized by a high flow of irregular migration, and thus harbor the most significance to future developments in immigration control policies.

While some developing countries have pursued labor-export as a national development strategy, the overall control of migration flows rests with the destination countries. As Ramamurthy (2003, 15) notes, "in the absence of [an] international regulatory framework, the ... labour-importing countries are *de facto* the policymakers, while the role of the ... labour exporting countries is ... that of a policy-taker." It is therefore immigration, and not emigration, policy that determines the scope of both legal and irregular migration (Meyers 2004, 3). Host governments legitimize control by using political rhetoric that portrays immigrants as a threat to national culture and to local employment opportunities, thus succeeding to invoke xenophobic and racist societal attitudes

7 There is hope for a revision on bilateral policies as the more recent approaches by the UK and Nordic countries on applying a more developmental emphasis on issues of migration show (see for example, Department of International Development (DFID) 2007). At the multilateral level, there have also been some efforts made by international organizations such as the ILO and IOM to keep the migration-development nexus in the international agenda which culminated in the General Assembly talks on International Migration and Development in 2006.

towards them (see e.g. Chang, G. 2000; Koser and Lutz 1998). Externally, the position of control is fortified by the dependency of developing states on the labor demand in the destination countries, and the foreign exchange revenue this brings through remittances (Hugo 2004, 90–91). The politicization of migration can therefore be more directly understood as predominantly characterized by securitization or immigration control both presently, and in the foreseeable future.

Processes of globalization, however, are challenging receiving states' position of control. The misalignment between increasing global economic exchange, where this necessarily involves labor, and the tightening of immigration controls has also produced an increase in irregular migration. As Jordan and Düvell (2002, 3) have put it, "[m]ore mobility plus more restrictions equals more breaches of migration law." This is particularly evident in the rise of transnational communities. While transnational communities have a legal component to them, with many flows occurring under tourist, student or business visas, they are also characterized by a significant membership of irregular migrants.[8] Studies in transnationalism (Appadurai 2000; Falk 1999; Portes 1998; Portes et al. 2001; Smith and Guarnizo 1998) have highlighted the latter characteristic, drawing attention to their position as the "migrant-underclass" and to their struggles against capitalism as "globalization from below." The migrant-underclass engage in survival circuits or informal recruitment networks. It is estimated that between 15 and 30 percent of irregular migrants employ traffickers or smugglers (Stalker 2000).

As mentioned earlier, these circuits respond to the demand for cheap and flexible migrant labor in the industrialized countries. In addition, labor unions, albeit not as powerful as they once were, have inadvertently contributed to moves by businesses to employ cheaper and often non-unionized migrant labor. Employing irregular migrant labor usually involves dealings in the informal economy and is therefore impervious to both formal business cycles and government regulations (Cornelius 1998; Tsuda 1999). Even when such dealings are exposed, they are generally not considered as a serious crime (Martin 1993, 5). As a result, a significant number of workers who migrate to undertake low-skilled work do so in undocumented situations. Due to what they call the "structural embeddedness of demand," Cornelius and Tsuda have thus argued that in the final analysis, immigration controls have failed and will continue to

8 Irregular migration, also interchangeably called illegal/undocumented/unauthorized migration, constitutes the crossing of borders without official authorization from the destination state, and/or the violation of the conditions for entering a destination state. It is important to note here, however, that the term "illegal" should be avoided as it conveys the idea of criminal behavior on the part of the migrant. In this book, I use the term "illegal" in inverted commas in cases where I want to imply the receiving government's treatment of the migrant worker as more reflective of the harsher meaning of illegality than of the more inclusive meanings attached to the terms undocumented/irregular/unauthorized.

fail as long as their success is dependent on the economic costs of *not* hosting such labor (Cornelius and Tsuda 2004, ch. 1). While this assessment is not entirely applicable to states such as Hong Kong, which, as discussed in more detail below, is smaller and therefore able to relatively succeed in immigration control, there is nevertheless a certain permanency for "temporary" migrants (e.g. Alegado and Finin 2000; Tsuda 1999) in its economy.

The Philippines, France, and Hong Kong: Following the Trends

Having looked at the characteristics of international labor migration, it is possible to focus the discussion on how both capitalist development and the current trends in international labor migration have been experienced within, as well as among, the individual countries used for the study—The Philippines, France and (China) Hong Kong. Together, they provide a good example of how a set of economies fared the global restructuring of the 1970s and 1980s, with the Philippines losing out and becoming a labor-exporting country, and France remaining, and Hong Kong becoming, a labor-importing country. In addition, they provide a good example of the relationships between sending and receiving countries in the current global political economy.

The Philippines became independent in 1946, and for a time until the deepening of corruption in the Marcos presidency (1965–1986), the economy displayed the fastest growth in Asia (Lucas 1993). Deregulation in the early 1960s, however, resulted in a devastated Philippine economy which has been made worse by successive governments' ready adoption of IMF and World Bank neoliberal development strategies, namely increased deregulation, export-oriented industrialization and SAPs. As Scipes (1999) has observed, "while [the World Bank] had provided the Philippines with only 326 million in loans between 1950 and 1972, it gave the Philippines more than 2.6 billion dollars between 1973 and 1981." Based on this type of development strategy, the Marcos administration responded to the new global demand in the service sector by embarking on a labor-export program. By 1978, it became clear that the Philippines had a comparative advantage in overseas contract workers against other developing countries. Filipinos, in comparison, had higher literacy rates and were more knowledgeable about capitalist processes and the English language. Labor-export thus became formally incorporated into the national development strategy (Battistella 1995; Gonzalez 1998). Its continued "success" has been apparent through the rapid rise in remittances—from over $US5.7 billion in 1997 to over US$8.5 billion in 2004 (POEA 2005), making it one of the largest source of foreign exchange for the country (Taylor 2004).

Despite this profitable labor-export program, however, both external and internal factors have impeded successive governments' drive toward industrialization. Externally, national debt is still high at over US$55 billion.[9] Moreover, there is increasing competition from other emerging labor-exporting countries such as Indonesia and Sri Lanka. Internally, high population growth, rampant government corruption, and the continued pursuit of neoliberal development have exacerbated poverty, under-funding the health and education sectors in particular. Almost half of the population lives below the income poverty line of $2 a day (UNDP 2004, 147). In addition, the long-term effects of SAPs have resulted in a "deficit in decent work" (ILO 2004a). This is particularly evident for women in the Philippines who McCulloch and Stancich have identified as "the "invisible adjustment factor" which makes SAPs bearable [for the country], working twice as many hours as men per week in order to satisfy their families' basic needs" (McCulloch and Stancich 1998, 432). In 2002, the Minister for Labour and Employment estimated that out of 33.7 million Filipinos of employable age, just over half (18.6 million) have full-time employment with the remaining 15 million being unemployed or under-employed. The majority of the un(der)employed are women (NSCB 2003). For the great majority of those who have employment, salaries are barely able to sustain a basic standard of living with many working families unable to pay for their children's education beyond primary schooling (Carroué 2003). These conditions, along with the increased global demand for feminized jobs, have contributed to the feminization of emigration from the Philippines (see here also, Parreñas 2003; 2005). In 1975, 12 percent of Filipino migrant workers abroad were women, rising to 52 percent in 1995, and again to 70 percent in 2005 (AMC 2000; UNDP 2004, 87).

By contrast, the French economy remained strong during the global restructuring. As with other First World states of the time, France imported semi-skilled male labor to aid its industrialization. From the late 1940s until the 1970s, it used labor from its less developed neighbors in Southern Europe, namely Spain, Portugal and Italy, to develop its manufacturing sector. Strong growth in this sector subsequently fuelled an expanding service sector whose operations and resources became centralized in its capital city, Paris. At this level of development, women were able to participate in the workforce. They quickly moved out of the reproductive and private work of raising families to the productive or public sector of raising capital. Women who had migrated with their husbands from Southern Europe filled the gap in reproductive labor by undertaking paid domestic work, to be later joined by women from France's former colonies such as Algeria and Morocco (Narula 1999). The immigration of women from the Philippines, most of which have been undocumented, began in the 1970s. In 1996, there were an estimated 17000 Filipina domestic workers

9 This amounts to almost 13 percent of Philippine GDP for 2004. The ousting of Marcos from the presidency in 1986 revealed the extent of his corruption and the damage to the national economy this had caused. He left the country with a national debt of US$27 billion, the highest it had ever been (Boyce 1990, 1993).

(Anderson 1996; Torrés 1996) which according to more recent estimates, has risen to around 50,000.[10] Presently, over 50 percent of immigrant women in France work as domestic workers (RESPECT 2000; Weinert 1991), reflecting a feminization in migration from the end of the receiving country.

As a NIC, Hong Kong's rapid industrialization quickly resulted in a lucrative service sector (HKLD 1992, 2). Like France, the increased participation of women in the workforce left domestic work and child care to be taken up by migrant women labor (Tam 1999, 265–6). Hong Kong-born female workers refused to undertake full time live-in domestic work, opting instead for more flexible hours or for other low-skilled jobs, or even unemployment (Constable 1997, 26). The Hong Kong administration therefore embarked on a labor-importation scheme of "foreign domestic helpers" (FDHs) to obtain a supply of live-in domestic workers. Again consistent with the trend in the feminization of labor migration, these FDHs were women. Demand for FDHs remains high in Hong Kong. At the time of the inception of labor-importation in the early 1970s, there were 881 FDHs. In 2005, over 220,000 FDHs lived and worked in Hong Kong (HKID 2005). An increasing number of workers from Indonesia and Thailand are competing with Filipina workers who have traditionally constituted the great majority of (85 percent in 1995 and 53 percent in 2004)[11] of the FDH population.

The acceleration of migration is particularly evident in the Philippines and France. In 1975, the total of deployed workers from the Philippines was just over 36,000. More recently, an average of around 900,000 workers per year are deployed (POEA, 2004 figures). Although France has recorded a steep decrease in net inflow of migrants in the last decade or so due to its "zero immigration policy" (discussed below), the numbers of migrants from Asia and Eastern Europe has been increasing since the end of the 1990s (IOM 2003, 29). As a

10 Due to the undocumented status of FODWs in France, the figures given here are questionable. For instance, despite a five-year lag, O'Dy (2001) uses the same estimate of 17,000 as used by Anderson and Torrés in 1996. In contrast, personal communication with Ms Estrada of the Philippine Consulate in France suggested the estimate of the Filipino population to number at around 50 000 in France, with 20 000 located in Paris, of which the great majority were women (Diary RPC, September 23, 2003).

11 The drop in the numbers of FODWs can be attributed to the after-effects of the 1997 Asian financial crisis which saw Indonesia as the worst hit in the region (with the annual rate of GDP dropping down to -15.3 percent in 1998 and unemployment rising to 20 percent from 8 percent and 4.9 percent respectively in 1996) compared with the Philippines' GDP drop of 5.5 percent and 2.1 percent rise in unemployment. The result has been a higher deployment of workers by the Indonesian government compared to that of the Philippine Government with Indonesian workers predicted to outnumber the Filipino workers by 2007 (AMC et al. 2001, 170—for figures see pp. 14–15). The increase in the range of destinations to which a potential FODW can go (Tyner 1999), may also be a factor for the drop in their numbers in Hong Kong.

receiving economy, France has also experienced the trend in the differentiation in migration. It hosts one of the highest immigrant populations in Europe with migrant types varying from refugees, temporary, legal, irregular and so on. *Acceleration* affects Hong Kong to a smaller degree due to its geographic and demographic composition. Its small size and geographical setting as part of China, the most populous country in the world, has meant that Hong Kong has always had to strictly enforce immigration control policies. In contrast to France, the main issues in Hong Kong involve only those of irregular migration and refugees, the numbers of which come to no more than a few thousand a year (HKSAR 2004).

The relationships between the Philippines, France and Hong Kong provide a good illustration of the manifestations of the globalization of migration. They show how the international division of labor—Paris and Hong Kong as the global cities and the Philippines as part of the survival circuit—is reflected in the interconnectedness of their economies. As the Philippines continues to depend on migrant remittances, so Paris and Hong Kong depend on migrant labor. In addition, the technological developments allowing better communication and lower cost transport are facilitating the expansion of survival circuits to reach beyond traditional countries of destination linked by colonial heritage, and beyond regional migration systems (Hugo 2004, 94–5). The expansion of survival circuits also implies expanded operations in the informal sector, which in turn facilitates irregular migration. The increasing population of Filipinos in France is but one example of this. Although this occurs to a much lesser degree in the unique setting of Hong Kong, some FODWs in Hong Kong nevertheless use its visa system as a stepping-stone to obtain entry into Canada. (Canada is considered a preferred destination for domestic work because it allows the worker to apply for permanent residency after two years of full time live-in employment).

The rise in irregular migration has led to the importance of migration issues in the politics of all three states. For the Philippines, as a sending government, this means less ability to monitor and protect its citizens. While, with the significant amount of remittances central to its economic solvency, many observers (Ball and Piper 2002; Gonzalez 1998; Parreñas 2001; Tyner 1995) have highlighted the financial rather than the social interest associated with protection, the Philippine government has nevertheless demonstrated considerable administrative effort to protect the welfare of its overseas workers. To date, it has the most developed laws and provisions of the countries that export low-skilled labor (Ball and Piper, 1020. See here also Chapter 4). The most important of these is the Migrant Workers and Overseas Filipinos Act of 1995 which sets out the welfare and protection measures for its overseas workers, including provisions for encouraging documented means of passage (POEA 1995). Despite some positive reports on the efficacy of these responses to the needs of overseas workers (Santo Tomas 1999, 2005), the Philippine government remains powerless to deter irregular migration as more and more of its citizens need, and are able, to migrate. In addition, and as shown earlier, the control of the politics of labor migration rests with the receiving country.

For governments of receiving countries, and as discussed earlier, the increase in irregular migration means tighter regulations in border controls. Again, due to its unique setting, Hong Kong immigration administrators were able to boast that "during 2003, ten illegal migrants were arrested each day, compared with a daily average of 15 arrests in 2002" (HKSAR 2004). In contrast, France has had little success in curbing irregular immigration. It is a country of much more complex immigration history, immigrant composition and volume (see e.g. Hollifield 2004). It was not until the early 1990s when a national recession hit France, and after failures by successive governments to control immigration since the mid-1970s, that then President Mitterand set a goal of "zero immigration." This effectively meant that since immigration control had proven futile, the next logical step was *immigrant* control—or to roll back the rights of foreigners.

Immigrant Policy: Domestic Work and Human Rights

Given the persistent flows of migrant labor into their borders on the one hand, and the growing economic pressure on their economies to use migrant labor on the other, what effects and consequences do the immigrant policies of France and Hong Kong present to the living and working conditions of FODWs in particular? As much of the existing literature on overseas domestic workers has shown, the response to this question cannot be divorced from the issues raised by gender, race/ethnicity and class ideologies in both immigration and domestic work employment policies (see here especially, Pratt 1997; Anderson 2000). As evident in the labor market segmentation by sex and race mentioned earlier, the effect of immigration and labor policies has been to keep women migrant domestic workers suppressed at the bottom rung of the production ladder, rather than to improve their positions.

With regards to immigration policies, this has meant continued operation under the male-breadwinner-female-dependent-spouse and family reunification models of migration despite clear evidence of the feminization of migration (Lee 1996). Feminist-structural studies have also underscored the intersection of gender with race and class in discriminatory policies. Migrant women domestic workers are "classed" not only as unskilled or low-skilled workers, but they are also viewed as foreigners or outsiders, and are thus made "invisible" by being forced into informal and unprotected employment (Mattingly 1999; Smet 2000; Zlotnik 1990). Similarly, domestic labor employment policies in destination countries have been inadequate in addressing the specific conditions of domestic work as isolated and personal or care work (Ramirez-Machado 2003). Domestic labor employment policies, too, have been shown to operate under gender, class and racist biased ideologies on domestic work. Domestic work is treated as reproductive or women's unpaid work in the private realm of the home, and as devalued and dirty work left for servants and "outsiders" to undertake (Anderson 2000; Bakan and Stasiulis 1995; Glenn 1992; Stasiulis and Yuval-Davis 1995). In addition, familial ideologies that designate the home as private, have meant that the state and other public bodies cannot readily intervene in cases of domestic worker abuse (Bakan and Stasiulis 1997b, 44). It is thus in the area of domestic work, that the pain of not just immigration control, but also immigrant policy is felt most.

In France, forms of discrimination are evident in a number of ways. First, French immigration policies fail to acknowledge independent female entry both by recognizing female entry mainly through family reunification, and by making it difficult for women to receive work permits (Misra et al. 2005). As a result, many female migrant workers in France have entered either through tourist visas, which many overstay, or by outright "illegal" means such as by using the services of smugglers and/or traffickers. Some arrive as escapees from the relatively harsh working and living conditions in the Middle East, or from wealthy Middle Eastern employers (many being diplomats) who either have settled in France as political refugees[12] or who go to France for their vacation. Once in the country, the "escapees" are able to remain hidden from immigration authorities by engaging in "invisible" employment such as domestic work. Hence, as mentioned earlier, over half of immigrant women in France work as domestic workers. Second, although France has among the most responsive labor regulations governing domestic work (Blackett 1998; Vaz Cabral 2001), these regulations apply only to those who are legally employed. The regulations do not address the need to issue work permits for domestic workers, leaving the status of legal employment to the discretion of the employer to register the worker. However, not many employers register their employees, further ensuring that exploitation in relation to their working conditions, pay, and social benefits, remains largely hidden (Narula 1999, 161).

Third, the French government has responded to the high numbers of undocumented migrants by granting visa amnesties to "illegal" migrants, a significant percentage of which were given to domestic workers (Lloyd 2003). In addition, the government also enabled employers to legalize their domestic workers. However, the French government's inadequate acknowledgment of the gender, racial and class biases in the domestic work immigration and employment system, means that many employers have been able to continue employing cheap and flexible labor, which if documented, would mean higher wages and taxes, and ultimately less control over their employees (see e.g. Mozère et al. 2001). For the migrant domestic workers, this ultimately means being relegated to a dependent immigration and employment status.

---

12 For instance, following the outbreak of civil war in Lebanon (1975), the fall of the Shah of Iran (1979), and the outbreak of the Iran-Iraq War in 1980 (see Anderson 2000, 77).

In Hong Kong, the Administration's strictly regulated FDH sector provides a set minimum wage, a formal labor contract which is contestable in its labor courts, and an Ordinance that provides for the rights of migrant workers to join/form trade unions. However, the contracts do not specify working hours, with workers on call for up to 24 hours, a situation exacerbated by their live-in conditions. The contract is bound to immigration control policies that limit such workers to two-year terms in order to deter claims to citizenship.[13] In addition, the New Condition of Stay (NCS), was introduced by the Administration in 1987 in response to a perceived increase in irregular activities by FDHs. It requires FDHs to leave its borders within two weeks of the termination of their contracts or at the expiration of their visa, whichever is earlier. This means that any labor conflict with employers has a strong likelihood of leading to deportation, and therefore loss of employment for the FDH. Constable (1997, 154) has noted that "the way that rules and policies are enforced and interpreted [in Hong Kong] reflect deeply ingrained cultural biases that favor the rights of the employer over those of the worker, and that devalue the domestic worker." Thus while in France, migrant domestic workers can be said to be literally invisible, in Hong Kong, the visibility gained through documentation[14] is cancelled out by societal preconceptions that deem migrant domestic workers invisible.

NGO Protection and Assistance

Migrant domestic worker and human rights NGOs in both France and Hong Kong have revealed how this invisibility makes migrant domestic workers vulnerable to slave-like treatment and other forms of violence. While NGOs implicate employer-inflicted abuse in migrant domestic worker enslavement, they have also revealed how illegal practices by recruitment agents/agencies can drive these women into slave-like conditions. These practices can range from extortionate rates charged by the agents/agencies that lead to debt-bondage, to collusion between employers and smugglers/traffickers to buy and control not just the worker's labor but her very personhood (see here especially, Anderson 2000).[15] In line with this, structural studies have pointed out the complicity of the

13 "Hong Kong citizenship" does not technically exist, but "permanent residency" is its legal and practical equivalent. I retain the term "citizenship" here for consistency in style. See here also Bell and Piper (2005, 199).

14 FODWs in Hong Kong are fully visible in their massive social, sometimes political, gatherings in the city center every Sunday. However, there have been many public complaints about their visibility in terms of their crowded numbers. Further, the political activities of FODW-based NGOs have been careful not to deviate too much from preconceptions of overseas domestic worker "invisibility" within Hong Kong society (Chapter 3).

15 There have been cases, too, when recruitment agencies have been known to operate as recruiters and smugglers and/or traffickers. Despite recent efforts to distinguish between traffickers and smugglers (see, for example, in ILO 2001), there is still

state in making "invisibility" synonymous to irregularity, and thus underscore the need to see the issue as "state-facilitated slavery" (Phizacklea 1998, 33). Similar studies have noted the same conditions in Hong Kong and other receiving countries with documented migrant domestic worker populations such as Canada, Singapore and the Middle East (e.g. Bals 1999; Constable 1997; Gatmaytan 1997). As Anderson (1997, 37) observes, "the need for ... [domestic] labor is not properly reflected in immigration and employment policies, making domestic workers who are already vulnerable to abuse and exploitation even more dependent on their employers by denying them an independent status ...."

Nevertheless, NGOs have been able to raise public awareness and influence state policies by promoting human rights, sometimes expressed as migrant worker's rights or women's rights (Anderson 2001a; Law 2002b). In the last decade or so, they have been able to broaden their influence at regional and international levels by forming transnational activist networks composed of similar groups fighting for justice for domestic workers around the world. While their efficacy remains questionable against more powerful state and international institutions, their potential to evolve into a stronger counterforce to state, regional and international control, is nevertheless upheld in the literature (e.g. Anderson 2001a; Ball and Piper 2002; Phizacklea 1998; Stasiulis and Bakan 1997). Piper and Uhlin (2004, 13–14) draw a correlation between (trans) national activism and democracy, noting that democracy is an issue of not only citizenship but also human rights. Human rights is an area which democratic states, like France and Hong Kong,[16] find problematic to control; they are more difficult than citizenship to legitimate as a concern of state sovereignty. Human rights, therefore, is one area in which migrants can counter state strategies (see especially here, Massey 1999, 313–14).

A further observation to make regarding these organizations is that they are mostly composed of migrant workers, including those with undocumented status. Indeed Jordan and Düvell (2002, 33) note how irregular migration itself can be seen as a means to counter state strategies. This points to an important characteristic of overseas domestic work migration which has received little attention in the literature: that of tenacity. Even in documented situations such as Hong Kong, this observation holds true for the many who stay there by renewing contracts or by successfully circumventing state rules. Further, FODWs seem willing to by-pass Philippine state regulations that protect them in place of securing employment overseas. For example, Yeoh et al. (1999, 11–12)

insufficient explanation of how, and when during the process of recruitment, they can be distinguished. In the present study, I will therefore refrain from distinguishing them.

16 Hong Kong, albeit under the administration of a non-democratic Chinese government since 1997, continues to operate under a nation-state and has maintained its liberal administrative systems as inherited from the British colonial administration. It is for this reason that I classify it as democratic.

observe that some FODWs enter Singapore, a destination country notorious for its strict policies on overseas domestic workers, through so called "tourist visas" which they overstay. This practice occurs despite explicit warning from the Philippine government that underscores the vulnerability inherent in such undocumented entry and work. It is thus not uncommon to come across FODWs who have been in Hong Kong, Singapore, or more generally in overseas domestic work, for as long as 20 years, sometimes more. Further evidence to this is the shift in NGO services which previously dealt with repatriation but now concentrate on livelihood support (see e.g. Roberts in Ball and Piper 2002, 1030). Thus, despite oppressive state policies, significant numbers of FODWs remain in France and Hong Kong.

The central issue addressed by the book concerns the ability of FODWs in Paris and Hong Kong to practise agency in overseas domestic work, and the ways in which this practice is affected by state immigration and labor policies as well as by global development processes. Given their persistent high numbers and their growing activism for the right to work *and stay* in destination countries, their participation in overseas domestic work cannot be explained only by the structural characteristics of the global labor market. Nor can their participation be explained through analysis of the voluntaristic orientations of the individual migrants. The consolidation of structural explanations with voluntarism in a structuration perspective (see below) may provide an important basis for understanding how migrants practise agency, but they say little of the migrant's "staying power." Indeed, what are the factors which determine the migrant's *ability to continue* in overseas domestic work, and how do they relate with the practice of her highly constrained agency? In order to contextualize this question within a wider conceptual framework, the next section reviews the main theoretical approaches to migration and their relevance to understanding agency and capability in overseas domestic work.

Structure, Agency and Capability in Migration Theories[17]

The dominant approach in migration studies is based on modernization theory and neoclassical development economics. Both theories explain population

17 Agency and structural-based migration theories have received comprehensive review by Massey and others (see especially here, Massey et al. 1993). Goss and Lindquist (1995) have also meticulously reviewed these theories in order to explain their structuration approach to international migration. Moreover, agency and structural based migration theories along with the structuration approach has also been reviewed (Lee 1996), as well as in the particular context of overseas domestic work (Abdul Rahman 2003; Phizacklea 1998; Tacoli 1996a). Rather than reproduce the extensive references to the agency and structural-based theories, and the integrative approaches of the households approach and social/migrant networks theories on international migration in this current review, I direct the reader to these reviews instead.

movements as a product of, as well as a solution to, imbalances in the spatial distribution of labor, capital and natural resources. Where people are "pushed" to move as a result of economic, social and political problems in poor parts of the world, they are simultaneously "pulled" by comparative advantages (such as higher wages for the migrant) to the wealthier parts. Underlying this push-pull effect is an aggregate of micro-social or agentic processes, underscored by individual decisions based on a voluntaristic and rational evaluation of the costs and benefits of migration. It is predicted that as competition between migrants in the rich countries eventually drive wages down, accumulated remittances and return migrants' skills will stimulate economic growth in the source region, thus eliminating spatial inequality along with migration. These theories are therefore also referred to as the functionalist theory and equilibrium theory. Because they are the theories used in policymaking for international labor migration, they form, what is termed in the literature as the orthodox model. While such predictions may indeed be plausible in a setting where the labor market is regulated (Ramamurthy, 2003, 7–8), much criticism made of this model rests on the very question raised by structural conditions that ensure the absence of such regulations. Within this body of theory, there is a lack of attention given to structural forces that shape and control both the course of migration and migrants' decisions.

The structuralist or neo-Marxist perspective on migration has been an important response to the limitations of the orthodox model, and is the perspective shared by the feminist-structuralist approach on overseas domestic work migration (discussed further in the next chapter). In contrast to the orthodox model, this perspective employs a macro-social approach that identifies underlying structural forces in migration. These forces have been explained through a combination of dependency theory, modes of production theory, and world systems theory. While the dependency and modes of production theories recognize inequality between core/receiving and peripheral/sending regions as an important precondition for the former's exploitation of the latter, world systems theory characterizes this core-periphery relationship in terms of capital-labor relations. Operating under the global market economy, capital and commodity flows are argued to be established between the regions under patriarchal and capitalist ideological structures, thereby commodifying the means of (re)production. Migration is thus an outcome of social and spatial structures which create the ideological conditions that produce migrants, rather than as an aggregate of individual decisions and actions. In contrast to the critiques on the orthodox approach, critiques of the structuralist perspective refer to its overly pessimistic view and marginalization of the individual's agency in migration, especially amidst positive experiences by migrants such as gained financial and social autonomy.

Building on social networks theory (as used in particular by Kearney (1986), Massey et al. (1987) and Singhanetra-Renard (1992)), Goss and Lindquist (1995) propose a structuration approach which articulates structure and agency as mutually integral parts, thereby reconciling micro and macro elements in migration processes. They explain the interplay of structure with agency through a concept of the "migrant institution," where "agents with particular interests and playing specific roles within an institutional environment, drawing knowledgably upon sets of rules in order to increase access to resources" (ibid., 345). (The structuration approach is further discussed in Chapter 3.)

On the question of an individual's capability to continue in migration, the structuration approach has been adept at keeping the functionalist orientations of the agent "to increase access to resources," while ensuring that it is bound by the structural considerations of "roles within an institutional environment." In this way, it is the more accurate tool for explaining migrant's decisions in migration. By itself, however, the structuration approach cannot explain the need for continued participation in the "migrant institution," nor the capability required to do so. Although the structuration approach identifies migrant institutions as spaces of control where "marginalised populations are … able to mobilize resources and rules in order to influence the actions of the more powerful towards them" (Goss and Lindquist 1995, 33), it provides little discussion on how this process may be conceptualized in terms of the collective but vulnerable resistance by migrant NGOs. In this regard, it fails to examine how migrant institutions fare against global, state, employer and recruitment institutions, thus neglecting more established institutional environments where "rules" render these spaces highly constrained and the continuity of the control uncertain. The structuration approach thus remains at best descriptive, without consideration of the macro-social, historical, materialist and dialectical process of the institution itself, nor of the institution's position against other institutions.

Moreover, it is not clear how migrant institutions differ from each other in both social class and gender positions. For instance, while both FODW migrants and highly skilled male labor migrants migrate to increase access to resources within the current institutional environment of labor migration, the latter's capability to continually access resources is more certain and less precarious than the former's. Furthermore, a skilled labor migrant is more likely to gain "increased" access to resources than a FODW migrant for whom access may not occur at all. To be useful in explaining capability in FODW experiences, the structuration approach will therefore need to more fully integrate the structuralist model. Similarly, structuralists' over-fixation on the role of constraints to capability could benefit from the more fluid and integrative structuration approach. The following chapters proceed to develop this structural-stucturationist approach, guided by insights from migrants rights NGOs and from the domestic workers interviewed for this study. Having raised here, some questions on agency and capability in the FODW context through Goss and Lindquist's structuration approach, it is possible to view the factors determining the practice-ability of agency from a dual perspective. That is, as composed of both constraining and enabling elements. In noting also the importance of fortifying the structuration approach with the feminist-structuralist approach, it is possible to gain a more accurate sense of the power relations—in which constraining elements are more powerful—that underscore the ability of the enabling elements to produce opportunities for the agent. This perspective is a crucial reminder that agency is first and foremost highly constrained in the FODW context, not only structurally but also in the agentic sense. As discussed in the previous chapter, this perspective is also an important basis from which to identify livelihoods, resources and human rights as integral elements for a concept of capability that offsets the unequal power relations.

The task of the following chapters will be to systematically show how FODW capability can be conceptualized and evaluated as an essential part of FODW agency.

Conclusion

This chapter has outlined both the material and analytical context for examining agency and capability in Filipina overseas domestic work. It showed that understanding FODW agency and capability requires an engagement with the structural context of Filipina overseas domestic work not only as an issue of immigration and domestic employment policies, but also as an issue of development. Characterized by constraints in processes of uneven global development, the structural context of Filipina overseas domestic work illuminates a second important area; that of FODW capability—what the FODW is able to do and be despite these constraints.

The chapter also reviewed the main theories of international migration to highlight the linkages between the structural context of Filipina overseas domestic work and FODW capability. It showed, however, that current theories are inadequate for addressing issues of capability in Filipina overseas domestic work. The chapter therefore identified that current migration theories need to be reworked in the form of a "feminist structural-structurationist" framework to enable understanding of the interplay of agency with capability in the women's labor migration for domestic work. It will take the following few chapters to elaborate on this revised framework. The next chapter firstly locates the analytical space for the framework. It does so by reviewing the extent to which current literature on overseas domestic work have incorporated the structural context of global domestic work migration, and the issues of capability it raises, into their analyses.

PART II
Agency and Filipina Overseas Domestic Work

Chapter 3
Empty Agency: The Oppressed Third World Woman

In Chapter 1, I used structuration theory as a point of departure to argue that FODW agency remains inadequately theorized without the concept of capability. This chapter sets out the current state of knowledge on the agency-capability connection with particular reference to overseas domestic workers. I review the literature on overseas domestic workers agency organized around the main migration theories of the functionalist, feminist-structuralist (hereafter structuralist) and structurationist approaches. I demonstrate that current approaches leave the agency of overseas domestic workers largely unexamined and have consequently failed to capture issues of capability. This knowledge base is essential from which, in the following chapter, I can propose a synthesis of the structuralist with the structurationist approach to correct the absence of capability in current analyses.

The Functionalist Perspective: Disembodied Agent

The orthodox understanding on migration is characterized by functionalism at both the individual and greater societal level; the individual's functionality, or exercise of rational action to migrate for better wages, aggregates into the functionality of a bigger whole that is the global political economy to eventually correct inequality, and hence eliminate the need to migrate in the first place (Chapter 2). Goss and Lindquist (1995, 320) note how this functionalist perspective "reduces migrants, a social category that is structured by gender, ethnicity and social class, to mere embodiment of labor power." They further observe that it is particularly in this way that "the functional approach has become a policymaking orthodoxy for international labor migration" (ibid.).

In this review, I focus this functionalist understanding of migration on the individual migrant. Individual functionalism is a micro-social process, underscored by the psychosocial orientation of the migrant. It implies the capacity for willed and voluntary action (e.g. Zelinsky 1971, as cited ibid.), and thus foregrounds the central role of agency within the orthodox model. This is an important basis from which to understand the theoretical framework that underlies the literature on overseas domestic workers' agency. By taking the individual migrant as the unit of analysis, this body of literature draws on the concept of human agency to illustrate how overseas domestic labor is a conscious and voluntary choice of the migrants to sell their own labor, for their own reasons, and for their own futures. The literature on overseas domestic workers agency has emerged as a direct response to the rigid structuralist view (Chapter 1), but they remain few and lack in-depth inquiries compared to structuralist-based works.

In a research note, Ebron (2002) reflects on the voluntary actions of FODWs in Venice. She considers the structural effects of the exploitative "maid trade" between sending and receiving states, a racist host society and "masters" for employers, from the points of view of the FODWs themselves. She argues that, on the whole, the FODWs don't find these constraints troublesome. Instead, FODWs see these constraints in light of the positive gains from their experiences of overseas domestic work. Employers find them hardworking, trustworthy and valuable employees. Their family and nation-state depend on their financial assistance. And they do not see the acceptance of the wider Italian community as important because they view their experience in Venice as a temporary process through which they achieve their financial goals. This is thus, Ebron contends, how FODWs "successfully negotiate living and working … in Venice for one or twenty years" (ibid., 8). While providing important insights into FODWs' "willed and voluntary actions," Ebron's brief paper leaves unexamined the nature of "negotiating" the living and working conditions in overseas domestic work, which are not always "successful." Ebron's account of FODW experiences is limited to Venice, one of the most affluent cities in the world, where it is more likely that a FODW can achieve her financial goals and find living conditions acceptable for up to twenty years.[1] She also leaves unexplored whether in those years, the FODW experience has been free of abuse, either in the context of Venice or in destinations previous to Venice. Thus, although there is earlier acknowledgement of the wider temporal and spatial contexts of the FODW experience, they receive no further exploration.

In a journal article, Gibson et al. (2001) take the singular case of Luz, a former FODW in Hong Kong, to analyse what they call "the multiple class processes" in Luz's experience of a migration trajectory. Prior to migration, they identify Luz's situation as a feudal agricultural worker in the Philippines. During the migration experience, they identify two class positions in which Luz finds herself: as a slave for the first of her seven years in Hong Kong while working for abusive employers, and as an independent overseas domestic worker for the remaining years for clients with whom she could negotiate working hours and working conditions. After migration, Gibson et al. identify further transformations in Luz's situation. With her accumulated savings, Luz had returned to the Philippines to buy a small business and some land with her husband. Gibson et al. regards this position as that of a capitalist, and of a feudal landlord. At the same time, however, Luz could also be identified

1 Importantly also, Venice is located in Italy, a nation whose Catholic faith finds much in common with mainstream Catholic culture in the Philippines. In addition, Italy is a country which is relatively, politically tolerant of undocumented overseas domestic workers from the Philippines.

as a feudal subject as she performed surplus labor for her husband within their household. Gibson et al. thus argue that class needs to be understood as process; neither singular nor static, but more importantly as insight into how FODWs' agency might be identified outside of discourses that construct them as victims. They extend this view of class by drawing on the activities of an NGO in Hong Kong that supports migrants' entrepreneurial aspirations to save capital and set up community-run businesses in the Philippines. They propose to view these activities as a collective representation of class transformation. That is, "the transformation of a slave class position into a potentially communal class position as a migrant worker moves from domestic employment in a household overseas into work within their home community in a cooperative set up by migrant savings" (ibid., 380). They go on to suggest that FODWs' agency can thus be "imagined" in terms of the role of FODWs "as economic activists with many capabilities and capacities to enact social and economic change" for themselves and for their home communities (ibid., 377).

While this less static concept of class is indeed a useful starting point for imagining FODW agency, it says little about how agency itself can be understood within class processes. Gibson et al. leave unexamined the relations between agentic orientation within this class fluidity and greater structures of capitalist production. Much focus is given on how class in its multiple form is experienced by FODWs, but little on how it is, or more importantly, *can be*, actually produced by them. This is surprising since Gibson et al.'s study is a response to the consequences such relations entail, where these involve FODW vulnerability and victimization by both receiving and sending governments. In Gibson et al.'s approach, therefore, class is static, remaining a pure category in itself. Class, itself, is not transformed. Rather, it is the FODW that moves through and across its many levels and forms. In other words, it is the agentic orientation by the FODW rather than class processes that allows analysis to "imagine" the agency of FODWs. The lack of attention given to this agentic orientation translates into an unsatisfactory account of FODW agency. This is most evident in their conflation of agency with "capabilities and capacities" as important terms which allow more accurate understandings of the efficacy of "agency," but which they leave unexamined. Indeed, what if, for Luz, the "class process" could not occur because she could not escape her first years of slavery? Or, what if, in the longer term, Luz finds herself enslaved as a domestic worker again as a result of losing her land and livelihood through the disruptive effects of modernization and capitalist development? Much like Ebron's reflection therefore, Gibson et al.'s inquiry shows how FODWs negotiate their structures (successfully), rather than negotiate *with* them.

It is important to note at this point how "negotiate" is used in these inquiries. It is used in a transitive manner. That is, agents negotiate structures in the sense that they move through or push pass them. However, without taking into account the power relations inherent in negotiations—as between at least two negotiating parties, "negotiate" takes on a meaning of "muddling through" or "getting by" structural constraints. In contrast, and also taking Giddens' theorization of agency as its point of departure (to be made more explicit in Chapter 5), the present study employs the meaning of "negotiate" in its intransitive form—to confer/negotiate *with*. In this way, it addresses power relations by recognizing that structures are indeed constituted by agents and their actions. It is agency that produces and reproduces structure. Thus, while agents negotiate structures (transitive), agents *negotiate with* structures/other agents (intransitive). I argue that using the intransitive, indeed transformative, form enables a more power-conscious understanding of "negotiate" as an exertion of agency through an act of bartering or "trading off," rather than as just an exertion of agency in the Foucaultian sense—fluidly but with no particular intended purpose or tangible achievement.

Inquiries into migrant domestic worker agency that do, albeit implicitly, foreground the agent in this intransitive way have been particularly useful in identifying the transnational context of overseas domestic work as an important site for the practise of agency, albeit in its aggregated form of collective resistance. Mozère (2001) demonstrates how through an established Filipino migrant workers' transnational network, undocumented FODWs use their agency to secure their position as the "Mercedes Benz" of domestic workers, and thereby monopolize the best paid and best employment positions among the wider migrant domestic worker community in Europe. Basing their study on FODWs in Paris, Mozére and Maury (2002) point out that through these networks, some FODWs, including those without formal employment contracts, have been able to successfully negotiate their terms of employment with their employers and achieve their financial goals of building a house or two and/or setting up businesses back in the Philippines. Mozère and Maury therefore conclude that FODWs are in effect *entrepreneures d'elles-mêmes* (self-entrepreneurs), indicating that they should perhaps be regarded as liberated rather than oppressed (Mozère 1999).

Tacoli (1996a) similarly found that FODWs in Italy choose to remain in a transnational status because such status enables them to become high-earning wageworkers in a rich country, rather than return home where wageworkers have a relatively poor earning capacity. Using a household strategies approach, Tacoli draws linkages between the Philippines as the country of origin and Italy as the host country to examine the causes, mechanisms and consequences of gender and life courses in Filipino international labor migration. Through this framework, Tacoli finds that the transnational-wageworker status enables the FODW not only to contribute financially to her family unit but also to exert control over this contribution. No longer financially dependent on their husbands, nor spatially confined within the oppressive structures of their own households, Tacoli shows how FODWs are able to negotiate their roles as dutiful daughters and/or self-sacrificing mothers on their own terms. Like Morokvasic (1984) found with overseas domestic workers of other nationalities working in Europe, Hondagneu-

Sotelo (1994) with Mexican domestic workers in the USA, and Gamburd (2000) with Sri Lankan overseas domestic workers in the Middle East, Tacoli found that FODWs are capable and rational actors who increase control over their own lives by seeing self-sacrifice and self-interest as not mutually exclusive in their decisions to migrate and work for the sake of their families (see especially, Tacoli 1996b; Tacoli 1999, 674–7).

In an article examining cultural politics, gender, and class relations in Filipina migration for domestic work to Canada, Barber (2000) extends the notion of FODW agency in terms of women's agency. Barber underscores the reproduction of achieved success in overseas domestic work among multi-generational FODWs. She uses the example of Christina, an FODW who is herself a beneficiary of remittances from older female kin (these can be mothers, aunts and sisters), to show that FODW agency is "embedded in layers of economic and social support flowing from and to female kin" (ibid., 399). Through this close relationship, FODWs gain "cultural capital," becoming well aware of the dangers of overseas domestic work, but also of transnational networks that act as safety nets in the event of unemployment and/or abuse in the workplace. These processes of women's agency enable a FODW diaspora to form (in Canada). However, Barber shows how this diaspora remains provisional in light of structural constraints, arising from historical processes of the global political economy, from states' emigration, immigration, and domestic employment labor policies, from employer dominance, but also from gendered constructions of familial obligations back in the Philippines. She thus highlights that understanding the practice of agency by FODWs must acknowledge that ""choice" is contingent and agency is culturally constrained" (ibid., 409). However, no elaboration is provided on how we may conceive of other, more materialist (as opposed to non-cultural) conditions that direct choices and that constrain agency. Nor, indeed, on the ways in which agency can overcome constraints.

Despite providing a relatively deeper examination of the concept of FODW agency, Barber's discussion on agency nevertheless shares a common thread underlying the other studies on migrant domestic worker agency: their conclusions on agency are based on the migrant worker's gainful and successful employment. A general critique of works on migrant domestic worker agency is thus their lack of attention to the constraining elements in the migrant worker's situation, and consequently, their lack of attention to explicitly theorize agency with—as opposed to within—its wider context of structural constraints. Tacoli's relatively comprehensive work (in the form of a book and two articles) is a particularly good example of how it is important in identifying (familial) constraint in the country of origin, but also of how it fails to explore this as a core constraint in a FODWs' life course. This omission is indeed perhaps "in the method," for Tacoli's use of a household strategies approach does not allow her to transcend the functionalist approach to understanding FODW migration. As Goss and Lindquist (1995, 327) have observed of the household approach, it is merely composed of the "effective substitution of the rational, calculating individual with a rational, calculating household ... and repeats the errors of voluntarism in [functionalist] approaches to social explanation."

Thus, much like the functionalist approach to the individual migrant, these works portray the migrant domestic worker herself as functional: she migrates for paid work to escape poverty and accumulate capital, eventually and inevitably placing her situation into equilibrium. How the migrant is capable of exerting agency for intended purposes, where this involves intrinsic relations with wider structural contexts and constraints, are left unquestioned, and in Tacoli's and Barber's case, unexamined. Parker (2005c, 3) notes that "[a]gency is often invoked by social scientists where they describe the ... emancipatory actions ... of individuals who are oppressed or severely constrained." This observation remains true for the agency-based works discussed here, and is both fortunate and unfortunate. It is fortunate because the focus on "emancipatory actions" is instrumental in identifying the FODW agent, as well as the site of their agency in transnationalism (the full value of this will become apparent in discussion on the structurationist approach, later in the chapter). It is unfortunate because the lack of focus on constraints leaves the agent disembodied; one whose functionings are not examined in direct relation to structural constraints.

The Structuralist Perspective: Absent or Latent Agency?

In contrast to agency-based works, structuralist analyses focus on constraints. The structuralist approach on overseas domestic work is characterized by a feminist interpretation of structuralist migration theories (Chapter 1). In particular, they identify three reinforcing structural layers, compactly sedimented by the globalization of capitalist production, that push and trap poor women within the precarious realm of domestic work in rich countries. These layers are the global, the national, and the receiving household.

Chapters 1 and 2 have already covered the global layers; neoliberal trade and development policies of rich countries have resulted on the one hand, in the contraction of welfare provisions and privatization of basic family services such as health, housing and education, and on the other, in the increasing inequality between nations and the impoverishing consequences of this to women's daily lives, particularly in developing countries. At the level of the sending state, structuralist studies underscore the Philippines' "feminized" position in the global economy (Tadiar 1997). These studies argue that the Philippines' incorporation into the global economy as a peripheral economy dependent on the core economies, makes the Philippine government ultimately powerless to make its overseas domestic workers' lives count outside of their economic value as labor-export commodities. Eviota (1992, 2004), for example, documents how structural adjustment programs have directed the Philippine economy toward export-oriented production, resulting in greater inequality among its citizens, and impoverishing women, in particular. Eviota (2004, 60) argues that not only have women been made more economically vulnerable in terms of their "multiple roles as producers of goods and services, reproducers of people, and maintainers of their family's well-being," overall economic insecurity has meant that in many cases, unemployed husbands have expressed their frustration either through physical violence or psychological abuse, or abandonment. Yet, it is on an export-oriented development strategy on which successive Philippine governments continue to depend. In the host state, structuralist studies show how overseas domestic workers remain hidden in terms of being women's unpaid or care work within the privacy of the home and/or in terms of denied documentation (see here especially, Anderson 2004c; Bakan and Stasiulis 1997a; Chin 1998; Lan 2006). At the household level within the host state, they show how capitalist relations of production permeate and reproduce the social relations between employer and domestic worker as consumer and producer of un/underpaid labor, respectively. It is in this way that the domestic worker's labor becomes caught up in the power structure of employer-employee relations that in effect translates into a master-servant/slave relationship.

In sum, structuralist works have clearly shown how the intersection of global development policies with host state labor and immigration regulations, as well as with increasing service-based work consumption, structures overseas domestic work. This has received ample documentation in accounts of overseas domestic workers' experience in host states around the world. Rather than provide a review of the power relations inherent in each of these layers, which can be found elsewhere (Abdul Rahman 2003), or review the current state of feminist migration research (Silvey 2004a), I focus here on the universally shared structure of overseas domestic work. Parreñas (2001) has identified this in terms of FODWs' "parallel lives" in the global economy. She (ibid., 247) describes "parallel lives" in the sense that FODWs "can cross-nationally ... identify with each other on the grounds of the similar effects of global processes in their lives." Parreñas (ibid., 248) identifies these similar effects in terms of "numerous dislocations of migration," but for the purposes of the present inquiry, I highlight the one dislocation of FODWs' migrant status as quasi citizens. Quasi-citizenship is described by Parreñas (ibid., 244) in relation to both the sending and receiving states:

> As the status of the Philippines as a sending nation ... leaves its government too weak to ensure the protection of its nationals, the incorporation of [FODWs] into the host society depends mostly on the cooperation of the receiving state. Yet racial and other forms of segmentation stunt the rights accorded to [FODWs] by the receiving state ....

In this context, I show how major structural works in the field either exclude or leave undeveloped discussions of agency within the more favored structural categories of race, class, gender, and citizenship. Building on this, I then show

how the structuralists' neglect of providing a fuller examination of agency results in a failure to explicitly identify poverty-induced migration as a fifth major category from which to explain not only structural oppression, but also as the basis for understanding capability in FODW agency.

Absent Agency

In Asia, Chin (1998, 2003) shows how the Malaysian state's drive towards economic development has mimicked global capitalist growth. She shows how capitalism in Malaysia has resulted in the rise of a modern middle class as a hungry consumer of the cheap and flexible labor of domestic workers from less developed regions. She shows how these workers are generally denied citizenship and other rights, and as with most other low-skilled migrant workers in Malaysia, are concentrated in jobs considered by citizens as degrading and demeaning. Cheng (2001, 2004) and Lan (2000, 2001; 2006) document the same situation for Taiwan, foregrounding issues of class, gender, race and citizenship as legitimizing categories for both state and employer treatment of overseas domestic workers as invisible workers. Strict state control, albeit recently abolished in Taiwan but still the case in Singapore (Huang and Yeoh 2003; Yeoh and Huang 1998, 1999; Yeoh et al. 2004; Yeoh et al. 1999), means that these women's bodies are highly regulated to the point where pregnancy tests are required every six months. If the test is positive, an migrant domestic worker may be immediately deported. In Hong Kong, although the working conditions for overseas domestic workers are comparatively more humane (Cheng 1996), overseas domestic workers still experience a wide range of abuse from employers and recruitment agencies as a result of the Administration's strict immigration laws (Chang, K. 2000; Constable 1997; Lowe 2000).

Likewise in the countries of the Middle East, strict immigration controls that limit contracts to three years along with inadequate domestic labor policies, render overseas domestic workers vulnerable (Shadid et al. 1992). Gatmaytan (1997) notes that reports of violence against FODWs, including rape and physical assault, have originated mainly from the Middle East. State gender policies that require segregation of the sexes outside of the home and restrict women's mobility are particularly problematic in that they contribute to the isolation of domestic workers, thus easily enabling violence and abuse against overseas domestic workers to go undetected (Silvey 2004b, 255). In Israel, too, Raijman et al. (2003) highlight the societal view of domestic work as degrading work fit only for "outsiders" or non-Jews. The intersection of this view with the highly exclusive immigration and immigrant policies of the Israeli state, despite being a democratic state, make domestic workers vulnerable to abuse. As Raijman et al. (2003, 733) explain, "[s]imilar to the Gulf states and to Taiwan, in Israel work permits are granted to employers, to whom the migrant worker is indentured, thereby maximizing employers' and the state's control over [them]."

Even in Canada's relatively "fairer" immigration-employment program (Stasiulis and Bakan 1997), overseas domestic workers are considered as commodities for trade among the sending and receiving states, the employers and the recruitment agencies (Bals 1999; England and Stiell 1997; Grandea and Kerr 1998; Pratt and the Philippine Women Center 1998, 1999 ; Stasiulis and Bakan 1994, 1996, 2000). Pratt (with the Philippine Women Center, 1998), in particular, shows how both the degrading class image of domestic work and an "othering" discourse based on racial/ethnic difference, has constructed the bodies of FODWs in Canada as no more than a cleaning and caring body. The construction of the FODW body in terms of its domestic servitude is also evident in other parts of the world, such as in the entry of *Filipineza* or Filipina in a Greek dictionary as "a domestic servant," in the manufacturing of FODW dolls in the 1980s in Hong Kong (Ebron 2002), and in the term "Filipina" itself as evident in childrens' discourse of the family in France (Anderson 2001b, 28):

> As a Filipina in Athens described, "I heard children playing, they are playing house. The other child said, "I'm a Daddy." The other child said, "I'm a Mummy." And then, "She is a Filipina." So what does the child mean, even the child knows or it's already learning, that if you are a Filipina you are a servant inside the house.

In the context of the United States, G. Chang (2000, 2004) shows how overseas domestic workers are trapped, on the one hand, by the United States' government's complicity with global political economic processes that force them to migrate to the United States in the first place and, on the other, by the United States' government's economic and political interests to keep them undocumented. Economically, overseas domestic workers are useful as shock absorbers of surplus, unpaid domestic labor crucial to national economic growth. Politically, the US government has done little to discourage xenophobic backlash against the few women who have managed to acquire documents after years of domestic service in the country. When they step out of their inscribed "domestic worker body" to access welfare benefits for the needs of their own households, they are labeled as "freeloaders." Chang underscores this as a "contradiction between the construction of immigrants as resource depletors and their very exploitation as resources" (Chang, G. 2000, 14). It is, however, those many more overseas domestic workers who remain undocumented that are the most disenfranchised, vulnerable and exploited in the United States. In the European context, Anderson (2000; 2001c) has shown that it is the undocumented live-in migrant worker who are the most invisible and therefore most vulnerable to abuse. Consistent with the findings of the other studies mentioned herein, Anderson argues that it is not only issues of race, class and gender, that oppress these women, but also the issue of nation, specifically, their lack of citizenship or independent status in the host states.

Feminist scholarship on domestic work (e.g. Cock 1980; Glenn 1992; Oakley 1988; Romero 1992) has been influential in providing the basis from which this multilayered structural oppression and commodification of overseas domestic workers has been expressed in terms of slavery. In particular, their identification of the "domestic woman" and her labor in capitalist modes of production as reproductive, invisible and unpaid, has in turn, allowed its identification as unfree labor (e.g. Bakan and Stasiulis 1997a; 1995, 161). Thus as Anderson asserts (2000, 128), "Slavery … has long been associated with reproductive labour, and reproductive labour with women."[2] In addition, she argues that much like the slave in the American antebellum south, "it is the worker's "personhood" rather than her labor power, which the employer is attempting to buy, and that the worker is thereby cast as unequal in exchange" (Anderson 2000, 2; 2004b).[3] This argument consolidates with abolitionist and human rights groups' findings on cases of domestic slavery in households headed by diplomats and corporate executives. Complementary to the structural feminist approach, neo-abolitionists and human-rights based migrant groups argue that the lack of independent immigration status given to the accompanying domestic worker(s) by the host state underscore their enslavement (see e.g. Anderson 1993; O'Dy 2001; Torrés 1996; Zarembka 2002).

Latent Agency?

While, as mentioned earlier, agency-based approaches have emerged as a response to the structuralist portrayal of overseas domestic workers as passive victims much devoid of agency, it is important to remember that some structuralist-based works do incorporate issues of agency in their analysis. Moreover, these works engage with the concept of agency at both the theoretical and praxis level.

Works that have incorporated agency into their theoretical analysis underscore the complexities of power in the Foucaultian sense and/or the multiple subjectivities in the overseas domestic workers' experience of both oppression and liberation. Constable (1997) uses Foucault's notion on the dialectic relationship between discipline and resistance to demonstrate FODW resistance against, but also conformity to, the disciplining power of the Hong Kong administration as well as those of employers and recruitment agencies. She asserts that because this conformity is actually based on the FODWs' conscious decision to use the disciplining tool of power on themselves, they cannot be understood as passive victims. However, in arguing against "romanticizing resistance," she concludes that FODWs' strategies of resistance should still be understood in terms of their weak ability to improve their subordinate positions. Thus, while FODWs cannot be viewed as "passive objects of oppression," neither can they be understood as "active subjects who successfully control themselves and their labour" (ibid., 13). Chin (1998) uses Scott's (1990b; 1990a) notion of

2 Anderson did not provide any references for this statement, but see similar observations made by other studies of slavery across history and across time with a feminist stance on the topic asserting that "the oppression of women antedates slavery and makes it possible" (Lerner 1983, 174). See also Turley (2000, 86).

3 See here also, Bakan and Stasiulis (1997b), Chin (1997, 1998) and Tadiar (1997).

infrapolitics or the politics of marginalized groups, to foreground resistance in the "hidden transcripts" of overseas domestic workers in Malaysia. She shows how overseas domestic workers can be conceptualized as political actors who "engage in different forms of resistance that challenge or renegotiate employer-employee relations" (Chin 1998, 128). These forms of resistance are often hidden from employers and the general public, and include the infrapolitical activities of footdragging, feigning illness and displaying non-deferential behavior during rest days. However, Chin (1998, 163) admits that "the hidden transcripts of domestic service ... is shaped mostly by the structure of work environments established indirectly by state authorities, and directly controlled by employers." Much like Constable's account of, and conclusion on, FODWs' resistance in Hong Kong, Chin (1998, 163) concedes that "[t]he overall effectiveness of [overseas domestic workers'] infrapolitical activities remains questionable."

Momsen's (1999a) edited volume, *Gender, Migration and Domestic Service*, is a collection of case studies on overseas domestic workers and their experiences around the world, at both national and international levels. Taking into consideration both global commonalities and local differences, it provides a balanced account of the oppressed but also liberating structural position of overseas domestic workers. Building on Bhabha's notion of the "Third Space" as sites of transformation through contestation, it identifies a multi-tiered space of resistance. The first tier consists of the domestic or household space where the domestic worker's dependency on her employer (for wages, documentation, food and so on) is eventually and inevitably reciprocated by the employer's dependency on the domestic worker's intimate presence in the privacy of their home and family. Intrinsically related to the household, the second tier refers to the physical and social mobility of the domestic worker in both the household and the wider society. While spatial and physical restrictions within the household parallel the constraints experienced in the society as a result of their sex, class, and race/ethnicity, they also present opportunities to the migrant domestic worker who, if not for the very act of labor migration itself, would more likely remain constrained by oppressive patriarchal structures in their places of origin. The last tier consists of socio-political spaces, characterized by meeting places in the host state. These places provide "sustenance and resistance" in terms of community centers, refuges, public parks, and also through organized networks that offer recruitment, legal services and when required, political solidarity.

Parreñas (2001, 30–35) confirms the equalizing interpretation of agency that characterizes the above works, this time, by underscoring the issue of subjectivity. In contrasting the "contingent freedom of the subject" with the "free will of the individual," she provides the contextual nuances of FODW agency, again consequently producing a less romanticized interpretation of Foucaultian resistance. Parreñas' (2001, 31) definition of FODWs' subjectivity allows her to "identify their multiple subject-positions ... or 'dislocations' [... in order ...] to emphasize the subordinate conditions of their migration." "Dislocations" occur as a result of the FODWs structural location as racialized women confined to low-wage immigrant work in the global economy. However, Parreñas suggests that FODW agency is not only limited but also enabled by the macro structural processes of globalization as well as by the meso-level institutional processes that constitutes the FODW subjection such as that of national governments, labor markets, the family and the community. She further argues that FODW agency is "conditioned" by its own subordination, and as such, "when acting against dislocations, [FODWs] do not necessarily impose interventions against structural processes but may also intensify and re-create [structural inequalities] (Parreñas 2001, 35). Hence, for instance, they hire poorer women back in the Philippines as domestic workers to care for their own children and households. Echoing Constable's and Chin's conclusions, resistance, then, "does not necessarily bring positive change" (Parreñas 2001, 34).

Having been careful to incorporate agency into their structural analyses, these works have been able to identify the rather weak nature of overseas domestic workers' resistance. However, because they either fail to sufficiently theorize the individual's agency to the larger socio-economic and political processes (Chin and Momsen et al.), or when they do (Constable and Parreñas), they fail to identify the transformative or capable aspect of agency, these works remain trapped in a purely symptomatic understanding of overseas domestic workers' resistance. Thus, while these approaches are more attentive to the complexities in overseas domestic workers' experiences, they fail to show how understanding these complexities can provide transformative or powerful resistance. In this respect, they explain no more than the *non*-functionality of these women's agency within their given exploitative structures, thus leaving the concept of structure static or "as a received notion" (Giddens 1984a, 16). In this way, therefore, these approaches describe a marginalized agency, rather than an agency capable of overcoming marginalization.

Nevertheless, in contrast to the functionalist view on agency, I observe that this structuralist treatment of agency actually provides a more appropriate—or indeed, *keeps,* the highly constrained—context for examining FODW agency. Could this marginalized agency then, be more appropriately understood as latent agency? If so, how is it possible to reveal and conceptualize it? And then empower it or make it capable? The remainder of this chapter addresses the first of these questions. It is in the next chapter in which the latter two questions are addressed.

The association of the structuralist approach with NGOs that advocate for the rights of overseas domestic workers can provide insight into the question of latent agency. In particular, I point to the examples of Bridget Anderson's work with Kalayaan and other rights-based NGOs in Europe, and Pratt's work with the Philippine Women's Center (PWC) in Canada. Anderson is a long-term member of Kalayaan, a London-based NGO which has been fighting for overseas domestic workers' rights for around 20 years. Her first book on the topic of overseas domestic workers, *Britain's Secret Slaves* (1993), was written in collaboration with Kalayaan and Anti-Slavery International. The rights-based activities behind this work eventually led to a policy response from the Home Office, which put into effect a regularization program for abused overseas domestic workers in 1998. However, reports of abuse remain high, indicating serious limitations on the efficacy of the program (Anderson 2004a). Nevertheless, the success achieved in the mobilization of migrant NGOs, trade unions and advocacy groups, provided the basis for addressing the problems of overseas domestic workers at the European Union (EU) level. Anderson's subsequent comparative research on overseas domestic workers in Europe (2000, see also Phizacklea and Anderson 2001) was instrumental in the development of the Europe-wide overseas domestic workers network, RESPECT. Although Anderson has analysed these works through a structural lens, she has more recently shifted with Kalayaan, from an understanding of overseas domestic workers' struggles in terms of slavery, to one that frames them in terms of women's and worker's rights (Schwenken 2005, 8).

The RESPECT network is unique in that it is primarily a self-help rather than an advocacy organization. The network's structure is composed of rights-based NGOs, trade unionists, researchers and overseas domestic workers of various nationalities. The organizational structure of the network ensures that policy directions are driven by the overseas domestic workers themselves, while the remaining members provide advisory and other support. While this does not mean that there is always consensus among the overseas domestic workers, they have been united in response to their identity as "victims." Whether Filipino, Moroccan or Columbian, overseas domestic workers in Europe call, instead, for their right to remain and work in the EU (Schwenken 2005).[4] Thus, while yet to appear more fully in her work, Anderson's practical association with overseas domestic workers has enabled her to learn and adopt a more agent-oriented approach to the problems of overseas domestic work. She has, for instance, begun foregrounding issues of livelihood (with O'Connell, 2003), documented resistance solidarity among overseas domestic workers of different nationalities in the EU (2001a), as well as acknowledged "hunger" as the driving economic factor for overseas domestic workers' labor migration (2001b, 29–30).

In contrast, Geraldine Pratt's nine-year collaboration with the PWC has been an academic rather than a politically active involvement in issues of FODW agency. In *Working Feminism* (2004), she tackles the problem of bringing feminist theory to practically engage with the daily struggles of overseas domestic workers. She shows, using Judith Butler's Foucaultian notion of agency, how these struggles are embedded in materialist processes within the global economy. In order to debunk critiques on the purely discursive and non-materialist undercurrents in Butler's notion of agency, Pratt highlights Butler's more "specific and concrete concerns" by citing what she identifies as Butler's "pressing question:" "what

4 That the network is based on self-help also means that it has been able to retain sustainability even after its funding ceased in 2002. The network is an expanded version of the network that Kalayaan, Anderson and others originally formed in the UK, with the additional membership of Solidar, a Europe-based international alliance of NGOs campaigning for global social and economic equality (see here Schwenken 2005, 6–9).

are the conditions under which agency becomes possible?" (ibid., 20). Identifying that Butler had left such a question undeveloped, Pratt proposes an insertion of a geographical perspective to understanding discourses more appropriately as "situated practices in particular places." As she argues, "if we understand discourses [in such a way], we can also understand agency and critique in more embodied ways" (ibid.). Learning much from her long-term collaboration with FODW activists in Canada, Pratt is able to identify issues of what she terms the "embodied pain of forced migration" to understand the conditions under which FODW agency nevertheless becomes possible. These conditions include those of familial duty and status which, she speculates, produces a "counter-discourse of responsibility … that may re-establish or maintain self-esteem and simultaneously empower [them] to demand higher wages" (ibid., 63). Related to the FODW's material(ist) existence and orientation, Pratt identifies another FODW counter-discourse that "emerges around the identity of consumer, as an individual with rights and freedom …" (ibid.). FODWs' desire for goods can lead them to challenge employers to comply with new minimum wage and overtime provisions in local labor laws. Further, Pratt (ibid., 64) shows how the conditions of possibility can also be found in the "border crossings between sites and discourses, by bringing one discourse into relation with another." Taking the example of FODWs' learned identity as exploited women in their time together at the PWC, Pratt (ibid.) explains how FODWs can use the very same discourse that underlies this exploitation, to their advantage:

> [t]he identity of exploited third-world women … is … introduced to Canadian employers within their homes...In some instances, domestic workers first role play in the safe space of the Centre. As [they] attempt to establish their rights as employees rather than family members or … immigrants, they … forc[e] employers to reconfigure their relations within the terms of labour relations, away from constructions of family or a type of liberal reading of immigration (which would see individuals entering Canada as lucky to be admitted into Canada, with no appreciation … of complicated webs of political economic relations and dependencies between Canada, the World Bank and the Philippines).

For Pratt then, these are examples of how "discourses are materialized … and … spatialised in ways that matter …" (ibid., 35).

Thus, while for Anderson, issues of agency have surfaced from structural constraints through actions against (political protest against overseas domestic workers' victimization) as well as with (to earn a livelihood through overseas domestic work) those constraints, for Pratt, understanding this double-sided character of agency (that is, simultaneously acting against and with) requires understanding agency in discursive and spatial terms. In this way, Pratt (ibid., 65) carves out that important theoretical space for agency—"making room" for it within structural analyses. While, in these ways, Anderson and Pratt's practical involvement in overseas domestic workers' struggles have done much to reveal latent agency in structuralist analyses, they remain unable, however, to provide insights into how this agency can be conceptualized and empowered. Understanding agency from the viewpoint of the conditions that make it possible, as Pratt does, enables an important beginning for the project of connecting structural with agentic analyses. However, it does not look into how such a connection might be conceptualized. For example, while the discourse and application of rights provides a way to empower the FODW, the lack of theorization on the relationship between rights and the limits of FODW agency renders the application of the rights discourse insecure in the long term (as discussed in Chapter 1). Moreover, the question of agency is still framed within strictly structural terms; agency is embodied in "situated practices in particular places." There thus remains a failure to honor embodiment as starting from, and with, the body rather than from/with the conditions of its existence. After all, as Pratt (ibid., 20) herself writes but leaves untheorized, it is the body that lives within, moves through and thereby creates the contradictions or double-sidedness "within and across discourses." For that central question of FODW empowerment, the question then is not what conditions make agency possible, but what conditions make it *capable*.

Careful to keep the important insights of power, and the politics of difference and mobility provided by the structuralist approach, the next section provides a conceptualization of how agency may be unearthed using a structurationist approach. This paves the path for the discussion on powering, or making agency capable, in the next chapter.

The Structurationist Perspective: Disembodied Agency

Goss and Lindquist (1995) argue that seeing the contemporary phenomenon of labor migration through a structuration lens escapes the determinism of functionalist approaches and corrects the absence of the agent in the structuralist approach. We are therefore given a richer understanding of labor migration, no longer reducing its social, cultural and political dimensions to purely economic determinants. They argue that labor migration is not the migrant/agent's articulation of demand and supply in an international labor market, nor is it their marginalization by inequality inherent in such processes. Rather, labor migration is a "complex articulation of individuals, associations, and organizations which extends the social action of and interaction between these agents and agencies across time and space" (ibid., 319). Drawing from contemporary Filipino international labor migration, they show how, in practice, these interactive processes, translate into "the complex of international and national institutions that transcend the boundaries of states and locales, linking employers in the developed or rapidly developing economies with individuals in the furthest peripheries of the Third World" (ibid., 335).

To capture the complexity of the interactive processes in the "migrant institution," Goss and Lindquist adopted structuration theory to allow them to integrate macro/structural and micro/agency scales of analysis in international labor migration. Goss and Lindquist argue that their approach to analyzing migration is different from other integrative approaches, like the household and social/migrant networks approaches (Massey 1990; Schmink 1984; Wood 1982), whose analytical categories are unable to "function as points of articulation between macro and micro levels of determination, or between structure and agency" (Goss and Lindquist 1995, 319). In particular they underscore the failure of these theories to keep the individual migrant, otherwise conceived as the agent, as the basic unit of analysis. The household approach takes the household as its unit of analysis, the needs, strategies, and actions of which respond and adjust to external changes and opportunities (Guest 1989; Rigg 1989; Stark and Levhari 1982; Wood 1982). But as symptomatic of Tacoli's analysis, mentioned earlier, no articulation of agency with structure in the household approach actually occurs, just the substitution of "the rational, calculating individual with a rational, calculating household." In contrast, they find the social networks approach more able to account for the individual and other social units such as the household, family and community. These units interact with each other through sharing information and other resources, thus forming social networks that can become migrant networks if the interaction is for the purpose of enabling and facilitating migration (Lightfoot et al. 1983; Massey 1990; Massey et al. 1987).

Like the analytical category of the household, however, Goss and Lindquist point out that social networks are not "coherent single-interest decision-making social units (Goss and Lindquist 1995, 345). As household members sometimes pursue their own individual interests over that of the collective family unit, so individuals and groups within networks may actually discriminate and compete against each other to pursue their own sets of interests. Furthermore, even when they become migrant networks, social networks are not specific to migration thus failing to fully identify the processes that lead potential migrants to pursue overseas employment. Migration is the sum of social interactions between agents (from migrants to recruitment agents, to immigration officials) and agencies (from recruitment agencies to labor trading states, to the World Bank) across time and space. Thus, theories that limit the analytical context of labor migration to household or informal networks strategies are unable to satisfactorily incorporate agency and structural determinations in migration (ibid., 327–31). In contrast, the migrant institution is based on a structuration process of migration in which structural properties of the migration system become recursively organized by agents and agencies across large distances and time, making migration both medium and outcome of these practices. In this way, migration becomes an institution or "an empirically identifiable social entity which incorporates both the intentionalities of individual agents and the structures of the social system (ibid., 332, fn. 1).

Abdul Rahman (2003, 2005) adopts this structuration perspective to provide an empirical understanding of the migrant institution in the particular context of overseas domestic work undertaken by Indonesian women. In her account of an Indonesian migrant institution in Singapore, she articulates the agency of Indonesian overseas domestic workers as structurally embedded in terms of their institution. As she observes, "although [overseas domestic workers'] actions are geared to the achievement of personal objectives, … their actions condition further social practices which are (re)produced … thus reconstituting the migrant institution in Singapore" (Abdul Rahman 2003, 144). She shows how, for Indonesian overseas domestic workers, this process of institutionalization allows "access to networks of interaction with other agents across time and space [that] helps them to mobilize rules and release resources in order to achieve their personal goals" (ibid.). Her identification of the agent's structural context from an institutional viewpoint is important in enabling a systematic articulation of the relations between agent and structure. The agent is thus no longer disembodied nor buried by the oppressive global economy. The agent instead can be viewed as "active subjects of migration" who draw selectively on institutional rules and resources in pursuit of their materialist interests, inevitably reproducing their agency through their migrant institution (ibid., 185). However, articulating the process of agency, in this way, does not necessarily lead to a migrant domestic worker's intended practice of agency:

> This is because the impact of the individual agency of situated actors is more local and has minimal impact on reconstituting more resilient structural features such as the inequities associated with the process of globalization and the politics of inclusion and exclusion of nation-states. (Abdul Rahman 2005, 182–3)

Thus for Abdul Rahman (ibid., 182), although possessing a degree of power and "capable of achieving their desired aims" through the migrant institution in Singapore, Indonesian overseas domestic workers ultimately possess weak agency. Much like the agency-based works discussed earlier, overseas domestic workers' agency is one that negotiates precariously through the more resilient and oppressive institutions, but that also becomes considerably weakened when detached from the migrant institution. As Abdul Rahman (ibid., 212) notes, "those … who serve their contracts almost in isolation, bounded by their employers' strict control…, may encounter serious barriers to the expression of agency and therefore empowerment."

To understand the limitations of Abdul Rahman's approach in explaining how the agent might be empowered, it is important to underscore the extent to which she applies the structuration approach to her analysis. Abdul Rahman uses the structuration perspective as a framework to "examine relations of domination and subordination within the migrant institution in Singapore" (Abdul Rahman 2003, 39). Specifically, she uses the structuration perspective to conceptualize agency in order to gain "insight into its impact on relationships of power between individuals and institutional power structures (op. cit., 185). She does not use it, however, as a framework for understanding the ontological existence of the institution itself. Nor does she use it for sufficiently theorizing agency with the constraints presented by "institutional power structures."

As earlier discussed, Goss and Lindquist have formulated the structurationist approach to be specific to migration movements. However, they do not formulate it as specific to the movements of those who have completed the migration process and have remained as migrants (Chapter 5). Likewise, Abdul Rahman does not question the need for specificity in understanding institutions as formed by specific actors with specific interests. She does not contrast the interests nor indeed, the socio-economic positions of those who have remained in overseas domestic work as different from those who are yet to undertake it. Overseas domestic workers are already migrants and are thus faced with a set of rules and resources that are slightly different in concept, but significantly different in practice, from potential migrants. Because Abdul Rahman's, along with Goss and Lindquist's, structurationist approach, is illustrated in the context of potential and returning migrants, they fail to sufficiently incorporate the transnational context of overseas domestic workers' agency and resistance as occurring not only between sending and host states, but also across host states. A transnational context, as demonstrated by the agency-based works in this review, is important not only for identifying the transitive location but also spatial and temporal possibilities of migrant domestic worker agency. On the question of the institutionalization of migrant worker agency, as in the "migrant institution," a transnational context can consequently provide a fuller understanding of not only how specific institutions form for the purposes of agents' survival, but also how they survive against other, more established institutions. These issues are taken up more fully in the discussion of an "FODW Institution" in Chapter 5. Suffice to stress here that while the structurationist perspective has given us an embodied agent, they have done so only partially, leaving the practice and process of agents' actions, including their aggregation—that is, their agency and institution—disembodied.

That agency remains disembodied in the structurationist approach is particularly evident in Abdul Rahman's treatment of structural constraints to individual migrant domestic worker agency. Her focus on "within" the institution does not allow a conceptualization of the agent in its wider structural context of unequal power relations in the global economy. In the migrant institution, the agent is empowered by resources and opportunities to control rules. The migrant domestic worker agent is therefore embodied by both possibilities and constraints inherent in their exertion of agency in, and as a result of access to, the migrant institution. Beyond or outside of the institution, however, overseas domestic workers' individual agency "has minimal impact." Agency occurs within the migrant institution but it is less clear if, and how, it occurs outside of the migrant institution. Thus, while Abdul Rahman theorizes the possibilities of agency through resource-use and rules-manipulation as a structuration process, she does not do so for the constraints on agency. She treats constraints as outside of (as in the case of abusive employers) or as distant from the migration institution (as in the case of more resilient structural features). This treatment of constraints goes against the grain of structuration theory that treats constraints as an intrinsic part of agency. In Abdul Rahman's work, this is particularly evident in her deviation from a structurationist approach to explain collective resistance, resorting instead to Foucault's notion of power and resistance. Her further understanding of constraints compares structural features with overseas domestic workers' individual agency rather than the structural feature or the aggregate of individual agency in the form of a migration institution. It is not surprising, therefore, to find that individual agency may indeed have less power than institutions. Here, Abdul Rahman conflates individual agency with the migrant institution. She fails to consider the migrant domestic worker's self-interest, and therefore orientation of agency, as intrinsically tied to structural/institutional processes beyond those of the migrant institution. Sukinah, one of the overseas domestic workers who Abdul Rahman interviewed, for instance, embarked on overseas domestic work in order to "lead an independent life" (Abdul Rahman 2005, 193).

Ultimately therefore, Abdul Rahman's undertheorization of constraints, and conflation of agency with the migrant institution, produces an understanding of agency as separate from, indeed terminator of, constraints. Agency goes on whether weak or powerful, but always despite constraints. In this regard, Abdul Rahman's approach shares much with the functionalist approach, both suffering from pre-given notions of the agent's power or *capability* to rationally and successfully partake in migration, and where thus power in the form of being capable to pursue personal goals is conflated with agency. Thus, as functionalist approaches conceive agents/actors as disembodied, so a structurationist approach leaves the process of their actions/agency, disembodied. This has further implications for Abdul Rahman's conception of power of the migrant domestic worker, on which I elaborate in the next chapter.

Conclusion

This chapter has reviewed the current knowledge on migrant domestic workers' agency. Since this agency is embedded in labor migration, it considered the analytical treatment of overseas domestic workers' agency within the functionalist, structuralist and structurationist approaches to the migration of overseas domestic workers. The review shows how current works on overseas domestic workers organized around these approaches, reveal, more than examine, issues of agency in the experience of overseas domestic work. In particular, the disembodied agents and agency of the functionalist and structurationist approaches, respectively, and the under-examined agent of the feminist-structuralist approach, results in a failure to identify the central role of capability in embodying the agent and agency on the one hand, and in enabling them, on the other.

Nevertheless, insights from agency-based works on the transnational context of migrant domestic worker agency as well as from the collaboration of structural feminists with FODW migrant rights NGOs have revealed a more embodied way of conceptualizing the agent, thus providing both a theoretical and practical premise from which to appreciate the central role that capability should play in currently analyses. This, together with advances made by the structurationist perspective on how we may theoretically conceptualize agency in migration for domestic work, enables the next chapter to elaborate on a structural-structurationist synthesis that can accommodate the inclusion of the central role of capability in current analyses.

Chapter 4
Beyond Rights: Embodying and Empowering Agency

This chapter proposes to unearth the "latent" status of agency within structuralist analyses, identified in the previous chapter. It does so with a view to synthesizing the structuralist and structurationist theories underlying the current analyses of migration for domestic work. I use insights from migrant rights NGOs' activities to illustrate the points of connection, demonstrating that it is at these points where the meaning of agency is embodied by the materialist meanings it holds for FODWs. These insights advance the conceptualization of power-exerting agents to empowered or capable agents. I use them to provide the outline around which assumptions underlying protection based on rights can be more fully informed with protection based on empowerment. As will become apparent in the following chapters, the synthesis between the structuralist and structurationist perspectives importantly provide the analytical paradigm for the study's proposed "capable agency approach," and more importantly, for the FODW's actual, practical empowerment.

Embodied Agency: From Power Exertion to Empowerment

As discussed in the previous chapter, a structurationist analysis of migrant domestic workers' agency as developed by Abdul Rahman, leaves the concept of agency disembodied. Here, I discuss the conflation of agency with power and its consequences, showing how the conception of power is thus also left disembodied. That is, while power may be exerted, used for resistance, or conceived of as central to "carving out of spaces of control" (Goss and Lindquist 1995, 333; Abdul Rahman 2003, 41–2), it is not clear to what extent it is effective in fulfilling these roles for the agent. Theoretically, the structuration perspective is useful in showing how agents "carve out spaces of control" through rules and resources. Curiously, however, Abdul Rahman conceptualizes power only in terms of rules and says little about the role of resources; she conceptualizes power with much focus on power relations and insufficient focus on power constitution. As she, herself, states (2005, 105), she uses structuration theory "to conceptualise agency [and gain] an insight into its impact on relationships between individuals and institutional power structures." But structuration theory gives equal importance to resources in the practise of rules in social interactions between individuals and institutional power structures. Abdul Rahman's over-emphasis on agency as something that individuals do/act/exert prevents her from acknowledging that it is resources that provide the material means to do so. Agency, as with power, is not just about doing, but it is also about having and being (discussed further in Chapters 5 and 6). Thus, while Abdul Rahman's (2003, 185, 214–15) agents are "capable of exerting "power"…[,] they remain disadvantaged and marginalized," and their resistance, ambivalent.

In contrast, this study seeks to depart from using structuration theory to explain how agency impacts on power relations.[1] Instead, it looks at how power impacts on agency. It takes one step back from looking at the power of the agent, to take up instead, the concern of how to empower the agent; specifically, how to make the agent capable. I want to look at how agents may be made capable of exerting power to overcome marginalization and succeed in resistance. In this sense, capability is not synonymous to the Foucaultian notion of fluid power,[2] but as a harnessed form of power specific to "situated practices in particular places" (Pratt in previous chapter)—in this case, Filipina overseas domestic work in, and across, Paris and Hong Kong. While the conceptualization of "capable agency" is the wider aim of the book, this chapter provides a preliminary discussion on why the concept of capability is integral to empowering or making FODW agency capable. I illustrate this point by using the example of the contradictory positions of FODWs rights-based NGOs in Hong Kong in their fight for rights, on the one hand, and for their livelihoods in overseas domestic work, on the other. Insights from these activities will provide examples of how a structuralist perspective can embody the structuration agent, and demonstrate the pivotal role that the structuration perspective plays in our conceptualization of empowering the embodied agent. The insights, in short, will provide the outline for a structural-structurationist approach to understanding FODW agency. Although I draw here specifically from the activities of FODW-based NGOs in Hong Kong, I will also draw parallels with those of the European RESPECT network and the PWC in Canada.

Despite its favorable working conditions in comparison to other labor-importing countries in the Asian region, the Hong Kong Administration's FDH employment policy has nevertheless come under attack, mainly from migrant worker-based NGOs and other associations which have burgeoned out of the activism of Filipino-based organizations in Hong Kong.[3] In 2000, the AMC[4]

1 In this respect, the present study shares much with Dales (2005), Mahmood (2001) and Parker (2005d) who assert that "we should discard the idea of agency as 'a synonym for resistance to relations of domination'" (Parker 2005b, 235).

2 Or indeed, a Foucaultian reading of power in structuration theory, as Abdul Rahman has done (2003, 41).

3 For a review of these NGOs see Sim (2002) and Swider (2006).

4 The AMC (Asian Migrant Centre) is an NGO in Hong Kong that acts as the hub for research on migrant workers in Hong Kong as well as in the greater Asia Pacific region. It advocates for rights as well as provides educational activities and support programs for the migrant workers. See http://www.asian-migrants.org/.

found that the lack of a government mechanism for monitoring contracts resulted in 15 percent of workers being underpaid, over 50 percent of workers being deprived of their mandated one rest day per week or statutory holidays, and around 9,000 subjected to sexual abuse, including rape (AMC and CMW 2001). In addition, the AMC (2001, 3) identified administration policies that promote racial, gender and class discrimination against FDHs. But it is the administration's imposition of the NCS or Two Week Rule, which the AMC identifies as the major cause of problems for migrant domestic workers in Hong Kong. The AMC (ibid., 2) asserts that this immigration rule "generally favours the interests of employers over those of [FDHs] as employers can dismiss migrants without justification while [FDHs] need to provide the proof of unfair treatment if they desire to win their case." This stance is supported by the umbrella NGO of the United Filipinos in Hong Kong (UNIFIL), which is composed of around 25 NGOs mainly run by FODWs (Law 2002b). In 1996, UNIFIL's campaign was joined by groups of domestic workers from other nationalities, forming the Asia Migrant Coordinating Body (AMCB).[5] This body became particularly vocal on the financial aspect of the abuse, underlining that

> an FDH is forced to contend with abusive employers for fear of greater loss to their livelihood ... While the employers can look anytime for a replacement, FDHs have to undergo ... a[n] expensive process just to be able to remain in Hong Kong if a labor or criminal case is pending. FDHs with labor cases are not allowed to work and are forced to borrow money ... to pay for visa extension fees and other necessary expenses to survive. (Asia Pacific Mission for Migrants (hereafter, APMM) 2003b, 29)

Although the response from the Hong Kong administration remains clear in the form of an unamended Rule, a sustained campaign for changing the NCS continues, involving the Hong Kong Committee on the Elimination of Racial Discrimination and the United Nations Commission on Human Rights (APWLD 2002). Moreover, the Administration's unamended rule did not deter the NGOs to curb the Administration's effort to cut migrant domestic workers' minimum wage in 1999. The AMCB (1999, 14–18), this time joined by the Hong Kong Council of Trade Unions, organized massive campaigns and mobilizations, asserting that migrant domestic workers were already burdened with

> the lowest [salary] for foreign workers in Hong Kong ... Even with the minimum wage for FDHs, a large number of Indonesians ... and other nationalities are ...

5 Namely the Association of Indonesian Migrant Workers in Hong Kong, the Friends of Thai group, the Far East Overseas Nepalese Association, and the Association of Sri Lankans.

> receiving wages below the minimum wage ... The decision to lower the minimum wage will further reduce the actual wage of many FDHs.

Although they were not able to prevent a wage cut, the group forced the Hong Kong government to reduce the wage cut from the proposed 20 to 25 percent down to 5 percent, thus claiming a victory of sorts (op. cit., 15).

As with RESPECT and the PWC, the issue of rights has been a central consideration in FODW NGO policies in Hong Kong. Hong Kong NGOs conceptually draw from, as well as actively contribute to the development of international human rights–based instruments such as the ICMR (for the AMC's adoption of this, see AMC 1995b). In 2001, a study of 20 major NGOs in Hong Kong found that almost half of them conducted seminars and training on rights education (AMC et al. 2001, 177). More recently, the AMC, along with the Indonesian Migrant Workers Union in Hong Kong, worked with the United Nation's Working Group on Contemporary Forms of Slavery to submit the case of "Forced labour and Exploitation of Indonesian Migrant Workers" to the United Nations Commission on Human Rights (Antislavery International 2003).[6]

Alongside their rights advocacy, however, has been the careful protection of their employment, which seems to provide a more appropriate understanding of rights as they matter to the FODWs. NGOs consistently protect their employment in Hong Kong through strong campaigns, on the one hand, and strategic silence, on the other. In a comparative study on the AMC and the Mission for Migrant Workers (MFMW), a member of UNIFIL, Weekley (2003) found that neither of their contrasting policies—the former based on a rather functionalist view of the "migrant entrepreneur" and the latter on the victimized migrant—were effective in promoting the rights of workers. Perhaps, however, the AMC and the MFMW have a different understanding from Weekley on how to promote rights for migrant domestic workers. Indeed those issues on which they have been particularly militant and strategically silent, but which do not seem to have a logical connection with their fight for human rights, gain sense when understood in the context of their interests in sustaining employment in Hong Kong. The more vocal issues include the campaign against the 1982 Philippine government Executive Order 857, the protest against the Aquino government in 1988, and the more recent massive wage-cut campaign led by the AMCB. The less vocal issues involve silence on issues that directly affect employment prospects, as well as on reintegration programs that underscore the primary importance of employment for FODWs in Hong Kong.

In 1982, the Marcos government's Executive Order 857 required 50 to 70 percent of FODW monthly earnings to be compulsorily channeled through

6 For the latest coalition and rights-based activities of the AMC, see http://www.asian-migrants.org/.

Philippine banks (MFMW 2000a, 4). The Order, deemed to "rob" the workers, became the reason for the formation of the UNIFIL alliance, then called United Filipinos Against Forced Remittances (Law 2002b, 212). Although UNIFIL did not succeed in abolishing the Order, it succeeded in removing the penalty clause, which meant in effect, that the workers could choose not to follow the Order without any penalties (MFMW 2000b, 3). In 1986, UNIFIL joined other groups to protest against the Philippine government's proposal to ban the entry of FODWs to Hong Kong. Then President Aquino imposed this ban as a means to curtail the increased cases of abuse among domestic workers in Hong Kong. Despite this noble cause, FODWs in Hong Kong were not willing to let the gates shut on their employment opportunities. Campaign approaches thus turned from the right to fair working conditions to the more immediate concern of the right and freedom to have work at all (Constable 1997, 207). In 1997, the AMCB's fight against the wage cut proposed by the Hong Kong administration again underscored the centrality of gainful employment for the FODW. As Law (2002b, 216) observed of the campaign:

> [T]hat [the coalition among different nationalities of FDHs in Hong Kong, along with the HKCTU)] came into being [due to the wage cut imposition] reflects the important perspective in Hong Kong of domestic workers as "workers," and attempts to build solidarity on this basis. It also reflects the financial imperatives of domestic workers themselves, who migrate to Hong Kong primarily for economic reasons.

Indeed, Law (ibid., 219) also found that some FODWs are now wary of the success of NGOs and their loud and visible activities "since they are seen to be jeopardizing their future employment."

Notwithstanding these fears from individual FODWs, NGOs have nevertheless kept silent on issues that could threaten employment. These issues include those of rights such as citizenship, unspecified working hours and gross structural inequalities in their employment sector.[7] The issue of FODW citizenship in Hong Kong is particularly interesting when compared to the situation in France. As Bell and Piper (2005) have observed, while "documented" in western liberal democracies includes access to citizenship, in East Asian societies, the status remains one of a strictly temporary contract. Even if contracts are indefinitely renewable, as in the case of Hong Kong, the option for permanent residence remains closed. The Immigration Ordinance[8] excludes FDHs from qualifying for permanent residence. While this does not mean that

7 Although the 1990s campaigns on maternity benefits for migrant domestic workers in Hong Kong were organized around equality of gender rights, it is important to note that the campaign was a response to changes made in the existing legal provisions for paid maternity leave for migrant women workers that would give employers the right to terminate contracts, paying off only a few month's salary (for details see Swider 2006, 125–7).

8 Section 2(4)(a)(vi).

the Ordinance has gone unchallenged, such as in the case of a FODW who has taken her case for citizenship to the High Court (*The Sun* 2003, 3), winning the case would certainly be the exception and not the rule.

For the NGOs, the key issue seems to be controlling the employment gates to Hong Kong, which could narrow if issues of citizenship were to be considered seriously by the Hong Kong government. As Bell and Piper (2005, 209) put it:

> For FDWs, the fact that the door is closed to [citizenship] does have one practical benefit—it means that there are more doors open to temporary contract workers. The only reason that so many FDWs are allowed to work in Hong Kong … is that all sides assume they will eventually return home. In Canada, by way of comparison, FDWs can become permanent residents after two years, but the government can afford to be relatively "generous" because it only lets in a few thousand such workers every year.

Similarly, NGO silence on long work hours, despite its obvious centrality as a source of abuse, points to an acknowledgment of market demand for 24 hours on-call service. With the advent of en masse and "cheaper" Indonesian labor, it becomes understandable why FODW-based NGOs would avoid the issue (ibid., 220). Arguably the strongest evidence of the central importance given to employment opportunities in Hong Kong, however, is the disjunction between the major NGOs' fight against structural oppression and its silence on challenging the inherent structural oppression in "domestic work" itself. As Constable has observed, "as long as domestic work is viewed as degrading … foreign workers will face little competition from local workers" (Constable 1997, 208). Indeed, this silence becomes all the more crucial in light of Hong Kong's integration with Mainland China, which increases the possibility of increased competition from numerous Chinese workers.

Further evidence to the importance of employment are major home-country reintegration projects, such as the Migrant Worker Re-entry Program (Migrant Savings for Alternative Investments), that depend on migrants' savings. The Re-entry Program is a long-term project of the AMC. The program encourages migrants to save and invest their earnings in the Philippines, in order to ensure a financially sustainable future upon their return. The AMC points out that one in five Filipinos in the Philippines depend on the income earned by Filipinos working overseas for their own livelihoods (AMC 1995c). The Filipino Migrant Workers Union (FMWU) notes how such programs provide "the most empowering experiences as they … enable migrants to return and remain in their home country" (cited in AMC et al. 2001, 198).

What these vocal campaigns, strategic silence, FODW-public indifference, and also more long-term focused projects point to, is that employment, and in particular, sufficient income from that employment, is the immediate matter for FODWs. Concerns of abuse in the workplace, and more generally, the lack of respect for migrant rights in the form of racist and discriminatory policies and practices in Hong Kong take secondary importance. In other words, FODW employment security in Hong Kong puts into context the political fight against discriminatory Hong Kong administration policies as second only to seeing Hong Kong as an economically desirable environment to earn a living, relative to that of the Philippines.

Providing support to this observation is a discourse pertaining to the "forced migration" in the Hong Kong NGO community. That is, "forced migration" of FODWs by successive Philippine governments through their neoliberal development programs (see here also, Chang 2004). In the early 1990s, the AMC (1995a, 52) had already began to identify the connection between FODWs' oppression and forced migration:

> There is no subtle pressure to accept difficulties or even "slight" abuses on pain of repatriation ... Their [workers] alternative is often less appealing—that of being sent home where there is no prospect for work.

The discourse of "forced migration" in Hong Kong became more clearly articulated when the MFMW released a set of magazine publications in 2000 and 2001, named *Migrant Focus*, for the readership of the FODW community in Hong Kong. Its titles alone provide a clear and chronological insight into the issues raised for FODW employment but also enslavement. *When the Only Option is Migration* (2000b) highlighted the Philippine government's inadequate national development strategy as the cause of deepening poverty in the country, and consequently of the increasing number of "willing victims" to migrate for precarious employment. In this view, the Philippine government is seen as "an adversary rather than a protector of its citizens ... peddl[ing] the notion that seeking overseas employment is a 'choice'" (MFMW 2001a, 5). Thus, the abuse and injustices experienced by workers are framed in the individual's lack of luck rather than as a structural responsibility of the government. *The Lucrative Business that is Labor Export* (2000a) discusses the Philippine government's elaborate set up of the state's labor export industry. This industry consists of the DOLE, POEA, OWWA and Philippine embassies and consulates worldwide[9] as well as private institutions, such as recruitment agencies. The MFMW argues that this labor-export system is geared to maintain the high numbers of overseas workers and thereby to

9 The Department of Labor and Employment (DOLE) has jurisdiction over issues pertaining to overseas contract workers. Within the Department are the Philippine Overseas Administration (POEA) and the Overseas Workers Welfare Administration (OWWA). The POEA oversees all issues pertaining to the deployment of workers while OWWA works closely with Philippine consulates and embassies to administer in-country services for Filipino migrant workers. These services include repatriation assistance, legal and counselling assistance, insurance coverage, and loan programs for housing, micro business enterprises, and education.

secure the "remittance business" of the government, which it uses mainly to repay international debts and to continue funding the system. *There's More to Migration than Money Problems* (MFMW 2001b) takes up the social costs of this economic focus on the gains of migration. It highlights the social problems caused by labor migration such as broken marriages, motherless families and vulnerability to trafficking, especially of poor women and children. The MFMW contends that these social costs are beyond the "personal" and are directly connected to the economic and political structures of Philippine society as a whole.

Finally, *Breaking the Cycle of Forced Migration* (2001a) highlights the role of migrant-concerned NGOs in bringing about political change not just in Hong Kong but also in the Philippines. This change is anticipated to break the cycle of forced migration through the establishment of labor unions and reintegration programs that guard the rights of workers to financial security. The MFMW argues that economic security will see the end of the need to migrate. The APMM (2003a) later extended the concept of "forced migration" to apply to other migrant domestic workers and their respective countries of origin, and in the particular context of global development (see here also, Luan 2005).

Indeed, the PWC, which has no official connection with these Hong Kong based NGOs, also ascribe the root cause of FODW presence in Canada to the political and economic crisis of their country of origin (see Pratt and The Philippine Women Center 1999, 39–40). Arguably also, an inverse approach to this concept of "forced migration" is the RESPECT network's fight for citizenship rights, which point to the importance of remaining in Europe for the purposes of retaining their livelihood. Alarmingly, however, politically powerful anti-trafficking policies largely ignore this concept of "forced migration," adopting instead, a definition that refers to forms of illegal recruitment such as through human trafficking. Given the relationship of the structuralist studies with anti-trafficking policies (Chapter 1), this oversight seems to be a reflection of the structuralist studies' use of issues of (uneven/under) development as a backdrop for, rather than as a crucial factor in, structural oppression. This important omission in current structuralist approach receives correction in Chapter 6.

Empowering Agency: Rights, Resistance and Capability

From the above account of NGO activities, it is possible to see how FODWs in Hong Kong "exert power," but also how the success of this, through NGO resistance, has been largely ambivalent. However, it would seem that the way they empower this exertion is evident not in their activities of resistance but in their fight to remain in employment in the host state.[10] This has both practical and theoretical implications. Practically, the transnational nature of their fight elucidates a more complete view of the constraints that embody them as including constraints of income-poverty in their home country. Theoretically, the issues silenced by NGOs in Hong Kong contextualize the FODW's practice of "self-discipline" (Constable 1997), hidden transcripts (Chin 1998), and multiple subjectivities (Parreñas 2001; Momsen et al. 1999) as a "trade-off" strategy; in particular, a trade-off to retain their *capability* to earn a livelihood. But whether silent or vocal, these NGO activities show how it is capability, and not resistance, that is intrinsic to power, and consequently, how it is empowerment rather than the advocacy of rights that can allow FODWs to act, resist, negotiate, and strategize. Resistance and rights advocacy is merely a functioning; a possible outcome of agency, and depends on the capability of agency to resist. It is through this premise that it becomes possible to understand not only what makes agency possible, but also what makes it capable (further discussed in Chapter 5).

Importantly, the NGO activities serve to illuminate, and define both the conceptual and practical parameters of FODW rights; rights cannot be achieved without firstly securing their livelihood opportunities. Chapters 6 and 7 provide a meticulous and narrative-supported account of how to understand these parameters using the concepts of agency and capability. The final chapter provides a discussion of how current efforts in empowering FODWs can work within, and beyond, these parameters.

Towards a Structural-Structurationist Framework

Given the limitations of current knowledge and approaches discussed in the previous chapters, with what framework do we begin to analyse these practical and theoretical insights, and their multidimensional relationships? I propose a synthesis of the structuralist with the structurationist approach, in which the structuralist approach is revised to include fuller acknowledgment and analysis of the situation in the home country. Despite myriad mention of "global" structural constraints, structuralist work has thus far largely focused on the situation within host countries. Integrated with the structurationist approach, this revised structuralist approach will provide a framework to better capture agency and capability in overseas domestic work. As will become apparent in the next two chapters, this will ensure that the agent's embodiment is fully accounted for, while keeping the agent as the basic unit of analysis. That is, as

10 Supporting this is Lan's (2006) comprehensive study of Filipina and Indonesian migrant domestic workers in Taiwan, and in which she observed that "most migrant domestic workers exercise overt resistance only when a contract's termination is inevitable" (2006, 55).

the structurationist approach reveals the dynamic, institutional constitution of FODW agency, the structuralist approach ensures that such a conceptualization is understood within the materialist constraints presented by the global political economy. Thus while, in this way, FODW agency is unearthed, a synthesized framework also allows us to see how their agency is embodied—as simultaneously constrained and enabled. To employ this framework is to ensure that discussions on FODW agency will necessarily involve an identification of her capability to overcome these constraints, and the associated issues of livelihood resources and security, human development and empowerment.

Conclusion

In this chapter, insights from migrant rights NGOs' political strategies to retain gainful employment in the host state at the cost of other human rights entitlements, such as that of citizenship, revealed a more appropriate understanding of rights as they matter to the FODW, both individually and collectively. For FODWs, rights seem to be more economic rather than politically oriented, ultimately defined in the context of a transnational livelihood strategy for the purposes of sustaining families and projects back in the Philippines. That on the one hand, constraints to the FODW thus extend to the structural impasse of poverty and un/underemployment in her home country, and on the other, her agency is ultimately oriented to safeguard against such constraints, reveal a more embodied use of agency by the FODW. It reveals, in conceptual terms, a structural-structurationist framework in which a revised structuralist approach that incorporates home-country constraints, provides the context of embodiment for the structurationist approach, while complementarily, a structuration approach unearths the latent agency buried in the structuralist approach.

This provides both a theoretical and practical premise from which to appreciate the central role that capability should play in analysis. Theoretically, it enables current analyses to more accurately define power in the context of capability rather than resistance; what the FODW can actually do and be to overcome oppression, and not merely her reaction against oppression. Practically, and as will become more apparent in Chapter 8, it provides current policy approaches with a theoretical basis from which to acknowledge that effective protection is based not only on measures against oppressive systems and structures, but perhaps even more importantly, on the very empowerment of agency in negotiating *with* its structures.

Having established, in this chapter, the centrality of capability for the understanding of agency in the FODW context, and having presented a structuralist-structurationist approach that lays the foundation from which the relationship between agency and capability can be conceptualized, the next chapter begins the detailed inquiry into this relationship by describing

FODW agency in its institutional context. Chapter 6 then builds on this by elaborating on the concept of capability in the FODW as empirically rooted in development-induced poverty of the country of origin, on the one hand, and as theoretically related to the concept of agency, on the other. This chapter has therefore provided the background from which the next chapter can explain the theoretical premise of agency in the study, and Chapter 6, the theoretical premise of capability. It is in Chapters 7 and 8 that the relationship between FODW agency and FODW capability receives full exploration.

PART III
Agency, Capability and Filipina Overseas Domestic Workers

Chapter 5
The FODW Institution

Chapter 3 showed how a structurationist approach is useful in revealing the individual agent and her central role in enabling the very existence of, or in "structuring," her immediate structures through a process of institutionalization. However, as discussed in Chapter 4, there is a need for a more specific and embodied usage of the structurationist approach to more appropriately account for capability in FODW agency. This chapter takes up the task of providing a more specific application of the structurationist approach. It presents a conceptualization of a "FODW institution" as a specific form of Goss and Lindquist's more general concept of the "migrant institution." In this way, it provides the backcloth for the conceptualization of FODW agency, onto which a conceptualization of FODW capability can then be juxtaposed in the next chapter, and finally related in Chapters 7 and 8.

I first outline Giddens' conceptualization of agency, structure and institutions. I then discuss how Goss and Lindquist have applied these concepts to explain Filipino international labor migration in the "migrant institution." This provides the theoretical background from which to conceptualize agency the "FODW institution." I will draw on data from the interviews to provide insight into how FODW's experience and reproduce this "institution." I discuss how this more specific application of the structurationist approach, in turn, provides a more appropriate concept of power in Filipina overseas domestic work. Finally, I conclude on the usefulness of this particular concept of power to highlight the importance but also precariousness of the FODW agent's participation in the institution, and hence raise issues of capability for the agent with regards to their continued participation in this institution.

Giddens on Institutions and the Structural

The "duality of structure" (Chapter 1) enables a conceptualization of structure as dynamically fluid, and as existing and operating in a "virtual order." Structure is at the same time composed of, and composed by, the daily recursive practices (which Giddens terms, "system(s)") of individuals (which he terms "actors/agents"). Being both medium and outcome of practices, structure is therefore both enabling and constraining of agents' actions (Giddens 1984a, 25). In this way, structure exhibits a dual character or a "structuration" process that reconciles the structure-agency dualism in social analysis, thus challenging uncritical acceptance of voluntarism or structural determinism (see here especially, Baber 1991, 229).

In their recursive practices, agents draw upon "rules and resources" to guide and enable their actions. Rules govern the conduct of social life. They can be conceived of "as techniques or generalisable procedures applied in the enactment/reproduction of social practices" (Giddens 1984a, 21). Resources are drawn upon "to make things happen, intentionally or otherwise" (ibid., 181). They are able to be reproduced in the course of social interactions (ibid., 15), and are of two types. *Allocative resources* "refer to capabilities ... generating command over objects, goods or material phenomena. *Authoritative resources* "refer to types of transformative capacity generating command over persons or actors" (ibid., 33). Together, and it must be emphasized, inseparably, rules and resources are intrinsic to the communication and justification of individual actions in social interaction, as well as to the exercise of influential power in social life.[1] When recursively reproduced by individual and collective actions, they become "institutions" (ibid., 375).

Agents operate at a certain level of "knowledgeability" that takes into account the opportunities for, but also constraints to, their actions within their given social institutions. Knowledgeability is "everything which actors know or believe about the circumstances of their action and that of others, ... including tacit as well as discursively available knowledge" (ibid.). Agents' "ability to know" operates within three dimensions of consciousness: while limited by *the unconscious,* where motivations for actions cannot be articulated, knowledgeability is effectively applied through their *practical consciousness,* and rationalized and verbally explicated through their *discursive consciousness* (Giddens 1990, 301). These latter two dimensions are informed by the agent's routine and holistic "reflexive monitoring" of their own and others' conduct; of their social and physical environment; but also of the very act of monitoring (op. cit., 5–7, 29). It is thus within these two dimensions that agents theorize and act upon the possibilities and constraints within their given institution.

Since social life is composed of multiple agents engaging with each other in an infinitely intricate matrix of actions, and therefore of knowledgeabilities, knowledge is not only constrained by unconscious motivation, but also by the simultaneous actions of others. Ultimately, then, any agent's intentions for their action are contingent to those of others, thus producing "unintended consequences of action" (ibid., 9–14). Here, Giddens' non-functionalist approach to social analysis becomes apparent. He asks that we understand "unintended consequences" by what agents *do* with rules and resources as separate from the outcomes of that doing—which may or may not be intended. Here, we are thus reminded that "agency refers to doing" and not necessarily to any achieved intentions through doing (ibid., 10).

1 Chapter 7 provides a more expanded discussion of rules and resources.

This has particular implications for Giddens' concept of power in the agent as intrinsic to agency (Outhwaite 1990, 65). He conceives agency or "doing" as basically the power "to do," and not in terms of power by whom. Power exists in action rather than in the actor. In structuration theory, therefore, there is no powerful and powerless—just power (see critique of this in Chapter 6). For Giddens (1982, 197; 1984a, 16), the important point to grasp here is that power/agency is inherent in every actor/agent, and because every agent's action impacts on another's actions, a "dialectic of control" occurs whereby agents become dependent upon one another's actions. Thus even those who may be in a physically/socially subordinate position, cannot be conceived of as "docile bodies" devoid of any impact from the actions of superior others.

As with the individuals who possess them, power/agency, and their institutional articulations through agents' recursive practices, exists in temporal-spatial contexts. The symbolic and physical manifestation of this time-space context are *locales*; socially constituted by its own sets of rules and resources (Giddens 1990b, 301) and where agents of various social positions, but also from various contexts of time-space, congregate (see here also, Chapter 1). Interaction is embedded in irreversible or finite time of the individual's lifespan (Giddens 1984a, 35). This does not mean, however, that "action" stops along with the "death" of an individual's body because social practices are situated in routine, or "reversible time." This includes the *durée* or day-to-day routine reproduction of social practices, and its institutionalized forms in the *longue durée* of institutional time, which continues to endure beyond an individual's existence (ibid., 34–7). Thus as individuals and their life paths in their *durée* are bounded in, and then unbounded from, institutions across time and space, social interactions continue on, "stretch[ing] across time-space "distances" (ibid., 127). "Structure" continues on fluidly across time and space, binding and reproducing these temporalities, and ultimately institutionalizing them. As institutions "stretch," annihilating space through time, the spatial limit of co-presence is transcended, enabling social interactions to occur across time and space where co-presence is unnecessary. Giddens (see especially 1984b, 127) terms the capacity of individuals and institutions for regularized interaction despite time and space distances, "time-space distanciation." It is the binding and reproducing of interactions through, and despite of, temporal and spatial constraints that individuals and institutions come together to form institutions, or structure, that span even larger stretches of time-space. As a general rule, the longer established the individual or the institution, the greater its capacity to span across larger stretches of time-space, and the greater her/its power for transformative capacity (op. cit., 259).

In sum, for Giddens, institutions are both composed of, and constituted by, complex and regular interactions among "knowledgeable" agents who strategically draw from "rules and resources" that are produced through their very interactions, and in which these interactions can stretch across time-space distances (see Figure 5.1).

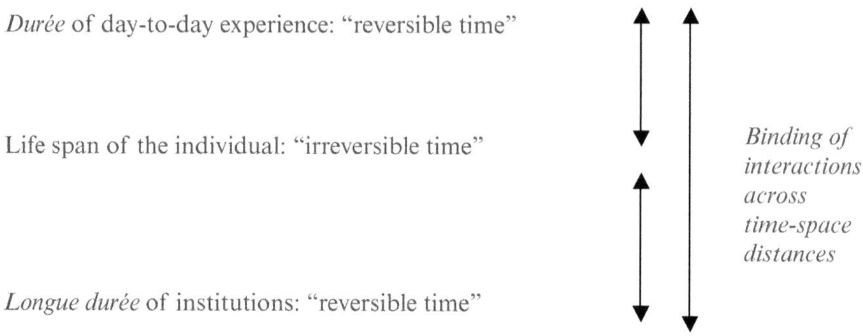

Figure 5.1 Structural properties of institutions

Source: adapted from Giddens 1984a, 35.

Through this concept of institutions, it is possible to see how structures are produced, as well as self-reproduce. This insight is instrumental in allowing the separation of the ideological from the practical dimensions of "structure." Thus, in practice or in action, there are many structures interlocking with others (see also here Chapter 7). In contrast, multiple structures can be regarded by agents in their totalities based on ideologies, or as Giddens (1984a, 24) terms them, *structural principles*—"the most deeply embedded structural properties, implicated in the reproduction of societal totalities." Rather than being an all-encompassing and static concept, structure then, is generic, multi-dimensional, and can be broadly conceived of as social systems which exhibit structural properties. Structure then becomes involved in, rather than the defining factor of, any explanatory framework requiring a structure-based discussion. Giddens (ibid., 185) provides the following "structural concepts" that may be involved in these frameworks:

- *structural principles*: principles of organization of societal totalities;
- *structures (or structural sets)*: rule-resources sets, involved in the institutional articulation of systems;
- *structural properties:* institutionalized features of social systems, stretching across time and space.

In the context of the FODWs, *structural principles* can be understood as the all-encompassing and static structure espoused by the structuralist perspective of patriarchal global capitalism, or in functionalists' terms, the global economy. In this chapter, this perspective is re-contextualized as *one of,* as opposed to *the one* structural feature of the FODW experience. *Structures or structural sets* in the FODW context are discussed in Chapter 7. The theoretical task of this chapter is to elaborate upon another *structural property*, which is equally embedded in the FODW experience, and in so doing, highlight the crucial agentic involvement in such structures. This structural property is the "FODW Institution." To discuss the "FODW institution," it is first necessary to understand how Goss and Lindquist adopt Giddens' concept of the institution to their analysis of Filipino international labor migration.

The Migrant Institution

Goss and Lindquist's structuration approach, discussed in the previous chapter, has already provided an empirical conceptualization of Giddens' highly abstract notion of institutions in the form of a "migrant institution." Here, the discussion will show how in particular, this institution is actually formed to become a social entity for Filipino migrants. Building on Giddens' notions of institutions, Goss and Lindquist (1995) take the knowledgeable agent as their basic unit of analysis. They take as their point of departure the "potential migrant" (ibid., 335) in the locale of Manila, where they interact with other agents, organizations and institutions involved in the operations of international labor migration from the Philippines (ibid., 340). These other agents and organizations include friends or family/kin members with knowledge of, or contacts, overseas, namely recruitment agencies; the Philippine state; and formal and informal associations who have interests in exploiting rules and resources within the "migrant institution." Within this institution, however, "the capacity for [self-interested] action is differentially distributed according to knowledge of rules and access to resources …" (ibid., 345).

According to Goss and Lindquist (ibid., 341), the agents who could be said to possess the highest capacities are those who are "established" enough to take the role of "gatekeeper" to resources desired by the potential migrant. In the migrant institution, these can include anyone who has contacts overseas or who has contacts with those who have such contacts, from friends and family members to current employers, local politicians, and recruitment agencies. To make contact, for example through telephones or email, usually involves transcending time-space distances, allowing "established" agents to network with others despite temporal and spatial limitations. Notwithstanding such power imbalances in the institution, potential migrants, by virtue of the "dialectic of control" in social interaction, can still act strategically to impact upon these positions of influence. Take for instance Goss and Lindquist's (ibid., 342) account of Evelyn Lopez's story:

> After separating from her husband ten years earlier, Evelyn Lopez needed to find income beyond her small earning from washing clothes. Eventually, she became a daily housekeeper for Eva Garcia, a government employee in the provincial capital. After several years of working for the Garcia household, she was able to approach Mrs Garcia about her dream of working as a domestic helper in France. Although Mrs Garcia would lose her housekeeper, she felt obliged to assist Evelyn

> by recommending her to a friend in a travel agency; Mrs Garcia even agreed to loan Evelyn the travel expenses, which would exceed 50,000 pesos. The employer-employee relationship in this case was long established and close enough that Evelyn could ask such a favour and be trusted to repay the cost.

An "institutional" understanding of migration importantly recognizes the sets of actors that constitute a given institution. Thus, not only is the agent foregrounded, but also those other agents of different socio-economic and political positions (for example, Evelyn and Mrs Garcia) who draw upon the same sets of rules and resources within the institution. This has led Goss and Lindquist to better articulate the role of the Philippine state, not as a passive structural fixture that recruits and exports labor, administers migrants' welfare, and legislates for their rights. Rather, the sending state is seen as an active participant that ensures the operational continuity of the institution in the *longue durée*, particularly as its very existence depends on the resources it can reproduce through its labor-export earnings (ibid., 338–40). An institutional understanding of Filipino migration has also led Goss and Lindquist to comment that employer and recruitment agents/agencies have largely been absent in analyses of international migration. Employers and recruiters play a crucial role in reproducing the migrant institution by providing and organizing the employment opportunities for the migrant worker at the particular level of the *durée* (ibid., 337).[2]

Giving primary importance to the agent/agents in institutional analysis produces a more apt and nuanced structural framework in which agents can be seen to exist in the *durée* or daily life, and of which they are knowledgeable participants in practical and discursive ways. This is particularly important for the current study as much is known of the "structural principles" that govern the experience of the FODW, but little of the structural set in which FODWs monitor themselves and their and others' actions, and in which they thus base their strategies for actions. As Cruz and Paganoni (1989, 100–101) had found in their study of 466 Filipina migrants and potential migrants:

> The respondents hardly understand themselves in relation to the nation as a whole. The government program to reconstruct the national economy certainly does not dictate their decision. Neither is it understood as contributing to the economic well-being of the host country. The national and international dimensions [that is, structural principles] are simply overlooked by respondents who are caught up in a process of fleeing from oppressive economic situations, or acting out their own desires for something different and more liberating.

While these findings may indicate limits to knowledgeability, it is important to recognize that it is in fact the migrant's actions, more particularly the extent or

2 Although, soon after this comment was made, the recruitment aspect was explored further through the concept of an "immigration industry" by Hugo (1995, also 2004).

capability of her intended actions, which face constraints. The issue for migrants is not about whether or not they know or aware of these constraints. Rather, it is whether their actions are capable of overcoming constraints, whatever this may entail for her intended purpose. Take, for example, my conversation about the idea of oppression with Gudilia, a respondent in Paris, as a demonstration of the ordinary FODWs' perceived irrelevancy of "having to know" about structural processes that impact on hers and others' situations.[3] After discussing issues of export labor, women and poverty in the Philippines, and how they can be seen as linked to migration for domestic work, Gudilia indicated that she spent little time thinking about these kinds of issues and more time thinking on what she was able to do *despite* them. As she explains,

> … "naapi" ["oppression"] … doesn't apply to me. Well, because if you're being oppressed, why would you let it happen? That's just up to the individual for goodness sake. Right? … With regards to the Philippine Government, in a sense, well I guess it's pretty hard to look after a country that is over populated. And I guess we have a very unfair system in the Philippines that runs on nepotism … So I guess this is why there are so many educated people in the Philippines with no employment opportunity. So this is also why some of these educated people just end up going abroad. I know so many here who have finished degrees in engineering and teaching, like that. Even though it's just domestic work, at least it's clean, decent work. And anyway, they seem not to regret that they ended up here. They're actually happy. So this is why people take risks and chances. But I can't really see this as oppression. Then again, I suppose if you really think about it, then yes, you can say that the Philippine government oppresses because it doesn't provide for its people. When all is said and done though, I don't think there's any point in blaming this and that because I really can't see anything changing with the Philippine government. Ultimately, it's up to the individual to do what they can with other opportunities presented to them. (Gudilia, Paris)

From an "institutional" perspective also, it is possible to understand just how the individual may morally justify their pursuits of opportunities to go overseas, even when this may involve "illegal" elements such as the use of fake passports. In an institutional setting, the presence of other institutions, both formal and informal, can provide support to the potential migrant. Thus, as Rodriguez (1996, 23) has pointed out, "[p]recisely because core institutions (legal, religious, local, governmental) support this migratory strategy, … [m]igrants may see their … migration as extralegal, but not necessarily criminal."

As knowledgeable agents in both practical and discursive ways, FODWs concentrate and build from rules and resources that are available for them to draw upon and manipulate. Limited though these may seem, Evelyn, for

3 Note my use of "ordinary" here in the sense that there are, of course, those few FODWs who are part of NGOs, and/or who may have had previous education and work experience relevant to understanding the global economy and its effects.

instance, could use her relationship with her employer to access resources such as a travel agent and a loan for her intended purpose to work in France. Gudilia provides a discursive rationalization of this in terms of doing the best with opportunities that come along. For the FODW agent then, constraints become relevant only if they restrict actions for intended purposes. Otherwise, knowledgeability is oriented towards opportunities rather than constraints.

While Goss and Lindquist are able to reveal the complex interactions within the migrant institution, and explain its existence as driven by knowledgeable agents, it is necessary for the current study to extend this structuration perspective more specifically to FODWs who are actual, rather than potential, migrants living the *durée* in a new locale. That is, as migrants with "situated practices in the particular places" (Pratt 2004, 20; see Chapter 3 in this volume) of host countries/locales. This allows the analysis to focus on the practices particular to the FODW situations as a separate set of institutionalized practices that exists alongside the migrant institution, but also with the more established, and hence more powerful, institutions of national and global economies (Goss and Lindquist, 1995, 336). In this sense, this "FODW institution" shares much in common with Abdul Rahman's theorization of an Indonesian migrant's institution in Singapore (Chapter 3). However, I build on Abdul Rahman's approach by not only providing an account of agency processes particular to FODWs within a migrant institution, but also by explicitly identifying issues of capability in the very practice of their agency. This allows a richer insight into what constitutes power for the FODW, not in terms of agentic exertion or resistance (previous chapter), but more specifically in terms of her ability to manipulate "rules and resources" around constraints, for intended ends.

The FODW Institution

Between the structuralist argument that migrant domestic workers are largely invisible, and the functionalist and structurationist approaches that call for the due visibility of agency in the workers, what remains unarticulated is the emergence of overseas domestic work as a FODW practice of increasing permanency in the contemporary global economy, albeit in the relatively shorter temporal context. In the particular context of FODWs, the *longue durée* of overseas domestic work has continued to exist for more than 30 years presently, and as current prognosis would have it (Chapter 2), is expected to continue long after the life spans of those who undertake overseas domestic work as life paths or "careers" (Giddens 1984a, 149–50). In this temporal-spatial context, it is possible to see how the practice of Filipina overseas domestic work has gained a degree of "solidity" across time and space. In other words, a structure or institutionalized form.

The FODW Institution: In Concept

In the FODW institution, the recursive and bounded practices that give systemic form to structure occurs as a result of the FODW's reproduction of day-to-day domestic work responsibilities in households overseas, and her interaction with relevant individual and institutions across time and space. This process can be understood as the institutionalization of Filipina overseas domestic work via particular sets of structural properties that bind together across time-space distances. Daily domestic responsibilities occur in "reversible time," repetitively and infinitely reproduced in the *durée*. The longer-term purpose of doing such work implies the life path of the individual. In the case of FODWs, this may be understood as "being a domestic worker;" or more specifically, as a means by which to fulfill her life role as mother, daughter, sister and/or a wageworker in gainful employment, and from which then, capitalist aspirations can be achieved. In contrast to domestic work responsibilities, the domestic worker and all the other life roles attached to her, has a more finite amount of time (until her life ends through death), and is thus located in "irreversible time." The further extended time-space character of institutions relevant to her situation include those of other institutions such as the migrant institution, state institutions, and global institutions, but of which the FODW institution displays the most directly relevant access for FODWs. Because institutions continue to operate with other life cycles or reproduced generations, they exist not only in the supra-individual or *longue durée*, but also in reversible or recursive time. This is shown in Figure 5.2, which builds on Giddens' diagrammatical expression of how temporalities in these interactions are bound together (see Figure 5.1).

Figure 5.2 Structural properties of the FODW institution

The broader time-space context of the FODW institution relative to the individual FODW is best demonstrated by the binding and unbinding or dropping in and out of FODWs from the institution through multiple contracts. Multiple or new contracts may be undertaken by different, or new generation kin/family members, or even through cases of those who hold one long term, or a series of various terms of contracts. Contracts can be formal. But they can also be informal, as in the case of undocumented or "illegal" work undertaken separately, within, or as an interim to, documented work. Other research have observed this characteristic of participation in Filipina overseas domestic work (e.g. MFMW 2001a; Piper 2003; Tacoli 1996a), but it is useful to draw here from the interview data to provide study-specific cases (Table 5.1).

Most of the respondents have plans to eventually and totally "unbind" from the institution by returning permanently to the Philippines, after they have saved enough to live a financially secure life there. As Ana in Hong Kong put it,

> My plan in the near future is just to be able to save enough to afford to go to Canada ... I know that the situation of a domestic worker is better there, especially that after two years, one has a chance of becoming a Canadian citizen ... In the longer term, I wish to accumulate enough capital and return to the Philippines to put up a business ... Even though the Philippines [government] is not very good to us, I still ... love our country and I want to retire and die there ... as soon as I have enough, [I'm going] back home. (Ana, Hong Kong)

On the other hand, Helena and Melanie who are currently undocumented, plan to eventually obtain legal residence in France and eventually unbind from the institution by living off their retirement pensions in France.[4] Here it is important to note that Melanie and Helena can make these plans by virtue of their particular locale in Paris, whose state institution, unlike that of Hong Kong, enables eventual citizenship. Helena and Melanie see citizenship in France as providing continued access to the FODW institution during and even after their lifespan has ceased. In particular, they see French citizenship as providing a mixture of allocative and authoritative resources which they identify as absent in the Philippines (and which similarly, are unattainable for

4 Some can unbind earlier if they marry a national, such as in the situation of a couple of ex-FODWs I met in Paris. Even then, however, some may choose to continue domestic work for extra income. As one Filipina married to a Frenchman there informed me, "Even though my husband has his own business, we have three children and I still do a little on the side so I can send some money to my family in the Philippines." In these particular situations, they may also move out of domestic work into factory and other low-skilled service jobs such as shopkeepers and production workers which require minimum competency in the French language. I did, however, meet one Filipina who was competent in the French language and who held a white collar job in a publishing company. Before her present job, and before she had met her French husband, she was a domestic worker (Diary RPC, 28/09/03).

FODWs under the "rules" of locales like Hong Kong). Thus, as Helena and Melanie tell of their plans:

> I don't have any plans to go home. When I get my papers, I will just bring my children over here ... So I will just continue to do domestic work for the rest of my life. This is the only way I know how to keep supporting my children ... Right now, what's important is I earn and save as much as I can because you never know what life is got ahead for you. If I should die earlier than expected, I want to die knowing that my children will be able to live on something. (Melanie, Paris)

> If [the Philippine] government ... helps the poor, well, do you think people would leave the country? ... I would never have had to leave my children ....You can stop Filipinos leaving, if you ensure they can earn a proper income there ... [F]or me, I have no more trust in our government ... That's why ... I will just visit the Philippines from time to time. I don't mean to be a traitor to one's own country, but what can you do if it gives you absolutely nothing in return ... if you grow old there ...—if you are poor there and you have no savings, how can you survive? Here, if you grow old, you have a pension. You are given something to live on whether you have had an education or not, rich or poor, as long as you've worked. I could always bring [my children] over here ... So [my children] ask "when will you stop that work?" "Well of course until I am alive!" I would respond. (Helena, Paris)

In contrast, Red in Hong Kong, plans to stay bound to the institution:

> ... I have friends doing domestic work all around the world. So it's my plan to move on after I've experienced Hong Kong. I have a friend in Paris, Germany, Austria, Switzerland, Italy and my Godmother is in the US. So I hear a lot about the lifestyle in these places ... It's better that I go home on vacation from time to time [rather than return permanently to the Philippines] and keep earning until I can because it's very hard to get a good job or to make your money last in the Philippines ... (Red, Hong Kong)

The respondents' use of rules and resources involved in these decisions are further discussed in the next section. What is important to note here is how together with the international experiences of domestic work, from Saudi Arabia to Paris; from Taiwan to Hong Kong and so on (Table 5.1), the above narratives provide insight into the nature of the locales in which the FODW institution operates. To elaborate on this, it is instructive to refer to Goss and Lindquist's (1995, 333) summary of how Giddens sees the relationship between social action and locales:

> All social action is contextual and is defined by a specific presence-availability, or potentiality of actors and institutions to come together, and by a specific "bundle" of allocative and authoritative resources. A given locale may then be specified by the rules and resources involved in social action and interaction within it.

Table 5.1 Characteristics of individual participation in overseas domestic work using FODWs' experiences in Paris and Hong Kong

FODWs*	Formal contract	Informal contract	Formal/informal
Alili	Series of 2-yr contracts in Hong Kong currently amounting to 17 yrs in overseas domestic work.		
Amity	One 2-yr contract in Hong Kong.		One 2-yr contract in Hong Kong: undertook "illegal" work within, and in contravention of, this contract.
Ana	One 2-yr contract so far in Hong Kong.		
Bernie	Eleven mths into a 2-yr contract in Hong Kong.		
Delia		Worked for several employers for 1 yr, and currently for 1 employer for 1 yr so far in Paris.	
Ellen	One long-term contract in Hong Kong.		
Felise	Two short-term contracts in Kuwait and Bahrain, respectively.	Continuing to work for 1 long-term employer in Paris for 8 yrs so far.	
Gemini	One short-term contract in Taiwan; 1 yr into a 2-yr contract in Hong Kong.		
Gudilia	Two consecutive long-term contracts in Paris.		
Helena			One long-term legal contract in Saudi Arabia; now undocumented worker in Paris for 3 yrs so far.
Indiana			Undocumented worker for multiple employers for the most part with 18 yrs in Paris; recently obtained papers, continuing on the same work.
JB			Undocumented worker for the first 5 yrs in Paris; recently obtained papers; continuing on the same work while undertaking some part-time work.^
Jinky	Seven mths into a 2-yr contract in Hong Kong		

Table 5.1 cont'd

FODWs*	Formal contract	Informal contract	Formal/informal
Lani			One short-term contract in Saudi Arabia; currently looking for undocumented work in Paris.
Lilia	One 2-yr contract in Hong Kong; planning to apply for a contract in Oman.		
Loveley	Undertook 2 contracts in Hong Kong but she terminated them early; she then completed another contract for the third time.		
Melanie			Worked under 5 abusive employers in Kuwait before settling on a 2-yr legal contract there; now working in Paris as an undocumented for 1.5 yrs so far.
Michelle	Four-yr contract in Saudi Arabia; then a series of 2-yr contracts in Hong Kong currently amounting to 19 years in overseas domestic work.		
Mila			Undocumented worker for the most part of 19 yrs in France; last 3 yrs of which is in Paris; recently obtained her papers and continuing to do the same work.
Minda			Documented worker in Lebanon; undocumented worker in Paris for 16 years; obtained papers in the last 5 years and continuing on the same work.
Nene			2-yr legal contract in Saudi Arabia; currently undocumented worker in Paris for 4 yrs so far.
Red	A few weeks into a 2-yr contract in Hong Kong, after her first contract was terminated by her employer after 10 mths.		
Sally			Undocumented worker for the most part of 10 years in Paris; recently obtained papers and continuing on the same work.
Virgo			Came to Hong Kong as a documented worker, but on arrival, was notified by her recruitment agency that her employment had been terminated. Currently taking the matter to court. While waiting for the outcome, undertaking part-time^ work.

* See Appendix 1 for individual biographies.

^ See Appendix 1 for notes on undocumented part-time work in Paris and Hong Kong.

From this, it is possible to understand Manila, Paris and Hong Kong, but also Canada, Saudi Arabia, Taiwan and so on, as specific locales with their own respective sets of rules and "bundles" of resources. It is also possible to understand that as locales, these host societies provide the setting within which the Filipina overseas domestic work social system coheres and reproduces in co-presence with others specific to the locale (such as employers, recruiters and state institutions), but also in virtue of achieving presence-availability, to, from and even across these locales.[5] The latter point is particularly indicative of the transnational characteristic of institutions; that "potentiality of actors and institutions to come together." However, because Goss and Lindquist interpret locales as "specific ... or physically bounded places," this notion of a transnational institution is left unexamined. Locales, they argue "are thus both arenas of interaction and containers of social power and may be conceived as the 'place' at which the individual literally faces the institution ... and where [their actions] connect[s] with social structures." But, without an explication of locales as taking a transnational, indeed a "translocale," form, they prevent understanding of power as transcending "physically bounded places." Further, although they acknowledge Giddens' notion of "time-space distanciation," Goss and Lindquist confine the application of this notion to social interaction, thereby preventing an identification of the institution as itself possessing such a capacity.

The FODW Institution: In Practice

Whether structuralist, functionalist or structurationist, the accounts of Filipino labor migrants' decisions to undertake overseas work form an implicit consensus. Filipinos are motivated to emigrate out of economic necessity, and more particularly as a result of unemployment, underemployment or insufficient wages in the Philippines. Given the context of a global economy that is conducive to the globalization of service work, and given also the context of an established immigration industry, it follows that a "migrant institution" would form, based around the desires of millions of individuals to obtain low-skilled service, albeit better-paying, work across the world. However, those who have achieved their potential as migrant domestic workers continue to draw upon rules and resources with more specific interests; this time, not the interest to obtain, but to retain overseas domestic work employment. Responding to this

5 Although this is not demonstrated in Table 5.1, it is worth noting that the possibility exists for FODWs to seek work in either Paris or Hong Kong. During fieldwork in Hong Kong, after Paris, a couple of participants suggested that they would keep their options open of trying to "get into" Paris since the pay was so much better and so, worth the risk of working undocumented. Just before I left Hong Kong, one of the participants had approached me for contacts in Paris.

specific interest, overseas domestic workers thus form a sub or co-institution: the FODW institution.

Although overseas domestic work employment for actual migrants can be said to have occurred through successful use of the migrant institution, this does not necessarily result in a successful time in the job. This presents the central problem for the FODW as their overseas employment depends on a successful time at work. FODWs thus concentrate their social practices and their use of rules and resources to ensure continued employment by institutionalizing practices that mitigate cases of unemployment and/or deportation. Because the FODW institution extends from, or is borne out of the migrant institution, the focus of this institutionalization process shifts from potential migrants to actual migrant workers. Successful retention of overseas domestic work becomes the focus of actions and is emulated by other FODWs, even to the point of enduring abusive working conditions as part of the strategy for remaining employed. In the institutionalization process, FODW social practices reinforce survival strategies and the social relationships on which they are based, by forming or joining networks. These networks are accordingly based around concerns of the FODWs and is composed of the wider Filipino migrant network/institution, including Filipino-based NGOs, sympathetic employers and other individuals, supportive state institutions (both by the sending and receiving states), and other human-rights based NGOs in their locales. Ultimately, the social practices existing among the actors within these networks, become routinized for the purposes of securing overseas domestic work employment, and with overseas domestic work thus becoming "structured by specific modalities of interaction, and [continued] access [to it,] ... conditioned by the operation of specific rules and mobilization of resources" (Goss and Lindquist 1995, 336). Thus is Filipina overseas domestic work institutionalized.

At this point, it is important to bring in narratives about two different experiences, and locales, to illustrate how the rather abstract account of this "institutionalization" can be seen to be transnationally/locally shared by FODWs. Here, the narratives of Sally in Paris and Loveley in Hong Kong can provide useful case studies. Sally and Loveley show the trajectory of their experiences from their decisions to undertake overseas domestic work in Manila, to their experiences in their respective host societies, and finally, to their future plans. In the following excerpts it becomes clear that while the "bundles" of rules and resources differ between Paris and Hong Kong, the process of routinization of social practices for the purpose of retaining, indeed, institutionalizing, overseas domestic work employment remains similar. Thus, as Sally's and Loveley's narratives show below, whether they are undocumented (for example, in Paris) or documented (for example, in Hong Kong), a similar process of institutionalization facilitates their use of specific rules to remain in employment, and mobilization of resources to retain employment (albeit not necessarily with the same employer, or in the same locale).

Sally (Paris)

I ... applied at the POEA ... to get a job as a caretaker [in Taiwan] ... You had to be a high school graduate to qualify for this [so] ... I had to get a fake diploma made ... Before I was about to sign the contract, I bumped into a recruiter for Paris. But this was an illegal recruiter. She provided the visa and everything ... "you see" she said, "if money is what you are looking for, you may as well go to Paris." It was the sound of money. She said, "you may as well give me the down-payment you are putting down for Taiwan, so you can use it for your visa and airfares to Paris, and then you can just pay the fee later once you are already working in Paris."

[When I got to Paris, I worked for Jewish-Tunisian employers] ... I was with them for four years ... all was fine for the first two years. They fulfilled everything that was in our agreement. But once they had my passport, that's when things went wrong. I gave it to them because they had promised to help me get my papers. Then they started taking money off my wages to pay for the administrative costs involved. But two years later, still nothing had happened. So I asked to be given my passport but they wouldn't return it ...

[*Sally ended up in the streets, surviving on "part-time" work*]

One day I heard from another [FODW] that my ex-employer was saying bad things to people about me; that I was mean to her children. This enraged me because it was not true. So I rang her and asked why she was spreading lies about me. She apologized and responded that she had to do so because the children were missing me and the only way she knew to wean them off was to tell them bad things about me. I said this was unacceptable, and that I wanted all those things to which I was entitled but for which I was too timid to ask when in her employment. So I said, "Madame, give me the money you owe me and my passport, and forget everything!" She then had the nerve to say, "I have nothing to pay you. I have nothing to give back to you" ... I was enraged. How can she think that she could treat me like that? So I said, without thinking and because by this time it became obvious that I had nothing more to lose, "ok hold my passport, keep your money. I'll see you in court!" And I slammed the phone down.

Now, I was undocumented and I knew very little about the city, yet I just threatened a diplomat with legal action. So I just walked and walked [to think things through] ... I was also sick at the time. I had just come out of the hospital a few days before because I had gotten sick from overworking for them [6] ... Luckily, I bumped into an employer for whom I was working part-time. She saw how down I was and asked me what was wrong? I told her what happened and she said "oh you must not lose hope. Call me tonight and I will give you the name of an organization that can help you with your case." She ended up making an appointment for me with

6 Although Sally was undocumented, she was able to avail herself of the Aide Médicale Etat service available for undocumented foreigners in France. This is a medical insurance provided by the state for access to medical care including examinations and prescriptions. Access for those who have lived in France for less than three years, however, is limited to hospital care.

the CCEM. And so it began; three lawyers looked after my case for three years. I received so much support from the French public and the people around me; from providing supporting statements to the courts, to a nice encouraging word here and there …

I won … at the labor court, but I was not satisfied with all the judgment. They didn't acknowledge all the other exploitation I experienced. So I decided to appeal. I even wrote to Madame Chirac and her office wrote back an encouraging letter to me! I said to them that it wasn't a question of money. I was interested in real justice. I ended up winning the appeal … The employers were not imprisoned but were made to pay a fine and compensation … I am now a legal worker here so I will work until I receive my retirement pension …

I became an organization within myself helping Filipinas here in difficult situations. You see because of my successful case, I got exposed to the legal and social world here and learned how to use them to help those of us in need … I can say that I have been able to achi*eve and do more things being here, overseas …*

Loveley (Hong Kong)

When I was 17 and still at school, my mother died and my father could not financially support my college education. So my aunties, who were here in Hong Kong, decided with my father that I should come here to work. [They already had an employer waiting for me]. I knew that I had to do domestic work, but I had absolutely no training in the area. So when I got to Hong Kong I found it really hard because apart from me not knowing how to do the work, I did not get along with my employer at the time … I really did regret coming here then. I didn't realize it would be so hard … So I went home without finishing my contract and I remember I did not want to ever come back to Hong Kong …

I decided I would then apply for Taiwan. But my aunties suggested coming back to Hong Kong … They offered to pay for my agency fees and this was an offer too good to refuse. Plus, my father suggested that perhaps Hong Kong was safer for me because at least … my aunties were here. So I agreed. [But again I did not like my employer and she was paying me below the minimum wage, so I went home and] … did not finish my contract … .

The third and last time I came to Hong Kong, however, was solely my decision. By this time, I was more confident with both the job, and myself. And I felt like I could do it … well this time. [Again, my aunties had arranged an employer for me]. I was also happier with my employer and I can say now that I don't have any regrets this time around … my last employer and I got along quite well. We would talk all the time about current affairs and things like that. But this is because she knows the employer-employee relationship. Not like those others who see this relationship as a master-slave one.

… But you see, this depends on yourself to ensure that you get a better employer. You can always leave bad ones and look for better ones … You have to know what is in your contract before you sign. The Embassy, the Labor Court and other offices too can help you understand bits of the contract you might need clarifying. You have to know that you are protected by the law …

> I'm going home soon. [*At the time of the interview, Loveley was in Bethune House*[7] *because she had overstayed her contract*]. I was hoping that I could secure another contract before I go home to avoid dealing with the recruitment agencies] I would like to come back again but I'm not sure if I can because there's now an age limit to work here … But I will keep applying in other countries. I will be doing this job for a while yet … .
>
> Oh there are many things I have planned with my father and brother, including investments at home. Because we don't really have any dependents, we can all put our money together and save for our future. In the short term, I want to apply for another contract in another country because when I went back the last time, I had a job there in the Philippine for nine months as a salesperson but I was really very bored and the pay was very low. So because I think it's better here, or in another country, then I see no reason why I shouldn't keep exploring …

Sally and Loveley demonstrate how rules are made, bent, but also broken by the FODW if the rules pose an obstruction or end to her gainful employment. Their narratives also show how resources are mobilized through networks. From the beginning, Sally was prepared to forge a high school diploma and choose a path of "illegality" to obtain higher-paying employment. Later, she retained employment by continuing to work without papers in "part-time" work, and by winning a court case against her employers that eventually led to a legalization of her status. Loveley, on the other hand, showed how it was possible for her as a domestic worker to leave her employers and terminate her contract. Later, she overstayed her contract in order to secure continued employment and to bypass recruitment agency fees. As with Sally, she was able to draw upon resources from informal networks that enabled her to obtain a job. Unlike Sally in Paris, however, Loveley was not so fortunate in securing her continued employment in Hong Kong. Despite this however, she does not plan to stay unbound from the "institution" for long.

Perhaps the making, bending and breaking of rules is more succinctly demonstrated by Virgo's story of an FODW she knew in Hong Kong:

> I know of someone who was imprisoned for one and a half months after surrendering herself, and was then deported back. Her visa had expired when she had not yet finished putting her four children through school. She needed a few more years of work here [and so she overstayed]. So after about three and a half years of being an ["]illegal["], and she had finally put all her children through school, she surrendered herself [to the authorities]. (Virgo, Hong Kong)

This type of control over their employment situation is often overshadowed by accounts privileging the power of state institutions, recruitment agencies

7 A shelter ran by the Mission for Migrant Workers. See Appendix 2 for more information.

and employers over that of the FODW. As evident from this story, and also from Sally's and Loveley's narratives, the "established" agents are not only the employers, and/or the people smugglers, the recruitment agencies, and state institutions (such as, immigration/labor/social affairs departments and courts in the case of the receiving states and Philippine consulates/embassies), nor even the growing body of human/migrants' rights NGOs. They can also be FODWs themselves. "Established" FODWs, by virtue of their long-term presence-availability in the locale have been able to accumulate knowledge and resources to, in turn, recursively redistribute them for the purposes of ensuring the continued operation of a FODW institution. In her narrative, Sally showed how she had become one of these FODWs, while from Loveley's narratives, her aunties could be said to take this established role.

There is an implicit importance in acknowledging the central role the individual FODW plays in her employment situation. For whether it's Sally's socially active approach to helping her compatriots stay in the institution, or Loveley's more personal insight into how to ensure success in the institution by choosing the right employers, it is this rather subversive process that enables the learning and thereby appropriated use of rules and resources by other FODWs. The Sunday gatherings of Filipinas in the parks of Paris and Hong Kong (and other host locales) may be more than just a gathering of "poor third World women domestic workers." They may indeed serve as the central generator that powers the FODW institution.

The excerpts above also demonstrate that employers use FODWs to further their own interests, but are also used by FODWs for *their* own interests. Thus, as the case with Sally, she used her employers as a means to obtain her papers, and when this did not work out, she used another employer to help her out of this problem. Other respondents in Paris also used their employers as a resource. JB was able to obtain her papers in only five years with the help of her employer,[8] Helena's employer is currently supporting Helena's application for documented status, and Gudilia was able to borrow a large sum of money from her employer to build a house in the Philippines. Likewise, Red was able to use her employers to remain in Hong Kong to find other employment. As she recounts:

> When [my contract] was terminated [by my employers] … I said to myself that I wouldn't get angry (at them) but that I would try to understand … After I was made to cut my hair shorter because I looked too pretty, I thought, ok that's fine. Then … one day … [she] said, "what's wrong with you?! Why is it that you just sit there quietly when I get angry at you?" I answered "because Ma'am I understand. I have to understand you. I am your "helper" and moreover, you are probably pressurized

8 At the time of interview, French immigration law required a minimum of ten years of living and working in France before such applications are considered. With currently stricter immigration rules, this is no longer the case.

> at work." I understood too that she was having trouble coming to terms with how her last husband left her for another woman, and at the same time, that her current husband and I got along well with each other … Anyway, when all else failed I held onto this relationship, and kept a positive attitude. So I spoke to them and asked them to at least support my immigration application so that I do not have to go home to reapply from the Philippines all over again. And they obliged. (Red, Hong Kong)

The point here is that although the dependency on the employer is certainly obvious, this dependency is not total but one that is governed by "the dialectic of control" where relations of domination-subordination operate reciprocally. There is a strong element of connectivity between employer and employee (see also the story of Evelyn Lopez above). Ellen's account illustrates this, showing in particular, the importance of her position within the employers' household:

> What I don't like at the moment is trying to discipline my wards. Now that they are grown up … they are hard to discipline. I want them to study because education is important. I tell them this like a second mother, but they don't listen. I really do care for them and I get personal here because I basically brought them up and I get really upset if they play *mahjong* with their friends instead of study. This is really unacceptable to me because we really do value education in our [Filipino] culture. I get so angry that sometimes I threaten to leave them for the Philippines. The parents agree with me and they also threaten the kids that I will leave if they don't study hard. So I suppose if they study hard and I continue to be happy with their treatment of me, then maybe I may even stay with them until my old age. (Ellen, Hong Kong)

Gudilia's experience with her employer in Paris also demonstrates this interdependent relationship between employer and domestic worker:

> Sometimes I would be in the kitchen and my sister would be visiting, and Madame would be bored because she has no one to talk to, and she would come in and say "Girls, let's talk." [*hearty laugh*] And my sister would jokingly whisper in Tagalog, "gosh she's a disturbance." Then Madame will say "OK stop working." And we'd say "OK Madame." And we'd just talk about anything and everything … Sometimes, when I have a personal problem, I'm a little more quiet than usual. But Madame is very nice and she can sense this, so she asks me if everything is OK. But if I stay quiet and don't respond, she knows to give me my space and she kindly says, "oh OK, maybe you're just tired." She also speaks to her children to respect me. She reminds them of how lucky they are and tells them that they must be more understanding of my situation since my own children are far away. (Gudilia, Paris)

Thus, employers may indeed treat the domestic worker like family for their own interests (see, for example, Anderson 2001c; Cox, Rosie and Narula 2003; Lan, Pei Chia 2001), but so does the domestic worker (Adams and Dickey 2000; Momsen 1999a).

Moreover, employers may treat FODWs as "commodities" in terms of being a part of the furniture to be moved and sold along with houses (Constable 1997). However, Mila's reflexive-monitoring and up to date knowledge of rules, beyond relationships with employers, to those of legal significance to her employment situation (in this case the recent work-hours amendment to labor laws in France), allows her to negotiate her employment situation on her own terms:

> I've noticed that work rules are changing for the better now. For example, if one is a live-in worker, you had to work 10 hours/day. Now it's down to eight hours/day. But not all employers follow this rule. However, one should try to negotiate with the employer anyway. When you negotiate you have to empathize with your employer's situation first of course. Like for instance, with my current employer, because they are a family I can see why they would need more work done. Soon, however, they will be selling the house and I have chosen to stay on because the new owner would like a housekeeper too. And I am comfortable where I am. I have my own space—own bathroom and kitchen in the house. And seeing that the new owner is single, then I suspect it will be less work and I can ask for the 35-hour week. (Mila, Paris)

FODWs also mitigate dependency on the employer through their knowledge of the translocale/transnational property of their positions. When asked if they would consider working anywhere else, almost all respondents in Hong Kong, except those who have worked there for more than ten years and have consequently achieved an acceptable level of financial security (Alili, Michelle and Ellen), expressed a desire to obtain work in what were considered to be better places/locales. Destinations which had reputations for better salaries and/or better conditions included Western Europe, North America and some parts of the Middle East like Oman. Other destinations in Asia such as Singapore and Taiwan, were, by contrast, negatively compared to Hong Kong for their unfavorable immigration and labor rules towards overseas domestic workers.

Correspondingly, the respondents in Paris were resistant to moving anywhere else, except perhaps to London, which seemed a "romantically" favored destination by some. Lani, in particular, having just escaped from her Saudi employers who were on vacation in France, was planning to look for work in London:

> When I was still in high school, I would hear good things about London. I had a classmate who ended up marrying someone form there and she said it was very nice there … I've always wanted to go to London. (Lani, Paris)

Another FODW ("Lolita"), who had recently escaped from her Middle Eastern employer with whom I spoke at a church gathering, said that she was using Paris as a transit to London. She informed me that she had left her employers not because they had been abusive, but because she wanted to work in a place where there was more freedom to move around outside of the house. "Of course," she said, "the pay is also better in London" (Diary RPC 28/09/03). However, as informed by the other Paris respondents, it is doubtful that after a little more time in Paris, they would still consider leaving. Indeed, Lani, also a recent escapee, has since found a stable job and remains in Paris (personal correspondence 16/09/05 with Nina Tuazon of the Euro-Pinoy Association). As Nene and Sally put it:

> I came across an acquaintance who is now in America, and when she heard I was planning to go to Europe, she advised me "do well in Europe. Take care of your job there because what you can earn there, you can't earn in America." On top of this, she said that France paid the biggest salary in all of Europe. (Nene, Paris)

> No [I wouldn't work in] ... Hong Kong; long hours, low pay, bad treatment. Especially now that I'm free in France. I'm free.
>
> From what I know, especially when I attended a domestic workers' forum in Belgium, in 2000, many said that out of all Europe and elsewhere in the world, we are lucky to be in Paris. Domestic workers in other places have to endure longer hours, bad treatment and lack of privacy. (Sally, Paris)

FODWs thus also consciously and strategically make the move to locales where the rules are more conducive to ensuring their *gainful* employment, or more specifically, to ensuring access to the allocative resource of employment. She leaves a "bad" and/or low-paying employer for another, as best demonstrated here by Mila:

> I worked in Monaco for most of the time. I came to Paris after spending six months with my daughter in Canada, because it was easier to find work here. I had promised my employers in Monaco that I would be away only for one month so I lost that job. I left my [very first employers] ... in Nice. I left [Nice] for Monaco because it was almost double pay in Monaco. (Mila, Paris)

But she is also able to mobilize authoritative resources, including at a transnational level to secure her employment situation and/or to improve it. Indeed, Lolita was using the resources in the church group in a similar way. Having transcended locales by achieving presence-availability through migrant networks or the migrant institution, FODWs continue to utilize them when employment situations/opportunities are too constrained by their respective locales. This is perhaps best exemplified by the mixture of formal and informal contracts that FODWs undertake within and across locales (see Table 5.1). In these ways, therefore, the FODW institution is one which is regularized by the workers themselves. Admittedly, regularization does not take the conventionally understood legal form, but the nevertheless active participation of the FODW in regularizing the work so as to enable her to go on as intended (discussed in detail in the next chapter), provides new insights to the current understanding of oppressive and constraining structures of state and global institutions as the major power-holders in the regularization of such work. As Goss and Lindquist (1995, 334) have observed, "structural constraint does not operate above or outside the individual but operates through the individual in the cumulative everyday and strategic decisions and actions that they make."

To summarize the concept of the FODW institution, I juxtapose it here with Goss and Lindquist's "migrant institution." Where they have used as their basic unit of analysis, the "potential migrants" who "employ their understanding of the rules of interaction and exploit their access to allocative and authoritative resources within the migrant institution to obtain overseas employment" (Goss and Lindquist 1995, 335), the current study takes as the analytical starting point, the FODWs who employ the same understanding and application of rules and resources, albeit this time, within the "FODW institution," to *remain in* overseas employment. The "potential migrant" from a bounded locale, becomes the potentially independent migrant in a translocale. The implication of this for the conceptualization of power in FODW experiences is discussed below.

Power and the FODW Institution, Power in the Institution

As the "potential migrant" domestic worker becomes the overseas domestic worker, there is a change in the nature of her dependency. She becomes less dependent on the Philippine state and the recruitment process/agencies, and more on the employer and the host state. In some instances, the FODW gains absolute independence from the recruitment agencies and the Philippine state. This is largely due to having paid off her recruitment fees successfully, thus enabling her to keep her earnings mostly for her own use. Moreover, absolute independence from her employers and the host state is also achievable once she has gained citizenship, as in the particular case of Paris, or once she has worked and saved enough capital to return to the Philippines to live a financially secure life. However, this kind of success depends on her continued presence in the FODW institution. In this sense, overseas domestic work employment can be understood as an incubator of her independence, or the elemental resource on which her potential for independence, and hence empowerment, hinges. This point is further discussed in Chapter 7, while the expansion of their choices or freedoms in terms of "capabilities" in the FODW institution is discussed in Chapter 8.

It is important to note for now, the bias towards authoritative over allocative resources not only in Goss and Lindquist's interpretation of Giddens' "institutions," but which also seems evident in others' interpretation of Giddens' notion of "agency" such as in Abdul Rahman's study (Chapter 3).[9] Because of the focus on agents and agency in the explication of the constitution of

9 Other notions include those of Long (1992) and Clegg (1989). Their notions of "effective agency" and "strategic agency," respectively orient understanding of resources about how effective or strategic agency orientates itself against more dominant social actors.

institutions, current structurationist discussions on resources have largely focused on its authoritative effects on other agents , such as through domination and subordination. This in turn has resulted in a failure to more fully account for allocative resources; more particularly, material resources or capabilities required for daily functioning. In particular, they have left unacknowledged the important issue of access to these types of material resources in cases where agents exist in a context of low income or allocative resource-poor societies. Although the FODW, by virtue of her migrant status in developed settings, is arguably in a context of allocative resource-rich societies, the fact that she could very well be undocumented and/or on a short-term contract, keeps that status insecure. This insecurity can lead to her being in an "employment" situation where employers and/or recruitment agencies can coerce her to endure slave-like working conditions, thus limiting, if not altogether denying, her access to allocative resources. Thus, until she has managed to obtain legal residency and thereby secure legal entitlements and access to allocative resources in the rich societies, or worked long enough to accumulate sufficient savings that in turn enables her to access allocative resources in the Philippines, she remains confined to a context of poor resource access. Sally's experience, as discussed earlier, is perhaps most exemplary of this vulnerability. Without the allocative resources in the health, justice and welfare systems of France, she would not have had the power to take her employer to court; nor helped her compatriots; nor secure for herself a retirement pension. Her independence hinges on the FODW institution, which is an institution that exists only in the allocative resource-rich (trans)societal context.

Giddens (1984, 256–62) himself provides little consideration of the possibility that allocative resources may be controlled beyond any dialectic resolutions, or are in such short supply that they become a significant factor in the analysis of agency. This leaves the question of how this myopic focus on authoritative resources impacts on the efficacy of agency for transformative action—in the case of FODWs, from dependence to independence. Also taking into consideration that "institutions are not themselves knowledgeable nor can they act … " (Goss and Lindquist 1995, 334), I proceed in the next chapter to explore and develop a more nuanced understanding of agency, and its capability for transformative action.

Nevertheless, the structural understanding of the FODW situation in the form of institutions presents a marked improvement in current analytical approaches. As a specific set of rules and resources kept in operation by FODW agents' interests in overseas domestic work employment in the *longue durée*, the FODW institution gives FODWs' experiences of overseas domestic work solidity/permanency/structure. As it gives systemic and solid form, and therefore tangible visibility, to those fragmented forms of power in hidden transcripts, and discourses, it transcends the structurally reductive approaches that "bury" such forms of power. The FODW institution reconciles the dualism of structure and agency in current analyses of FODW experiences by showing how agency creates structure through institutionalization, and how thus structure is both medium and outcome of agency. Furthermore, an institutional form enables comparability—and complementarity to other institutions, especially the current global and state institutions, which have achieved greater time-space distanciation, and therefore power, due to their extended existence. This has implications for the long-term project of FODW empowerment as embedded in the continued time-space distanciation process of the FODW institution itself. As the FODW institution continues to evolve in time-space, operations of power within it will continue to be harnessed by an increase in the number, but also forms, of "established" agents who become increasingly knowledgeable of the rules by which to exploit more resources within the institution. Indeed, this process seems to have already begun; in the three or so decades of the institution's existence, overseas domestic work employment continues to flourish, along with a hoard of human rights and migrant workers' rights-based NGOs, and of researchers. Like Loveley's experience here, which alludes to the "replacement migration" of older FODWs who have gone back to retire in the Philippines by younger FODWs (Chell-Robinson 2000), researchers who are offspring of Filipina migrant workers who have taken up jobs in the domestic services sectors of the destination country (such as myself and Rhacel Parrenãs) reflect not only the transgenerational property of the institution, but also increasing knowledgeability within it.

Conclusion

Drawing from Giddens' structuration theory, Goss and Lindquist have been able to reveal the intimate interdependence of migrant worker agents within broader time-space contexts in which their strategic actions take place, to form "their institution"—the migrant institution. Drawing upon the same sets of theoretical concepts, the current study has likewise attempted to demonstrate their applicability to FODWs in Paris and Hong Kong, a particular set of Filipino migrant workers, in "trans"locales. In doing so, the study has extended the migrant institution, in which agents' main purpose is to *obtain* access to the allocative resource of overseas employment, to that of the FODW institution, in which agents' primary purpose is to *retain* access to the resource.

This specified context provides the basis from which to gain a more complete understanding of power in Filipina overseas domestic work. As discussed in Chapters 3 and 4, an unspecified account of the process of institutionalization produces an understanding of agents' use/exertion of power that says little about the greater role of power to enable such an action in the first place. Indeed, Clegg (1989, 218) observes that "organised networks of power," such as the FODW institution, "are an achievement of power, not its generative principle." The question then, is how the agent remains powered so as to be capable to use/exert/act. As shown in this chapter, the specific understanding of the migrant institution in the form of the "FODW institution" enables an understanding of not only exertion of power by FODW agents but also the role of power in enabling their agency to "institute" overseas domestic work. It has also been shown that this role is conditional to the FODWs' access to allocative resources, which in turn, exists in a transnational/locale context. This insight is important in revealing another dimension to questions of struggles in FODW experiences as not only about resistance or "struggles against what" (that is, against authoritative resources that take the form of structural constraints), but also "struggles for what" (that is, for allocative resources). Through the concept of a FODW institution, it is possible to see how the struggle for allocative resources occurs through individual FODW's knowledgeable negotiations within the institutionalized actions and interactions of their connected interests used to maintain control over these resources. These allocative resources, as will become apparent in the remaining chapters, serves as means or functionings for the FODW to gain and maintain capability in achieving her valued ends.

On the whole then, the focus on the attainment, but also retention of, the migrant worker status enables a clearer view of the transnational/locale and differing capability context for the FODW's exercise of agency. In this way, it also highlights the need to see the distinction between "potential" in terms of the "capability" required to reach that potential, and "attained" in terms of actual functionings or exercise of agency within the FODW institution. This distinction clarifies that it is in the institution (attained capabilities) that FODW agency can function/work/be practiced.

But much is still to be said about how FODW agents fare against constraints within, but also out of, the institution. Looking at the issue of constraints will require incorporating feminist structuralist analyses that foreground FODWs' structural disadvantage. This structuralist inquiry, and its role in explaining the notion of "capability" as the theoretical framework that informs a theorization of constraints in FODW experiences, is discussed in the next chapter.

Chapter 6
A Capability Approach to Agency

The previous chapter provided a structurationist account of Filipina overseas domestic work. This allowed a conceptualization of FODW agency as both constituted and constitutive of her most immediate structural context, that which I termed the FODW institution. In extending the analysis on FODW agency, this chapter examines constraints to FODW agency, both within and outside of the FODW institution. It does so by drawing from the feminist structuralist perspective on overseas domestic work along with structural constraints caused by underdevelopment in the country or locale of origin (Chapter 3). Indeed, what about those who remain outside of the FODW institution? An explication of Sen and Nussbaum's notion of the capability approach (CA) in this chapter provides the theoretical ground from which constraints in relation to the FODW institution can be understood, and from which a fuller account of constraints at the structural level to FODW agency becomes possible. In this way, this chapter provides an account of the "structuralist" in the structural-structurationist framework outlined in Chapter 3.

Firstly, I look into key components of the CA with particular relevance to agency. These components consist of a family of concepts: capability, capabilities, functionings, freedom, well-being, quality of life, and agency. However, because, as I show, the particular concept of agency in the CA is economic-centric and insufficiently developed, I fuse the CA concept of agency with Giddens' sociological concept of agency in his structuration theory. This in turn allows discussions to identify a complementarity between Giddens and Sen and Nussbaum's concepts of agency that is useful for explaining constraints to agency. Drawing on respondents' narratives, I then show how a fuller understanding of structural constraints in FODW agency rests on a foregrounding of the development-induced constraints raised, albeit left unelaborated, by the feminist structuralist approach. It also shows how this fuller understanding both informs, and is informed by, a conceptualization of capability in FODW agency. Finally, I conclude with a discussion on the role of capability as crucial to the practise of agency by FODWs.

The Capability Approach

The CA is a comprehensive theoretical body that has grown since the 1990s, and is popularly associated with the Human Development school and policy section of the United Nations Development Program. As mentioned in Chapter 1, the

CA foregrounds the humanist aspect of development, which was previously and totally understood from an economistic viewpoint. Rather than assess standards of living through income, goods and utilities, it looks at how people actually live, and at their freedom to choose how to live. While many others have contributed to further developing the CA with its original theorist Amartya Sen (1980; 1983; 1984; 1985a, 1985b; 1987, 1990; 1992; 1993, 1995, 1999; 2003; 2004), I particularly consider, in this study, Martha Nussbaum's contributions (1988, 1992; 1995; 1998; 2000, 2003; 2004, 2006). Gasper (2002; 3003) and van Staveren (2003) note how Nussbaum's more explicit concept of the CA is an essential complement to Sen's relatively abstract notion. Nussbaum provides a more satisfactory account of agency in the CA through her "richer" theory of the person on meanings, actions, and emotions (Gasper 2003, 9–10).

Essentially there is strong philosophical agreement between Nussbaum and Sen on the evaluative value of the CA as "an account of the space within which we make comparisons between individuals and across nations as to how well they are doing" (Nussbaum 2002, 122). Between Nussbaum and Sen, the individual, or agent, as the basic unit of analysis of this capability space, can be understood not only in terms of Sen's "choosing and rational individual" but also Nussbaum's more socially embodied individual. Having said this, and despite the primary importance Sen (with Drèze, 2002; 1999) gives to the role of human agency in enabling the larger paradigmatic change from viewing development as not only the means but also as ends to a person's freedom to lead a valued life, agency remains largely untheorized in the CA (Crocker 2004; Gasper 2002; Menon 2002). In the next section, I attempt to improve on its theorization by fusing it with Giddens' theory of agency. To prepare the discussion however, there is the need to elaborate on the CA through an explication of its key concepts, with particular emphasis on their relevance to the analysis of agency.

Functionings is the concept on which the CA rests. Functionings are various realized or achieved components of a person's way of living. Working for wages and spending of income are examples of functionings. In light of the diverse and complex content of components within a person's life, Sen suggests that functionings be seen as particular sets. A set of various functionings make up a person's life. Thus for example, a FODW has a particular set of functionings specific to her life paths, as different to say, my particular sets of functionings as a researcher. A person's *capability* is the encompassing set of alternative functionings sets that she could or has the freedom to attain. Sen calls this *a capability set*. Thus when speaking of capability, Sen sometimes refers to it as the set of life-paths attainable for a given person. Note that whereas functionings are attained aspects of how a person lives, capability is the potential aspect of how a person *could* live. Or put another way, while capability refers to the ability to do various things, functionings refer to what is actually (being) done. For evaluative purposes, the CA thus identifies the range of life options that agents have (capability set) and their agency in terms of what they actually do and achieve (functionings).

To explain agency processes in a capability set, Sen proposes to look at agent's actual objectives vis à vis their personal *well-being.* For Sen, a person's well-being consists of achievements she has reason to value. To measure well-being, Sen proposes that we examine what agents can do in terms of what they are free to achieve—*agency freedom*, and what they can be in terms of how much person well-being they have attained—*agency achievement*. With such information, it then becomes possible to understand what is meant by having capability, the extent to which it can be practised, and its meaningful purpose. Having capability can be understood as the freedom to choose or in Sen's terms, an agent's *well-being freedom*. While Sen has contextualized his notions of freedom in the CA in both its positive and negative aspects (discussed further in Chapter 8), Gasper (2002, 25) points out that the "CA has always been oriented towards positive freedom, the possibility to do." Thus, with respect to freedom but also constraints, capability can be more specifically understood as "the extent of an agent's positive freedom" (ibid., 4). Finally, the meaning and goal of having capability can be seen to lie in the agent's practice of agency and well-being freedom on the one hand, and possession of agency achievement, on the other, which on the whole, constitute the agent's *well-being achievement* or *quality of life*.

While in this way, Sen provides a neat and clear categorization of the doing and being aspects of the agent, much critique has been leveled at his "reasoning," hence rather utilitarian, agent, and more generally, his insufficient picture of the human being (see especially ibid., 20–24). Sen writes of the human concepts of sympathy and commitment to explain how agents relate to others. *Sympathy* refers to an agent's feelings of well-being brought about by others' well-being achievements. *Commitment* refers to an agent's support of other's achievements even without such impacts on their own achievements. These concepts, however, say little of how others, including institutions and structures impact on the agent and her agency freedom.[1] While Nussbaum's richer concept of the individual helps to humanize the rational chooser, she does little more than comment on Sen's unnecessary distinction between agency and well-being—that is, she sees his distinction between functionings and capability as sufficient (Gore 1997; Nussbaum 2000). Nor does she depart from seeing practical reason as the main site of agency (Robeyns 2005).

In the CA then, a concept of agency retains a largely economistic flavor. Importantly also, the analytical importance given to positive freedom in the

1 Although Sen (especially, 1999) recognizes the impact of social institutions (such as those related to the operations of the global market, governments, NGOs, the media and so on) on the capabilities of individuals, he does not analyse the role of institutionalized power and its constraining impacts on individual opportunities to achieve intended ends (see here, for example, Hill 2003).

CA prevents Sen (and others) from articulating agency-constraints or indeed, agency-capability (Alkire 2002; Corbridge 2002; Devereux 2001; Gasper 2004; Giri 2000; Qizilbash 1997). Gasper (2002) suggests here, that the CA needs to engage with other disciplines in the social sciences to expand understanding on the actions and content of being "human" in human development. In this chapter, and explained in more depth in the next chapter, the present study attempts to fuse the CA concept of agency with Giddens' sociological account of the agent as "actor." The rationale behind this is that between Sen's economic-oriented interpretation of agency (human choices/opportunities), Nussbaum's more explicit ethical angle in terms of personhood, and Giddens' extensive account of human action, agency can be understood more fully, and in more humanistic terms. This is particularly relevant to the FODW case, where being "human" does not necessarily or automatically follow on to being "developed." The fusion, in this way, allows agency to be better understood in terms of its constraints but also how constraints bring about issues of capability in FODW agency analysis.

Capability, Constraints and Giddens' Agency

The previous chapter outlined Giddens' concept of agency and constraints in terms of their relations with structural principles. Here, we focus constraints to see how they relate to capability. Constraints here are viewed as the node of agency and capability; neither agency nor capability can be theorized without them. To understand constraints to agency more fully, it is important to elaborate on the elements of power, choice and intentions in agency.

Power, Choice, Capability "to Do" and the Absence of Intentions

As discussed in Chapter 5, for Giddens, power in agency is conceptualized not as what people intend but in what people do. More recently he has reiterated this in these terms: "agency … is the *capability to do* … and that is the basis of power, no matter how large scale any given structure of power may be" (Giddens 1984a, 84, my emphasis). In this way, he locates power not only in the context of "doing" but also in the dyadic relationship between choices and constraints, hence his use of "capability." To Giddens (ibid., 84), "choice isn't between what people say about why they act as they do, on the one hand, and some kind of causal force that makes them act as they do … it is the capability to do otherwise." This is also illustrated in his observation on the limitations of choices, even to the point of no choice. Giddens provides the rather extreme scenario of "a person pointing a gun at your head, [as] subjected to the "presumption of motivation." Contextualizing this within the broader scheme of the politics of choice, he asserts that "all social constraints are only constraints in terms of motives or interests [agents] have." Thus for instance, "if you didn't value your life at all, it would be of no significance that someone is pointing a gun at you" (Giddens and Pierson 1998, 84–5).

It is important to argue here against this rather reductionist notion of choice, and how it is a direct result of Giddens' apolitical conception of power as what one *does*—or in CA's terms, a functioning individual. Agency is seen as readily, if not naturally, capable action. Therefore power is about what one *does (or doesn't) do*—capability intact—rather than what one might or could have done. Giddens' explication of agency within a constraints-choice dyad as simultaneously constraining and enabling may be useful in explaining agents' continued participation in say, a structure that oppresses (or indeed kills) them. However, it is not at all helpful for the many of us who do value our lives. Giddens (1984a, 3) does say that "[t]o be a human agent is to be a purposive agent …." He goes on, however, to caution the reader of

> terms such as "purpose," or "intention," "reason," "motive" … since their usage in the philosophical literature has very often been associated with a hermeneutical voluntarism, and because they extricate human action from the contextuality of time-space. Human action occurs as a *durée*, a continuous flow of conduct … Purposive action is not composed of an aggregate or series of separate intentions, reasons and motives.

To base these terms in response to representations of the person from a certain body of philosophical thought, and on a time-space context of human action rather than human existence, is to lose the actor in the action. Indeed, "hermeneutical voluntarism" is not necessarily an incorrect paradigm from which to view FODWs' actions (as perhaps most evident in Chapter 7). Nor does having "purpose," "intentions" and so on necessarily lead to an extrication of "human action from the contextuality of time-space." This was particularly evident in the discussion in Chapter 5 which showed how the time-space context of FODWs' agency could be conceptualized in a "FODW institution," and in which their actions could indeed be shown to compose "of an aggregate or series of separate intentions, reasons and motives" (see also here the discussion on a "capability set" in Chapter 8). In this regard, Giddens' separation of agent's intentions from what they do fails to acknowledge how an agent's intentions may indeed be important in the decision to participate in the first place, or in the choice to improve the(ir) situation. Intentions are important if actions are to be meaningful to the agent, for intentions are both descriptive of, and guidance to, agent's valued actions.

In over-focusing on agency as human action, Giddens' structuration theory treats capability as an element of agency, but agency is not at all considered as an element of capability; agency and "doing" is explained, but not the capability "of doing those things in the first place" (see here also, Baber 1991; Layder 1997; Mouzelis 1989). His unquestioned view of capable or achieved actions (in Sen's terms, *agency achievement*), leaves agency untheorized in the context or degree of its freedom to be practised (*agency freedom*). In the particular context of FODWs, agency exists in life situations where, as individuals whose situations embrace elements of the stereotype of the "poor Third World woman," they do confront strong structural forces that constrain and oppress them; that prevent them from achieving quality of life or a standard of living, as intended and valued by them. In these situations, therefore, a focus on the "capability to do" needs to shift to a focus on the "capability to do *and be*." While from an evaluative (as opposed to a theoretical) perspective, Giddens (with Pierson 1998, 64, and as also evident in his later work in "the third way" on welfare politics) does relate the "being" as essential to capability—he has for instance suggested that ""as far as possible, rather than give people goods we should give them capabilities ..."—he has nevertheless left the connections unexplored.[2]

Capability and Agency

It is fortunate then that Sen and Nussbaum (see especially 1993) have taken up this exploration in their policy formulations on the quality of life and standard of living. Sen's (1983, 160) story of the use of a bicycle in assessing standard of living, is useful here for both a theoretical and practical illustration of the relationship between agency and capability in the FODW context. In Sen's analogy, which I reproduce below, I substitute the "bicycle" for "overseas domestic work," "the characteristic of transportation" for "the characteristic of paid employment," and the act or functioning of "moving about" for the act of "living." Note here that for Sen, the standard of living more specifically refers to "personal well-being related to one's own life" (Robeyns 2005, 13).

> Take [overseas domestic work]. It is ... a commodity. It has several characteristics, and let us concentrate on one particular characteristic, viz., [paid employment]. Having employment gives a person the ability to [live] in a certain way that [s/]he may not be able to do without employment. So the employment *characteristic* of [overseas domestic work] gives the person the capability of [living] in a certain way. That capability may give the person utility or happiness if he seeks such [living] or finds it pleasurable. So there is, as it were, a *sequence* from a commodity (in this case, [overseas domestic work]), to characteristics (in this case, [employment]), to capability to function (in this case, the ability to [live a certain way], to utility (in this case, pleasure from [living a certain way]).
>
> It can be argued that it is the third category—that of capability to function—that comes closest to the notion of standard of living. The commodity ownership or

2 It is worth noting here, however, that Giddens does qualify his theorization of agency in structuration theory in the context of a sociology of the "'advanced' or more modern societies" where highly constrained life situations are not as salient (Giddens 1984a, xvii).

> availability itself is not the right focus since it does not tell us what the person can, in fact, do. I may not be able to [undertake overseas domestic work] if—say—I happened to be handicapped. Having [overseas domestic work]—or something else with that characteristic- may provide the basis for a contribution to the standard of living, but it is not in itself a constituent part of that standard. On the other hand, while utility reflects the use of [overseas domestic work], it does not concentrate on the use itself, but on the mental reaction to that use … So the constituent part of the standard of living is not the good, nor its characteristics, but the ability to do various things by using that good or those characteristics …

Sen's articulation of agency here as the "capability to function," is important for building on Giddens' notion of agency as "capable doing"—as functioning through unquestioned presence, accessibility and use of characteristics and commodities. The CA illuminates what valorizes an agent's actions; that is, "the ability to live in a certain way." It also underscores what enables or empowers actions or functionings in the first place—capability. Agency might imply power, but it is only a means through which power is exercised. It is capability that is the source of power for the agent; it is the basis of a standard of living that cannot otherwise operate or "go on" without the actor's "ability to do various things" towards that end. A CA approach to understanding agency thus shows how valueless and powerless "doings" are without "the capability to function." Put tangibly, because a FODW's capability to function comes closest to the notion of her standard of living, being without capability denotes being without her valued standard of living. In the same regard, however, although the CA is useful here in the evaluation of agency efficacy, it is Giddens structuration theory that can explain how it is that agents "do" or "go on" in order to be.

It is particularly in the area of agent's knowledgeability from which Giddens' contribution to the CA comes. For the actor's ability to do things but also to go on as intended (or valued) in doing those things is governed by what agent's know to monitor and know tacitly to live life. But while the agent's knowledgeability is an important undercurrent in the agency-capability relationship, so is the CA's articulation of commodities or capabilities (or as identified in Chapter 5, allocative resources) with which FODWs achieve their agency. Thus, where structuration theory presumes that it is the knowledge of rules and use of resources that makes people capable of action, the CA complements this by identifying that it is the presence of readily accessible resources/capabilities that makes people's actions capable. The next chapter looks more closely into agent's knowledgeability and the role of capabilities in the FODW's "capability to function" by analyzing constraints to her agency at a micro level. For now, the following discussion looks at the nature of constraints to the FODW's standard or "certain way of living" at the meso and macro levels.

Constraints in FODW Agency

The previous chapter showed how FODW agency constitutes its structures in the form of the FODW institution. It also showed how the institution is one of several structures that impact on FODW agency. But while the FODW institution is one in which FODW agency is practised, it is also where it can encounter constraints. As an institution that exists side by side with those that have greater time-space distanciation and therefore greater influence, such as the global economic system, the FODW institution is not impermeable. External processes necessarily affect the practise of agency within the FODW institution. Thus, FODW agency analysis also requires acknowledging constraints from outside of the institution. The previous section showed the importance of capability or the "extent of an agent's positive freedom" in conceptualizing but also in intervening against constraints to "doings" of value to the agent. In the FODW's case, she values her doings of undertaking paid domestic work transnationally (Chapter 5) because they provide her with the "ability to live in a certain way." For the FODW, her valued doings are therefore intrinsically tied to the FODW institution, and by the very nature of this relationship, are therefore also tied to external processes.

Internal Constraints

Albeit transnational in characteristic, FODW experiences of domestic work in the FODW institution physically occurs at the host locales. As discussed in Chapter 3, feminist structuralists have identified the constraints to Filipina overseas domestic work in terms of abuse and enslavement at these locales. To draw here from respondents' views and experiences of these constraints, illuminates how these internal constraints arise out of, or are an extension of, constraints outside of the FODW institution.

In order to obtain the respondents' stance on their work situations, I drew on their knowledgeability to classify their positions within the given dualistic paradigm of slavery and wagework. I also introduced the category of "oppressed worker" to encourage thinking beyond this dichotomous paradigm (Appendix 1). Most respondents (19 out of 24) kept within the dualistic paradigm, with the majority positively seeing their situations as that of "wageworkers," and with a small few classifying their situations as that of "slaves." However, because the criteria for determining who is enslaved, oppressed/abused or contentedly employed rested on the FODWs' own classification of their situation, variations to the three categories emerged, such as oppressed/abused wageworker. See Table 6.1.

The respondents' definition of wagework generally adheres to the liberal view of the free labor wage contract, regardless of their self-classification. Neither was there any essential difference in this definition between the respondents in Hong Kong and Paris, except what seems a more pragmatic view of freedom

Table 6.1 FODWs' own classifications of their work situations in Paris and Hong Kong

FODWs in Paris	
Delia	Wageworker
Felise	Wageworker
Gudilia	Wageworker
Mila	Wageworker
Nene	Wageworker
Indiana	Wageworker
JB	Wageworker
Minda	Former slave now wageworker
Melanie	Former slave now wageworker
Sally	Former slave now wageworker
Helena	Former slave now abused wageworker
Lani	Slave
FODWs in Hong Kong	
Michelle	Wageworker
Red	Wageworker
Virgo	Wageworker
Bernie	Wageworker
Loveley	Wageworker
Lilia	Wageworker
Ellen	Slave wageworker
Jinky	Abused wageworker
Alili	Oppressed wageworker
Amity	Oppressed/abused wageworker
Gemini	Slave
Ana	Slave

attached to the contract in Hong Kong. Amity in Hong Kong who considers herself as an oppressed/abused wageworker, for instance, describes wageworkers as "those whose contractual agreements are fulfilled, no matter how hard or demanding the work." Responding to how she understood the difference between an "employed" and an "enslaved" FODW, Red, also in Hong Kong, elaborates on how contractual agreements are fulfilled:

> The difference starts with the domestic worker and the relationship that [she] build[s] with the employer, the master … The pillars on which this relationship stands is

> your knowledge about your rights as stated in the contract. In particular, should the employer not honor something that has been agreed, and you have calmly brought the discrepancy to their attention, you must accept the consequences and act according to the contract. It's important that you are aware of your rights and working conditions and that you communicate this to your employer quietly, timely and clearly. You're an adult and usually with some education, or if not, there are plenty of professional and free help available .... If they abuse you once, then it's their fault. But if they abuse you twice, it's yours. You see the employers are aware that they have their obligations to the law and contract too. However, when there is physical, violent contact, no negotiation should take place. You must leave straightaway. (Red, wageworker, Hong Kong)

In Paris, Minda, who classified her situation as a wageworker despite previous experience of enslavement, simply describes the difference between the wageworker's and the slave's situation as when "one is happy and free. One is unhappy and not free," respectively. Indiana, a "wageworker" in Paris, elaborates on this connection between "freedom" and "work:"

> before you even start work, you agree on your salary. If I am not happy with the pay, then I tell them that I will leave them as soon as I find a higher paying employer ... You see being enslaved means you have no rights, you have no choice—it's as if your life is owned by your employer. Here we are free—we can choose to work or not. We can choose to earn money or not, it's up to us ... (Indiana, wageworker, Paris)

It is important to note here, whether in Paris or Hong Kong, that "contracts" do not necessarily imply legal validity. As Delia explains of the situation in Paris:

> We don't [all] have contracts here because we are [mostly] undocumented. So it's just all verbal. If the employer doesn't want you anymore, they can just fire you like that. Likewise, if we don't like their treatment of us, we can just leave. (Delia, wageworker, Paris)

In Hong Kong, although the great majority are documented, there are nevertheless instances when FODWs work undocumented, such as when overstaying or to supplement their full-time documented work, but also as a means to survive the interim when waiting for the outcome of labor and immigration judicial cases. In such "illegal" work, contractual agreements in Hong Kong echo those forged in Paris. Thus, as Virgo recounts of her "aerobics" or undocumented work in Hong Kong:

> … I can get up to HK$5000/month rather than the standard[3]because I work for several employers in different domestic work capacities. I am not live-in so I can provide ironing service for one employer for a few hours a week and general domestic duties for another. I can also negotiate my time and pay. I am also free to negotiate how fast I work … [Employers prefer] part time work … because they don't have to pay the monthly levy [as required in the official contract]. (Virgo, wageworker, Hong Kong)

In addition, the "wagework" experience can occur across host locales. Nene in Paris and Michelle in Hong Kong demonstrate the continuity of their experiences from their previous employment in the Middle East and the United States:

> In Saudi, my first job was to cook for a diplomat …. Then … I replaced [the Tailor] ….I could find any job I wanted within my employers' domain and he would pay me for it … He … always paid me on time. I was happy with the amount too. But I am much happier here [in Paris] because the pay here is about five times more! (Nene, wageworker, Paris)

> I [worked in] … Saudi … for four years … I was paid well. But I had to go home to the Philippines when my father fell ill. My Saudi employers were expecting me to go back, but once my father had recovered, I decided to apply here in Hong Kong because it's closer to home. When my American employers in Hong Kong returned to the United States, I moved there with them. (Michelle, wageworker, Hong Kong)

In contrast, definitions of enslavement were more fluid. Overall, the narratives on slavery were reflective of the feminist structuralist perspective that sees slavery in contravention to the labor rights attached to wagework, such as violence, non/underpayment, debt bondage and other similar abuses to liberty. As discussed in Chapter 3, employers, recruitment agency practices and host state immigration policies are identified as the main perpetrators. Among those who had previously experienced employer-inflicted enslavement, Melanie, Helena and Minda recount their time with abusive employers:

> When I first arrived in Kuwait, I went through five abusive employers: they wouldn't feed me on time; they wouldn't let me take a daily shower; they wouldn't let me sleep on time. Like that. I even experienced an employer pouring hot, newly cooked rice over me. (Melanie, former slave now wageworker, Paris)

> I'm in Paris because I escaped from my abusive Saudi employer when they came here for a holiday. I would sleep at 1am because they would make me work the whole

3 At the time of interviews, the minimum wage for FDHs in Hong Kong was HK$3,250 per month. At the time of writing (May 2005), it was HK$3,320 per month.

> day and night … [even w]hen I would get sick … the pay was very low … and we had no days off … I was so scared [when I was escaping] because our employer is a murderer. I know for a fact that he has killed people who have wronged him … back in Saudi … (Helena, former slave now abused wageworker, Paris)

> … my Lebanese employers treated me like a slave; [I was made to work] long hours [and] clean the carpet by hand … being made to clean the carpet like this … instead of using a vacuum cleaner, is the worst experience I have ever had in my life. (Minda, former slave now wageworker, Paris)

Ana in Hong Kong, who classified her situation as "a slave," and Lani in Paris, who at the time of interview also classified her situation as a "slave," point to various other ways in which employers inflict enslavement. They show in particular how the act of enslavement is made possible by the extent of employers' control over their labor and their personhood, but also over the most basic types of freedoms such as physical mobility both within and outside of the employer's household.

> Slaves are bought so they are owned; so they can be abused easily. I can say that I have been a slave physically because in a sense I have been "bought" by the employer … ' (Ana, slave, Hong Kong)

> As a slave … you are a victim; first, you are underpaid. Second, you are maltreated. Third, you are overworked. Fourth, they [the employer] are violent towards you … Fifth, we are not able to go out of the house … You kind of feel like an animal- they don't listen to you. You have no voice and you just do what they tell you. (Lani, slave, Paris)

With regards to recruitment agency-inflicted abuse, Gemini in Hong Kong and Sally in Paris, demonstrate the different modes of recruitment for documented and undocumented settings, where in the case of the latter, recruitment agencies become hands-on businesses that smuggle and/or traffic potential workers. They also show, however, that despite the differences, both modes of recruitment entail elements of enslavement:

> Usually here [in Hong Kong], that's what slavery is about; slaves of recruitment agencies, financiers and banks. You can fight and leave your employers, but how can you fight the loan sharks. (Gemini, slave, Hong Kong)

> [The recruiters] took me and another eight Filipinos through forests …, we crossed rivers … They are killing Filipinos ah. I don't know how to swim—what if I had drowned in the river? Are they obliged to do anything for me in that situation? No, because they already had my money [deposit] … Yes, this practise is called "trafficking"—which is a kind of slavery. At the time, I was really innocent … Had I

> known that it was that dangerous ... I would not have left [the Philippines] ... There was a time during those weeks of journeying when I really felt that it was time for me to die ... These recruiters don't really care about your life ... (Sally, former slave now wageworker, Paris)

Finally, Alili in Hong Kong, and Felise in Paris, provide accounts of how the host state, through immigration regulation, can facilitate migrant domestic slavery:

> I would say that I am oppressed because there are times when I've ... wanted to stand up for my rights against my employer's abusive ways, but I couldn't for fear that my contract would be terminated. Especially with the Two-week rule, this makes me feel even more insecure to fight for my rights because I have to race against time and this is not possible in court cases which always takes time. I would fear being terminated because for instance, there was a time when my mother was sick and without the income I am earning from this job, she had no chance of living. The hospitals in the Philippines would refuse to treat her unless we can present them with cash. In this situation, I couldn't afford to be without a job for more than a day. So this oppression through oppressive policies are like prison bars that prohibit you from escaping enslavement and abuse. (Alili, oppressed wageworker, Hong Kong)

> I would say that I have been enslaved because I am no longer in my own country ... I am in another country, I have no choice but to follow their own rules and regulations, so in this sense you are their slave here. ... Because of course when you want something very badly—like getting your papers ... you can't do anything about this. So you just have to painfully wait, not months, but ten years. (Felise, wageworker, Paris)

For Felise, the pain from this slavery arises from the long-term, possibly ongoing, endurance of a forfeited freedom to see children and family back home. That she classifies her situation as that of a "wageworker," however, is due to her satisfactory employment situation of eight years in Paris: "I am happy because they are nice employers and have been good to me ever since." Alili, too, despite being well aware of the exploitative constraints imposed by the Hong Kong administration, has remained in Hong Kong for 17 years. When asked how much longer she planned to stay on the job, she answered "until there are opportunities here for another contract, I suppose."

To date, there has been little exploration of this simultaneously occurring wageworker-slave situation. Ellen's classification of her work status as that of a "slave wageworker" further reveals a definition of slavery as a type of paid work which is absent in current structuralist accounts. As Ellen explains of her situation:

> [I'm] a "slave wageworker." You see this is the way I think about my situation: abuse, enslavement, whatever—they are those negative things natural to life; natural to looking for money. It's a fact that it's hard to find and earn money. If you don't

> move or act or do, neither will money fall into your lap. So that although destiny has put me here in domestic work it has likewise put office workers in office work, say. But essentially, it is just work and we still have to work hard for our money. Enslavement is natural to my type of work, so that I can say, I am a slave—but I am not abused. My employers are higher in status but they still give me my pay and look after me when I'm sick. Just like other employers out there. (Ellen, slave wageworker, Hong Kong)

Ellen demonstrates here not only how wagework and slavery can be inseparably experienced but also philosophically accepted by the FODW. However, it would seem that slavery is seen as acceptable on the conditions that one is remunerated for the work provided, and that one is not subjected to violent abuse. Indeed, this perspective of "slavery" is implicitly shared across the range of respondents' situations, from those who classified themselves as slaves to those who classified themselves as wageworkers. Thus, for instance, Ana who classified herself as a slave explains:

> My first employer would feed me just one boiled egg and noodles a day for a week ... Of course I have my limits for when I think there is an unacceptable form of abuse. That's when I will fight back and take them to court and leave them. But if it's just the long hours and the unreasonable verbal scolding, well that's just part and parcel of the job. (Ana, slave, Hong Kong)

Recall also the earlier point made by Amity who classified herself as an abused/oppressed wageworker, on the honoring of contractual agreements (such as, being paid as agreed) "no matter how hard or demanding the work." Those who classified themselves as wageworkers also share the same conclusion on the slave-like nature of their work. As Lilia puts it,

> My employer stays at home so I wake up at 5.15am ... and work the whole day through. The workload is so much so it can be really difficult ... her presence makes me feel uneasy; knowing that she is casting her eyes on my work ... For me, this employment situation is not really acceptable, but we [overseas domestic workers] can't do anything about it. We have no choice. I mean, I have the discretion to leave but it's hard to get another employer. It's hard and so you can't really do anything about it ... The way she treats me is OK. She has never complained or scolded me ... Anyway, they are paying me above the minimum wage so I'm happy. (Lilia, wageworker, Hong Kong)

Similarly, Gemini in Hong Kong, who like Ana classifies herself as a slave, but who unlike Ana, separates the meaning of her slavery from her relationship with her employer, demonstrates an accepting experience of "slavery," albeit conditional to receiving sufficient pay.

> I call myself a slave because of the nature of the work—there to serve another person and 24 hours on call. But my employer ... treats me well. And I'm satisfied

> with my pay … especially if I compare it to Taiwan, I'm so much luckier here. I could say that they super-exploited, abused, enslaved me in Taiwan … (Gemini, slave, Hong Kong)

These accounts of the intersections of slavery with work beg the question of when is, or isn't, abuse enslavement? Helena's experience as a former slave now abused wageworker, and Jinky as an abused wageworker is particularly representative of how "abuse" is understood and accepted by the rest of the respondents. When Helena was with her Saudi employer, she had seen her situation as that of a slave, since although she was being paid, she had felt imprisoned, particularly because of the threat of violence from her "murderous" employer . Since she has been with her French employer, "abuse" has taken the form of non-violent but nevertheless overworked and underpaid conditions:

> I'm only paid F6000. This is not even E1000 [which is the standard pay among FODWs in Paris] … however, if I compare it to the pay in the Philippines, then I'm way ahead.
>
> I do complain about my long hours … sometimes my hours get taken up by listening to her stories … my relationship with my employer … is as if we are sisters … [But s]he says "I'm sorry I can't give you a pay rise because I am building a house at the moment, so I hope you will just receive these [gifts] in kind …." She knows how to handle me. When I am complaining that there is too much work and my head is aching, she gives me … things that will help relax me; a radio for music, a TV … But … what I really want is … proper hours and days off … (Helena, former slave now wage worker, Paris)

Jinky, in Hong Kong, similarly underscored the failure of the employers to honor a relationship which she believes should be based on mutual respect between human beings:

> … if you're a slave, you are both made to work harder than usual and given hard work. For instance, you would have to work 24 hours a day, without sleep. But if you're abused, there is more of a limitation to the enslavement. For example, I was abused but not enslaved. They didn't make my work hard for me, or make me work harder than what was in the contract, but they did abuse their responsibilities as both employers and human beings to treat me the way they did. When they would come home late, they would make me wait outside in the night and in the cold over and over again, simply because they didn't trust me with the keys to their apartment. (Jinky, abused wageworker, Hong Kong)

But while Helena, Jinky and other accounts are reminiscent of feminist structuralist views on the subordinate position of overseas domestic workers in the employer/master-worker/servant relationship, the point of concern shown here by FODWs is not so much the abuse, or how, why and to what extent, it occurs. Rather, the respondents here, and as reinforced by the examples of

Helena's escape from Saudi Arabia to Paris and Gemini's move from Taiwan to Hong Kong, show determined endurance to stay in overseas domestic work. Whether abusive or non/less abusive, cases of slave-like conditions seem bound to happen as long as they are in the FODW institution—yet they remain in it. It seems crucial then, in the context of understanding their slavery and/or abuse, that analytical attention turns, but also gives primacy to the FODWs' reasons for such endurance: money or income on which to live a decent life. Thus, even while she considers herself "a slave," when asked what overseas domestic work means to her, Ana explains that it means

> to survive. To earn enough so that ... I can afford to live a decent life [on my return to the Philippines] ... you realize that it's actually a precious type of job because it can be your ticket to a better life for yourself and your family if you play it right and persist long enough. You can even use the money you save to invest in a business back home and then actually help people there. (Ana, slave, Hong Kong)

As both Gemini and Helena also assert,

> *Masarap ang buhay sa Pilipinas pero mahirap ma buhay* [Life is sweet in the Philippines but the catch is to be able to lead one in the first place] ... I just refuse to work in the Philippines. There's even more abuse there and you don't even get paid for it! I would earn around P5000/mth in the Philippines whereas abroad I can earn around P20 000/mth. When you are used to bigger pay, it becomes impossible to look back ... I may as well be a rich slave here than a poor one in the Philippines. (Gemini, slave, Hong Kong)

> When I left [my children] they were seven and five years old. Now, my oldest is 21 and my youngest is 18 ... When I was working in Saudi, I got to go home every two years with the ticket paid for by the employer. Here, unless you have papers you can't leave the country ... You know the children blame me for escaping ... if I hadn't escaped I would be able to visit them. But ... if I hadn't escaped, we couldn't have afforded our house in the Philippines ... ; my salary for three months in Saudi is only one month's work here ... So, I say to myself, I can handle it here ... my family needs my help ... especially now that ... life is even harder in the Philippines. So even though I am very tired ... , I keep on working ... even though sometimes I am treated a little like a slave ... I have to accept (cries). (Helena, former slave now abused wageworker, Paris)

Here, Helena's escape to Paris, where there is more money, and not back to her family in the Philippines (and particularly seeing that she was able to return home every two years under her Saudi contract), is particularly demonstrative of how "slavery as paid work," is accepted in the particular context of its desirability compared to unpaid or poorly paid slavery seen as synonymous to working in the Philippines.

Thus whether the FODW is a wageworker, an oppressed/abused one, or even a "slave," what remains constant, and what she ensures is constant about her situation, is that she stays in the FODW institution where she is sufficiently paid for her labor. However, there must be caution in prematurely accepting the internal constraints presented by abuse and enslavement as a conclusion of the FODW situation. As the respondents here have demonstrated, harsh tradeoffs are necessary to achieve their valued ends of earning a livelihood. Gemini for instance highlights the need to deal with recruitment agencies and other "loan sharks" in order to gain the preferable status of a "rich slave" to a poor one. For Felise, it's a long and painful wait as an undocumented worker until she can obtain papers that secure her right as a resident of France. These and other constraints are as Ellen put it, "natural to making money." Or as Lilia has earlier explained, constraints are nothing they can do much about except to endure in order to get paid. Given these rather hopeless rationalizations of their situations, it is important to underscore the reasons that "shackle" FODWs to the institution in the first place, and often, for a long time. These reasons arise out of structural constraints that lay outside of, but that have a direct impact on her participation in, the FODW institution.

External Constraints

In discussing external constraints to FODW agency, it is important to go back to the beginning of the FODWs' journey as "potential migrants" (Appendix 3). As individuals, FODWs originally come from outside of the FODW institution. While rather obvious, there is nevertheless a need to chronologically reorganize an understanding of the FODW situation since so much literature, and much of the discussions on her situation, are located within the FODW institution (in host locales). For the purposes of the current discussion, this perspective is also useful in providing the basis from which to underscore the continuities in their forced migration (as argued by NGOs in Chapter 4) and their shackled positions to the FODW institution. JB's rich account of the reasons for why one might "forever" stay within the FODW institution provides a good illustration of this:

> Those with papers have to pay tax … So one earns more if one doesn't have papers. [Even if you have papers] … there are ways you can get around the tax system so you don't have to pay so much. I have my formal work but I also take on another job over the weekend [undeclared]. In this way, I can earn up to E2000/mth and I don't have to pay for my room, board and food. But the price you pay for the higher income is that you can't go home because it will be near impossible to get back in here again … Those who don't eventually get papers will just have to stay here forever. Anyway, they are looked after here better than they would be in the Philippines. If they should get sick here and need an operation, they don't have to spend a cent, if they can't afford it. That's the policy here … Come to think of it, it's probably

> a good thing not to go home. When you go home, you end up dead broke because you spend all your savings! And this results in us just cleaning toilets here forever to keep refilling our pockets! *Ooh la la*! … I could even say that my family back home, because I feel so guilty if I don't send them money, "enslaves" me. I wouldn't work two jobs and get so tired if they could look after themselves. But I feel so guilty when I have the latest fashion clothing here and good food, when members of my family do without them. (JB, wageworker, Paris)

It is important here to foreground that JB's reflections on the financial decisions behind remaining in Paris on the one hand, and her endurance of working conditions that she sees as akin to enslavement on the other, say more about the bigger problems of (economic) development in the Philippines than on her feelings of slavery. It is also important to make the connection between experienced slavery in the host locale, and cause of the experience as arising from the locale of origin. As JB explains, she works two jobs and gets so tired precisely because her family is deprived of material and nutritional needs without her earnings. Unlike JB, they are in a setting of underdevelopment, and are thus unable to earn sufficiently to buy good food and clothing to live a certain way. While JB's orientation towards her family is a stark example of Sen's explication of sympathy and commitment in the agent, it also illuminates how materialist structural conditions, and the financial and livelihood constraints arising from them, directs her practise of agency.

This brings the discussion back to structuralist theories that explain underdevelopment in peripheral countries like the Philippines, as a direct cause of global economic development processes. On the one hand, feminist structural accounts overshadow the issue of underdevelopment with victimization in the host locales. On the other, agency-based inquiries frequently mention the need to avoid reducing FODWs' reasons and motivations for migration to structural oppression in terms of poverty. It was, however, clear in my conversations with the respondents that poverty was indeed *the main reason* or cause for their emigration (see also here Agustìn 2006, 25–6; Campani 1993, 197–201). The "special" cases of Mila and Virgo who deemed their incomes sufficient to live comfortably in the Philippines, and whose primary reason for migrating was to leave their husbands,[4] become less special when they are considered in the larger process of global economic development. Both Virgo and Mila look at their reasons for embarking on overseas domestic work as exceptions to the rule. As Virgo elaborates here:

> I think the number one reason [for why so many Filipinas go overseas] is economic—the pay here is much better. There is work overseas instead of just being unemployed in the Philippines. They want to earn a living for their family. I would say that my case would be in the most minor of cases. Life is just too hard in the Philippines …

4 Divorce is socially, religiously, and legally unacceptable in the Philippines (see here, for example, Chant 1997).

> this is also why when they go overseas, they just put the thought of the consequences aside because their main focus is to earn and save for the survival of their family. It's the ultimate sacrifice for a better future … [For me,]—I am reluctant to reveal this, but I'm here because I had a problem with my husband … [so] it's not for economic reasons because I actually had a good job … I was a project manager for an engineering firm, … [I needed to leave the Philippines because] I feel so ashamed about my broken family … (Virgo, wageworker, Hong Kong)

However, Mila shows here, economic reasons are not necessarily separate from personal reasons for migration:

> Oh you know Filipinas, they are like ants. They have to get out of the Philippines. You block their way and they will find their way out. They want to get out because the salary there is so low …. Personally for me, when I decided to go overseas, I didn't want to become a domestic helper. Because I had [marital] problems in the Philippines, I just wanted to get out of there as fast as I could … I should have decided not to leave because now that I look back, I see how I have missed being with my children as they grew up … [But] when I started to realize that I made the wrong decision [about my children], I couldn't go back because by that time, my children were about to go to college. If I went back I would not be able to afford to put them through college. (Mila, wageworker, Paris)

Indeed, all the other respondents said they would not have left the Philippines had they been earning enough to support themselves and their families. When asked if they would do the same job back in the Philippines for the same pay as they earned overseas, the respondents said that they would not have left at all. As Alili puts it:

> Even if the work there is still domestic work and it paid enough to support their families, they would not leave. I would not leave! … I seriously would be satisfied if I was being paid even half of what we are getting paid here! (Alili, oppressed wageworker, Hong Kong)

Experiences with recruitment agencies are particularly illuminating of the centrality of poverty in the decision to migrate for overseas domestic work. Behind feminist structuralist accounts of recruitment agency-inflicted abuse, as demonstrated earlier by Gemini and Sally, lays the need of FODWs to use them. Although, as part of its Migrant Workers Protection Act, the Philippine government devotes significant resources to ensuring the legality of recruitment practices from the Philippines, there is still much non-compliance of the set legal limit on recruitment fees. The legal limit for fees is no more than one month's salary (POEA 2004). However, the limit excludes other administrative fees such as issuance of passports and visas, and airfares, all of which remain under the sole discretion of the recruitment agencies to charge. Accounts of recruitment agency-inflicted abuses abound not only within the interview sample, but also amongst the wider FODW community in both Paris and Hong Kong. As part of my participant observation, I would sit with different groups of FODWs[5] and would ask of their main concerns about their employment situation. Most of the time, FODWs would cite problems with recruitment agencies more frequently than problems with their employers. A common reason given for the proliferation of abuse by agencies is the vulnerability of the individual who is desperate to escape the poverty in the Philippines. As many would put it, *alam kasi nila na iyong mga Pilipina ay kakapit sa patalim* [it's because the recruitment agencies know us Filipinas will hang onto even a sharp blade just for the chance to earn here] (Diary RPC September 20/November 2, 2003).

To connect recruitment abuse to this desperation is to correct a common view that FODWs do not generally come from the poorest of the poor. Indeed, as the argument goes, FODWs use recruitment agencies because they are able to raise the large costs of recruitment fees. On the contrary, the recruitment agencies earn well beyond the one months' legal pay limit precisely because most of the applicants do not have the money to pay them in the first place, and therefore have to take out loans from them. In addition to other fees for travel costs, recruitment agencies charge applicants high interest rates for loans (Lan 2006, 55). As Amity tells of her experience with having to loan from an agency: "if I had the P80,000 to begin with and I did not loan it, then I would have just used that for capital to put up a business in the Philippines."

Other respondents, such as Bernie and Jinky, experienced abuse beyond the actual payment of fees. In effect, the high fees made them work for longer, not for themselves and their families, but for the agencies' profits. This was true too for Gemini who ended up taking a whole year to finish her repayments, and Ana who loaned P70,000 but ended up paying P100,000. At the same time however, Ana concedes the necessity of agencies to finding work, "I don't think much of agencies, but if they weren't around I'm not sure how easy it would be to find work." Recruitment agencies are so necessary that only Ellen and Lilia in Hong Kong did not have to use them. Others who used an agency reported that they handed over large sums of money loaned from other sources to avoid the agency interest rates. But, as Bernie shows, sometimes the money raised is enough only to pay for the required deposit:

> My agency told me to prepare for a P70,000 fee. This would amount to P100,000 with the interest. I took the risk; I borrowed some from my cousin who is only charging me a little interest, and my mother had a little. On top of this, I took up the agency's financial assistance program. Once you are qualified—that is, you have an employer waiting for you, then they are happy to lend this service to you. I thought

5 For a good account of these groups, usually bonded together by virtue of their respective common regional heritage in the Philippines, and to a lesser extent by common social, and in the case of NGOs, political interests, see Law (2002a).

> this was fair since it would only take three or four months to pay it all off. (Bernie, wageworker, Hong Kong)

Amity, Red, Ana and Gemini, who could not afford to raise even the deposit amount, signed away the loaned amounts without being given a receipt. Red explains,

> I knew the details of the deal. So I knew that I wouldn't get a receipt from them. I knew this before I signed up. But this was fine with me because … [M]ore important was my desire to get the job. (Red, wageworker, Hong Kong)

In Paris, the many who either did not escape from their abusive employers or came directly hired,[6] used the services of a recruitment agency. Since there is no official bilateral agreement on overseas domestic work between the Philippines and France, recruitment takes the form of tourist visas issued by "travel agents" which are overstayed, or as Sally demonstrated earlier, in the form of smuggling/trafficking. Delia and Indiana had, like Sally, experienced being smuggled/trafficked, while Nene, JB, and Melanie used "travel agents" (see here Appendix 1). But Mila, who had come to France once before, and who has experienced both forms, shows how tighter immigration controls in France leave smuggling/trafficking as the only current option for entry:

> The first time I came as a tourist. It was so easy in 1984—just packed my bags with my visa. The second time in 1988, it was more difficult so I had to come the clandestine way. It took me four months to reach France. I had to stay two weeks in [a city in Europe], then around three months in [another one]. (Mila, wageworker, Paris)

Mila also adds, however, that "I had my own money to pay the agency, although I know that a lot are now borrowing money for this."

That poverty is consistently the underlying reasons for FODW migration is also important in correcting the common view that most FODWs cannot come from the poorest of the poor since they are "educated." Perhaps the most prominent suggestion of this is in Parreñas' (2001, 150–96) notion of a "contradictory class mobility" experienced by FODWs. Parreñas argues that migration for domestic work by Filipinas with high levels of education and/or who have held professional occupations back in the Philippines, results

6 The term "direct hire" has a double connotation in the recruitment business in Hong Kong. The first is used more commonly among recruitment agencies and refers to recruitment agency-facilitated hiring of interested Filipinas directly from the Philippines and who have never worked in Hong Kong. The second refers to the hiring of interested Filipinas directly from the Philippines by the employers themselves, usually referred through familial/social networks. This second connotation is the case for those going to Paris and other destinations without bilateral labor programs with the Philippines.

in a decline in their social status as it increases their financial status. From the experiences of the respondents in the present study, however, only Mila's experience suggested that this was so:

> Before, being a domestic worker was shameful to me because in the Philippines I had my own maid … So being a domestic worker in the first years, I felt belittled. I felt that my mind went backwards … Anyway, I felt better by thinking that I earn more than office secretaries here. I know this because I had an employer before to whom I complained about my salary and he replied: "No Mila! Don't tell me that. I pay you more than I pay my secretary!" (Mila, wageworker, Paris)

Virgo, on the other hand, who out of all the respondents had the highest educational qualification and well- paying job in the Philippines, said that,

> … compared to my engineering job, [domestic work] is just as clean, honest and important a job to do. People may laugh at me because this is what I've ended up doing, but I've learned to become stronger and be more practical … [Having this job also means that] I could escape [my family problems in the Philippines] quickly while I can earn enough to continue supporting my children. (Virgo, wageworker, Hong Kong)

Apart from Mila, therefore, many did not experience any degree of "contradictions" as they either began their labor migration with very limited income as in the cases of Alili, Amity, Ana, Bernie, Delia, Gudilia, Helena, Indiana, Lani, Loveley, and Sally; or with insufficient income as in the cases of Ellen, Felise, Gemini, JB, Jinky, Lilia, Minda, Nene, Melanie, Michelle, and Red; or as in the case of Virgo, comparably sufficient income to her high-paying engineering job in the Philippines. Indeed, the respondents' experiences provide support more to reports on the situation of the majority of women in the Philippines that underscore experiences of poverty and high unemployment as a result of SAPs (see here for example, Chant 1996; Chant and McIlwaine 1995; Elson 1991; McCulloch and Stancich 1998), than they do to accounts that highlight their educated backgrounds. Thus, for instance, Delia tells of the impact of the decline in earnings of small agriculture in the Philippines to her situation:

> Life in Baguio [a city in the Philippines] is so hard. Where would I get the tuition fee for my three children? Two are about to go into high school. And my husband and I don't have jobs. We are just vegetable farmers and these produce are not priced very well these days. (Delia, wageworker, Paris)

Nene recounts her struggle to survive on two jobs at once:

> Even after my Saudi job, which enabled me to save a little and put up a little business of my own in the Philippines, I still had to get another job as a tailor. Even then, the income from these jobs were not enough ….
>
> In the Philippines, I used to get up at 4am in the morning, I would already be out of the house to buy stock for my shop. That takes me until 9am. At 9am, the store is ready to open and my siblings keep the shop while I go and sew some cleaning cloths … So here I am working like a dog, and still, my income is nowhere near as much as I earn here. (Nene, wageworker, Paris)

Finally, Alili tells of her experience in an export manufacturing company, and how such companies reduce women's work in the Philippines to disposable labor:

> I worked on the production line of a company that manufactured semi-conductors. I was part of a union but we weren't strong enough to stop the retrenchment, and I eventually found myself without a job. I decided to be a union member because it was obvious how the company would exploit us workers; we were given tough quotas, made to work overtime, and we were underpaid … I remember … one night when we held a picket-line … the bosses hired goons to scare us off. So there were guns and some people got hit … the company [in the end] changed their name to protect their reputation. These are the kinds of tricks that they get away with … When I applied at another semi-conductor company, they rejected my application because apparently I was over-age at 22! … I tell you, the recruitment process [in the Philippines] is rotten. So then, I started applying at agencies for overseas work. (Alili, oppressed wageworker, Hong Kong)

The very notion of many FODWs being "educated" ignores the politics of education in the Philippines. Only the few who can afford an education in prestigious universities are also the few who are able to secure the more gainful employment in the country. Thus, speaking of educated FODWs can be misleading since being educated doesn't mean that they finished (as in the case of Bernie) or could afford to finish their studies (as in the case of Alili), or if they did, that they could secure gainful employment afterwards, as in the case of Amity and Ellen.

> I would have liked to pursue my nursing career so that I could apply to go to America. But I haven't been able to pass the board exam so I can't practise it. I can't do anything about it I suppose, if I can't pass. So I've just decided to do overseas domestic work. At the very least, I am still earning good money … (Bernie, wageworker, Hong Kong)

> When I first came here [to Hong Kong], my plan was to stay … only until I've been able to pay for myself to continue my studies. I was a self-supporting student. I managed to complete one year [of college], but after that, it just became too hard.

> You see, I was also expected to help my family because we weren't very rich. So I had to concentrate on working for income. (Alili, oppressed wageworker, Hong Kong)

> I had just graduated from Teacher's College and I could not find a job. At the same time, my children were growing up. So then I thought of applying abroad and within three months, I was here. I could earn. (Amity, oppressed/abused wageworker, Hong Kong)

> I graduated from college [in my province] with a Bachelor in Industrial Technology. I thought I would go to Manila to find a job. It wasn't that easy, so I got a domestic worker job there with a Visayan woman and her Chinese husband who ran an auto-supply shop … One day, one of their nephews visited from Hong Kong. I was [encouraged] to go [and work for him as a domestic worker in] Hong Kong … When my contract papers came, I … really didn't want to go to a foreign land. But then at around about the same time, family problems entered my life—my mother died and my father was put into hospital and so there were lots of hospital bills to pay. So then I thought to myself "what am I going to do? I couldn't afford to pay these bills with my current income. I was only earning around P1000/mth. My siblings were all married and so they had their own financial obligations. I felt like I was the only one who could really help … this offer to work in Hong Kong was still going through so I just agreed, and here I am. (Ellen, slave-wageworker, Hong Kong)

Capability in FODW Agency

It would thus seem that the lack of valorization of poverty in FODW analyses leads to an under-examination of an important, if not the most important, space within which to understand FODW vulnerability—as primarily driven by conditions of poverty. As the narratives show here, it is not sufficient to identify that it is development and the mixture of financial, personal and geographical reasons this entails, that determines migration (Massey, Sassen, and Ehrenreich as discussed in Chapter 1). There must be a more explicit use of development in terms of its negative consequences that creates the "push" factor in overseas domestic workers' migration. For the particular case of the FODW, *it is* underdevelopment that causes migration. And in this way, is the very source of FODW vulnerability in the host locales. For the FODW, it is underdevelopment in the Philippines which makes her agency "incapable," hence her tenacious participation in the FODW institution to make it capable (this is explored further in the next chapter). Further, and as demonstrated earlier, this external origin of her vulnerability can directly lead to her oppression/abuse/enslavement within the institution.

If the CA, in Nussbaum's words, "allows comparisons between individuals and across nations as to how well they are doing," then the FODW institution provides the framework from which to make these comparisons for FODWs. As economically disadvantaged individuals from an economically disadvantaged nation, they are not doing so well. They remain deprived of commodities, incomes and other resources, but more specifically of "combined capabilities." "Educated" Filipinas, for example, share much in common with many educated women in Kerala who cannot find jobs other than sex work in Delhi (Nussbaum 2005, 180). As Sen also emphasizes in his work (see especially, 1999, 189–250), to have capability means to have a set of them rather than just one of them. Having a capability in terms of having an education, for example, is sufficient only if one also has the capability of a job that can in turn, transform education into a functioning. The FODWs' standard of living is thus precarious and largely dependent not only on their maintained presence in the FODW institution, but also on their "capability to function" within the institution. In contrast to conceptualizing FODW agency within the context of structural opportunities (such as, through networks and institutions as discussed in Chapter 5), conceptualizing FODW capability therefore requires conceptualizing FODW agency within the context of her structural constraints, primary of which is poverty in her country of origin. Before discussing this further in Chapter 8, however, it is necessary to understand how capability works with agency at the micro level. This is the task of the next chapter.

Conclusion

In this chapter, an articulation of the "structuralist" in the present study's "structural-structurationist" approach reveals the constraints both within and outside of the FODW institution. Internal constraints were identified to be consistent with feminist-structuralist accounts of oppression, abuse and enslavement. External constraints, on the other hand, involved identifying the grave limitations to livelihoods brought about by underdevelopment in the FODWs' country of origin. Importantly, this structuralist perspective also underscored the importance of seeing these constraints as related. FODWs endure constraints within the FODW institution as an extension, or result, of the external constraints. Whether internal or external, FODWs view constraints as a threat to their agentic orientations towards earning a livelihood. This understanding pointed to the need to revise the under-valorization of poverty in current agency-based analyses of FODWs, on the one hand, and its under-representation in feminist-structuralist approaches, on the other.

The theoretical association made between the conceptualization of agency in the CA and structuration theory was particularly important in illuminating the centrality of constraints in analysis; as the node from which agency-capability relations occur. This enabled a fuller conceptualization of constraints at the meso (FODW institution) and macro structural level, demonstrating how in turn, a meso and macro conceptualization of capability in FODW agency is rooted in underdevelopment in the country of origin.

There is a need now, in the next chapter, to focus discussions on FODW agency itself to allow a conceptualization of capability at the micro level. This is important because not only does it provide insight into how constraints and capability are actually experienced by the individual agent, it also provides the last theoretical piece in the puzzle of a "capable agency approach" that will be articulated in the final chapter.

Chapter 7
Agency, Capability and the Migrant Domestic Worker

Chapter 5 showed how agency works in the FODW context. Chapter 6 then discussed FODW agency in terms of its conceptualization with issues of capability. This chapter focuses on the FODW's experiential level of agency to determine what it means for FODW agency to be capable. Drawing from interview data, and extending from the theoretical framework on agency and capability discussed in the last two chapters, it employs the reformulation of structures by Sewell (1992), and of agency by Emirbayer and Mische (1998) in structuration theory, to illustrate how FODW agency can be conceptualized at the micro level. These reformulations of structure and agency focus analysis on the processes within the constitution of structure and agency themselves rather than on how they constitute society (as in Giddens' framework of structuration theory) or institutions (as for instance, in the FODW institution in Chapter 5). This microanalysis is crucial in two ways. First, it allows a more grounded identification of how agency is constituted (agency *in* the FODW) rather than exerted (agency *of* the FODW), allowing thus, focus on the "subject" rather than on "subject effects" (Chapter 1). Second and consequently, it forces analysis to contemplate agency "out" of the FODW, which is a necessary informational base for determining the nature, degree and indeed, absence of capability in her agency.

The FODW Agent

To physically conceive of the FODW as an *actor*, requires a presupposition that she possesses an agent's most basic composition—a socio-biological body. As Giddens puts it, "you can't be a human agent without having a body …." Giddens (with Pierson 1998, 90) proceeds to qualify this by underscoring the ontological context of the body: "… a body occupies a physical space and it orients itself towards others in a physical context." Given that the FODW is of a physical and social body, how does this translate into the conceptualization of her body as an agent? In structuration theory, the body *is* the agent, in the sense that it is the "'locus' of the active self" (Giddens 1984a, 36). Giddens (in Giddens et al. 2001, 266) does not separate the body from the mind, and asserts that such a body-mind existence is governed by reflexive knowledgeability:[1] "one has to understand our relationship to our bodies in terms of the whole flow of action and structure." Take here, for instance, Jinky's experience:

> I would like to save some money. Accumulate capital to invest for myself. Then I will go back to settle in the Philippines … [and] … to put up a little business, and not to work anymore. But this will require working overseas for as long as possible; *hangang sa kaya ng katawan ko* (as long as my body can take it). (Jinky, Hong Kong)

Jinky illustrates here that for the FODW, the flow of action and structure is one which involves the continued existence of her working body and of overseas domestic work, necessitating her to use her body as an agent, as a conduit for exerting her agency, for acting, to achieve a desired goal such as "putting up a little business." However there is also the issue of "irreversible time" for the usage of the FODW body (Chapter 5). As Jinky points out, the extent of this usage is only so far as the body "can take it," until it is terminally sick, or indeed dead. Hence, as structuration theory would have it, the need for the mind and body's mutual (indeed, dual) existence.[2]

Jinky illustrates here also how she may be conceived as an agent: she works, she saves, she plans, but she is embodied by her demanding work, her finite body and her social environment. As an acting and embodied agent, she is, in other words, a "(social) actor" (Emirbayer and Mische 1998, 1004). The following discussion uses Sewell's reformulation of "structure" to discuss the means by, and through which, agents or actors use and acquire resources. This in turn provides the conceptual basis from which Emirbayer and Mische's theorization of agency and its implications for theorizing agency in the FODW can be discussed.

---

1 "'Reflexivity' … should be understood not merely as 'self-consciousness' but as the monitored character of the ongoing flow of social life" (Giddens 1984a, 3).

2 I take the opportunity here to clarify the study's stance on the FODW "body" amidst other, differing stances. In the present study, analysis is not based on how the agents feel, nor how they are socially viewed, nor indeed, used (the majority of works on the Filipina overseas domestic worker already deal with this). Rather, analysis here is based on what they are capable "to do." This does not mean that my approach departs from works that highlight the constraints on the body, in particular, those that problematize female and marginalized bodies in social life (for example, Nast and Pile 1998). Similarly, this does not mean that I disagree with critiques of "the body" in structuration theory that assert that its concept of duality obfuscates the analysis of the sensual and carnal bodily properties (for example, Butler 1990; 1993; Shilling and Mellor 2001). But I do focus my use here of structuration theory to highlight the dynamic association between "constraints on," and "transformative properties of," agents' actions.

Sewell on "Structure"

Extending from the duality of structure, Sewell asserts that "agency is implied by the existence of structures" (Sewell, 1992, 20). Different from Giddens, however, Sewell provides a relatively tangible reformulation of the composition of structure. He replaces Giddens' institutional concept of "rules" with *cultural schemas*, and replaces Giddens' virtual authoritative and allocative resources with "actual" *human and nonhuman resources*, respectively.[3] *Cultural schemas* are basically the "rules of social life" which agents know and live by. In this way, knowledge of schemas "makes people capable of action" (ibid., 7). Schemas are virtual because they are generalisable and transposable, meaning that the agent can extend or transpose them to new situations and under a range of different circumstances. Resources, on the other hand are "actual." They are of two types: nonhuman and human resources.

> Nonhuman resources are objects, animate or inanimate, naturally occurring or manufactured, that can be used to enhance or maintain power; human resources are physical strength, dexterity, knowledge and emotional commitments that can be used to enhance or maintain power, including knowledge of the means of gaining, retaining, controlling and propagating either human or nonhuman resources. (ibid., 9)

Resources exist in time-space as specific characteristics and possessions of ontological agents. In the more abstract case of human resources, they are actualized through the agent's body-mind. However, while being "actual" in character means that resources are fixed and tangible entities, this does not mean that they are immutable or unchangeable. Their utility in "enhancing or maintaining power" makes them vulnerable to manipulation by agents. Sewell (ibid., 18–19) locates these vulnerabilities in the "unpredictability of resource accumulation" and the "polysemy of resources." The former is directly connected to the agent's transposition of schemas, which, depending on the new situation upon which they are transposed, can result in a modified composition of resources. When resources are modified, they can either diminish or improve in quality and/or quantity. In effect, the change in resource composition simultaneously modifies schemas, and thereby produces actions with unintended consequences. Unintended consequences of actions are also products of what Sewell terms the "intersection of structures." Here, "structures or structural complexes intersect and overlap" (ibid., 19), enabling multiple interpretations in the meaning of resources, depending on how the agent assesses their

3 For ease of reading, I reproduce Giddens' definition of rules and resources here from Chapter 5. For rules: "… techniques or generalisable procedures applied in the enactment/reproduction of social practices." For resources: "Allocative resources refer to capabilities ….generating command over objects, goods or material phenomena. Authoritative resources refer to types of transformative capacity generating command over persons …."

advantages for her purpose or in empowering herself. Because there are other agents and therefore actions being exerted within these intersections, unintended consequences ensue. This is explored later in the chapter.

Retaining Giddens' structuration perspective, Sewell (ibid., 13) explains how schemas and resources are intrinsically related, and how sustained and recursive use of them produces the effect of structures:

> Schemas not empowered or regenerated by resources would eventually be abandoned and forgotten, just as resources without cultural schemas to direct their use would eventually dissipate and decay. Sets of schemas and resources may properly be said to constitute *structures* only when they mutually imply and sustain each other over time.

This is how, as stated earlier, "agency is implied by the existence of structures:" structures exist because agents exert agency, through schemas and resources, which (re)produce structures.

Sewell's reformulation provides a more precise account of agents' knowledgeability in terms of their knowledge of schemas and their use and control of resources. In this way, it is important in identifying the particular sets of schemas and resources relevant to the context of Filipina overseas domestic work, and by default, the conceptualization of agency in the FODW. It is important here, however, to note that the sets of schemas and resources differ from rules and resources discussed in the context of the FODW institution (Chapter 5). Whereas rules-resource sets are relevant for theorizing agency within a given structural set, such as the FODW institution (that is, *of* the agent in that structural set), they are less useful in theorizing agency *within* the agent. To explain this, it is important to retain Giddens' (1984a, 377) original separation of the concept of structure from the concept of structures (refer back here also to Chapter 5):

- *structure*—rules and resources, recursively implicated in the reproduction of social systems. Structure exists only as memory traces, the organic basis of human knowledgeability, and as instantiated in action;
- *structures*—rule-resource sets, implicated in the institutional articulation of social systems …

"Structure" and "structures" are terms which Goss and Lindquist, and also Sewell, use interchangeably, but whose conceptual separation prevents a fuller understanding of agency in the agent. Although Goss and Lindquist look at agency in terms of its mutual relationship with structure, they look only at the exertion or "doing" aspect of agency. Similarly, Sewell's understanding of agency in terms of its constitutive relation with structures does not say much about the ontological agent herself as the do-er/actor, nor the exertion of agency amidst constraints brought about by a complex of structures, and the pertinent issues this raises for the agent's capability to exert agency. Nevertheless, Sewell's reformulation of structure/s allows analysis to focus understanding of the agent's structural context to its agentic context. This microscopic shift is crucial for theorizing agency in its full embodiment; from the inside out and the outside in. It therefore allows integration of Emirbayer and Mische's (1998, 973) conception of agency that "viewed internally, ... entails different ways of experiencing the world, by means of which actors enter into relationship with surrounding persons, places, meanings, and events. [And] viewed externally, ... entails actual interactions with its contexts."

Together, Sewell and Emirbayer and Mische's conceptualization of agency also enables understanding of how the more informal rules of social life (schemas) presuppose—in concept, but necessarily co-exist with—in practice, resources. This is later illustrated in Figure 7.2, and will be an important framework for theorizing capability/ies with agency. First, schemas and (non) human resources are explored below.

Schemas in the FODW Context

Sewell's (1992, 7) cue in understanding "the rules of social life" as consisting of "all the varieties of cultural schemas," allows rules or schemas to be conceptualized in the FODW context. If the "FODW" composite is for the moment, divided into its components: "Filipina," "overseas," "overseas domestic work," and "overseas domestic worker," it becomes possible to see that schemas cannot, by Sewell's definition, be identified with the agent being overseas, nor doing overseas domestic work, nor in taking up the position/role of overseas domestic worker. All these are "resources," as say, apparent in their availability in the FODW institution. Rather, schemas can be identified with the agent "being a Filipina." "The rules of social life," in other words, are bound up with the agent's knowledge of what it means to be a Filipina. Note that the schema is not the Filipina person, but the knowledge of the cultural rules that define a Filipina.[4]

4 This finds resonance with Nussbaum's concept of culture in her theorization of her Capabilities Approach. Nussbaum has a progressive or working view of culture; not as a static, romanticized, traditional entity and practice but one that is *made* by present peoples in present and changed/changing circumstances and contexts. As Nussbaum (2000; see also 1999) shows of the contestations and re-workings of traditional and established cultural beliefs and practices by Vasanti and Jayamma in their struggles as poor women in India, so the FODWs in this study find themselves in a dynamic context of their experience and re-making of culture, especially as they live with, and learn from/ about, on a daily basis with relatively prosperous women and men as employers , and who are from cultures different to their own. Correspondingly, I address the role of culture in the CAA as a functioning (that is, facilitating a certain practice of agency, rather than as a governing concept) by employing, here, Sewell's use of culture in the form of schemas. Far from claims that Nussbaum in her Capabilities Approach has conceptualized

As Emirbayer and Mische note, "there are no concrete agents but only actors who engage with their environments."[5]

In Filipino culture, the Filipina is idealized as a "good woman" whose goodness is exemplified through her roles as "dutiful daughter" and/or "sacrificing mother" (Medina 1991; Mulder 1997, 18–44). These roles often involve "helping her husband" to provide for the family in the event of his sickness, un/underemployment or absence (Ogaya 2004b). They can also involve helping parents and other family members who require financial assistance. Several studies have found that these roles not only play a major part in the reason for the potential migrant's decisions to undertake overseas (domestic) work (Arnold and Abad 1985; Asis 1995, 2002; Lauby and Stark 1988; Medina and Natividad 1985; Root and Dejong 1991, 1984, 1988), but that they also remain influential in her decision to stay on the job (Tacoli 1996a). For Filipinas, "the personal is also the family" (Asis 2002, 74). The respondents in the present study, composed of eight daughters and 16 mothers, echo these observations. As Nene, a daughter, illustrates, familial obligations are intrinsic to "cultural rules" that define her as a Filipina:

> … I remit even though I do not have a family of my own—my mother and siblings and their families need my financial support. This is not an obligation for me per se. It's my choice. I say this because I respect our culture in the sense that this is part of our [willing] obligation to our parents. Parents are very sacred and important to the Filipino. (Nene, wageworker, Paris)

And as Lilia, a mother, in Hong Kong states:

> There are so many things good about a Filipina … She is beautiful, kind, amicable, sweet, loving. And she is helpful. And we give our all to our family. Our best. This is why so many of us women work hard overseas … Instead of the man who should

culture away, I argue that her premise (along with others such as Narayan, 1997) of constructed and constructing cultures actually "bring in" culture into the individual and practical level, as I hope my discussion of agency and its institutionalization here shows. Furthermore, "universalist" values—when, as Nussbaum has stressed, they are understood in the certain context of cross-cultural applicability—is necessary for the political and policy administration of the CAA, where this will involve cross-cultural or international/cultural considerations to account for the dynamic transnational lives of migrant domestic workers (Chapter 8).

5 The Filipina cultural schema can also be explained through McKay's (2004b, 10) identification of "the Filipina" as a performative practice (Butler 1997). As McKay suggests, the "Filipina" (in the particular context of overseas domestic work) is an identity borne out of "naming practices that both enable and constrain individual agency as they simultaneously make personhood possible." For a general discussion on agency as a cultural construction see Parker (2005a: especially 230).

> leave, no it's mostly the woman that do so because we are the ones in particular who really hold our families closest to our hearts. (Lilia, wageworker, Hong Kong)

The "family" also extends to other female roles within the family. Among the respondents, there were also sisters and aunties who sought to assist family members in need. This was exemplified in JB's narrative in the previous chapter, for instance, which showed how she found living relatively comfortably in Paris impossible without thinking of her family's livelihood survival back in the Philippines. Ellen's experience provides a further illustration of this role:

> [I will remain working here] until my nieces and nephews have finished their college studies. I am giving financial support to … them … I also have a nephew who has leukemia, and so I help my sister with the hospital bills for that … I know that it's the obligations of the parents to look after … their own children … Others say to me that I shouldn't [help] because then they become dependent on me. But you see, in our province … [W]hat they earns is enough only for buying food. For hospital and other unexpected bills, what are they to do? I guess to help like this is embedded in our culture already. (Ellen, slave-wageworker, Hong Kong)

In these narratives, it is also possible to highlight how it is through their knowledge of the rules of being a Filipina (their cultural schemas) that Nene, Lilia and Ellen move into action; into undertaking overseas domestic work. This concurs with the observation made earlier that it is the knowledge of schemas that make people capable of action.

Important also to observe of schemas in the FODW context is that they are transposable. For the FODW, the transposition from being a Filipina living in the Philippines ("potential migrant") to one working in overseas domestic work (actual migrant domestic worker), occurs in response to the availability of resources. As observed earlier, schemas need resources for their continued existence. As Nene, Lilia and Ellen illustrate, remaining in the Philippines means not being able to practise the schemas of familial responsibilities because of a lack of nonhuman resources (of which the most primary is income) and human resources (that enable the gain, retention, control and propagation of both types of resources) as a result of un-/underemployment. Such schemas, in other words, would lose their power if Nene, Lilia and Ellen remained in the Philippines. The resources used to re-empower or regenerate these schemas, are, on the other hand, found in the FODW institution. The characteristics of these resources, and how they work with schemas to reproduce structures—and therefore agency—in the FODW context, are discussed below.

Resources in the FODW Context

If, as observed earlier, schemas and resources imply and sustain each other, then the regeneration of schemas must necessarily involve the regeneration of resources. As shown in the previous chapter, it is indeed for this very reason that Filipinas undertake overseas domestic work. For the FODW, regenerating resources involves being in the FODW institution, and finding there, sufficient income through employment in domestic work to support themselves and their families. More specifically, the access to employment and earnings regenerate the FODWs' nonhuman resources, whose accumulation in turn, regenerates the human resources that re-establish her status as good mother, daughter, sister, and/or aunty. This simultaneously re-empowers her schemas.

It is therefore a characteristic of resources, whether they are allocative/ nonhuman or authoritative/human, that they are "media through which power is exercised" (Giddens 1984a, 16). Power, in this sense, can be more accurately understood as "the capacity to achieve outcomes" (ibid., 257). Power is thus not a resource, but requires resources to operate—"to achieve outcomes." Indeed, Giddens originally referred to resources as "capabilities" which generate command over objects and other material phenomena (allocative) or over persons (authoritative) (Giddens 1979, 100). He thus places power "at the very origin of the capabilities of agents to bring about intended outcomes of action" (op. cit., 173). This is why Giddens (ibid., 33) refers to capabilities as "forms of transformative capacity." Without them, power cannot operate and therefore schemas are left powerless, making capabilities also redundant. Thus, whereas schemas make one capable of action, resources play the central role in enabling or making agents' actions capable of achieving intended outcomes. "Indeed" as Sewell (1992, 10) points out, "part of what it means to conceive of human beings as *agents* is to conceive of them as *empowered* by access to resources of one kind or another." What this, in turn, shows is that where power is the capacity to achieve outcomes, agency is the capability to use power *through access to resources/capabilities* to achieve intended outcomes.

Another characteristic of resources which has so far escaped Sewell's observation, but which is made possible through the present study's empirical grounding of his theory on resources, is that resources consist of two components:[6] elemental and generic. In the FODW case, schemas have an origin in their practice in the Philippines, and are then transposed to the overseas domestic work institution for the purposes of gaining the resources to ensure the existence of her original schema. This suggests that an aspect of resources is to provide the means by which individuals are empowered to exist or act. In ensuring the basic existence of the agent, these resources can thus be understood as *elemental*. Once transposed into the FODW institution, schemas are faced with a new array of resources and constraints, suggesting an aspect of resources that provides the means by which individual actions are facilitated and constrained within that institution. Because these aspects of resources address

6 Compare to Sewell's two types of resources: human and nonhuman, which show what constitute resources, rather than how they are constituted.

the external conditions necessary for that agent's continued function in the new context of overseas domestic work, they can be regarded as *generic*.

Conceptually, original schemas can be said to presuppose, albeit in practice necessarily coexist with, elemental resources, as is the case between transposed schemas and generic resources. In this sense, a new dimension is added to the conceptualization of structure, providing an insight into the structure of structure, so to speak (see Figure 7.1).

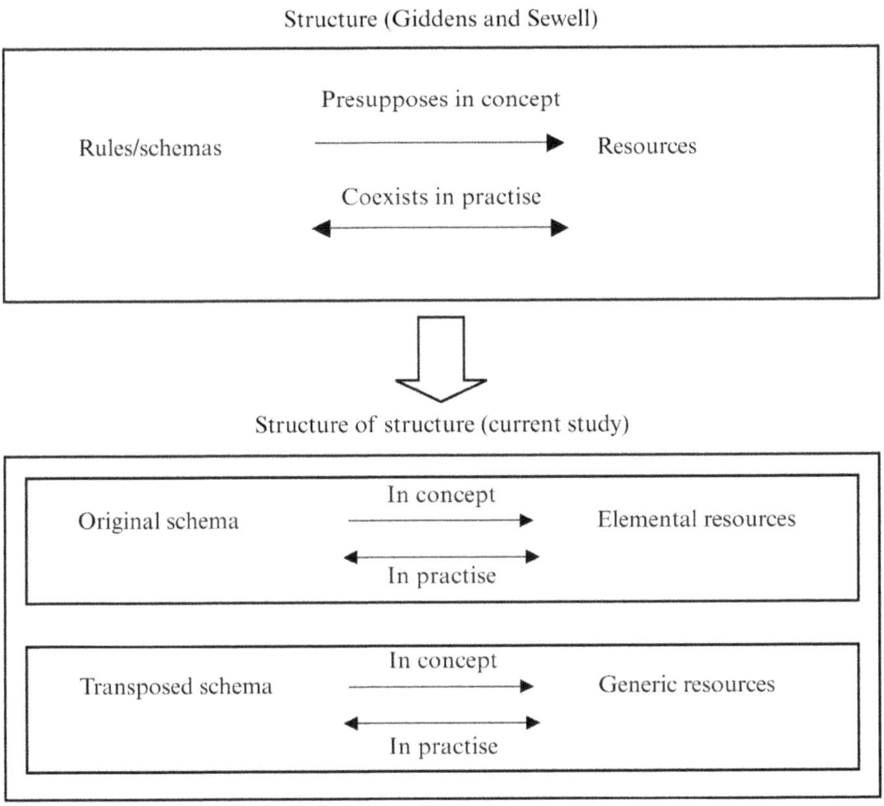

Figure 7.1 "Structure of structure"

This additional knowledge provides a further reformulation of the understanding of structure and agency as both means and ends, and thus suggests two interconnected paths to consider for the present study. The first is the need to look at resources or capabilities at two levels simultaneously. Such an approach complements and reaffirms the study's use of Nussbaum's concept of *combined capabilities*. The parallels are such that her definition of combined capabilities as "internal capabilities combined with suitable external conditions for the exercise of [a] function" (Chapter 1), can be directly applied to define the relationship between the two components of resources illuminated here: elemental resources must combine with generic resources to produce the capability to exercise a function. In the case of the FODW, her internal capabilities or elemental resources are useless without the suitable external conditions or generic resources that enable them to function, as do her generic resources without the presence of the elemental resources from which to generate. For the FODW then, the "capability to function" or "the ability to live a certain way" (Chapter 6) requires the operation of combined capabilities/resources. The FODWs' means to live a certain way, in other words, must coincide with the ends of that way of living.

The second path looks at how these "combined capabilities/resources" feature in the combining processes of schemas. That is, how original schemas fuse with transposed schemas to produce a more temporally and spatially dynamic understanding of structure (as demonstrated in "the structure of structure" diagram above), that thereby produces a more complete understanding of agency. This is fundamental for one of this chapter's main tasks of theorizing agency *in* the FODW. Emirbayer and Mische's reformulation of agency provides an important basis for this theorization, and is discussed below.

The Process of Agency in the FODW Context

Using the new knowledge of structure to extend from Sewell's conceptualization of the relationship between structure and agency, it is possible to specify that *temporally-spatially* located agency is implied by the existence of a *temporal-spatial* structure. The study takes a structuration perspective of time and space, and thus interprets Emirbayer and Mische's reformulation to necessarily include the dimension of space as indissolubly linked with the dimension of time.[7] That is, although they do not mention the spatial aspect in their study, this is assumed to be already included in their paradigm of the temporal aspect in agency. The assumption is made because firstly, they neither explicitly nor implicitly state that the spatial dimension should be treated separately from that of time. Secondly, the conceptualization of agency thus far has strongly suggested that beginning from the transposition of schemas, it is through the re-organization of time-space that the Filipina is able to overcome her period of crisis in the Philippines and lay the foundations overseas for a new period of accumulating resources to regenerate her cultural schema, now transposed.

7 I refer here to Giddens' conception of time-geography, as he draws on Heidegger, to characterize the agent's day to day conduct, and particularly to one of its main elements that suggests "that movement in space is also movement in time" (Giddens 1984a, 110–19).

This new way of seeing structure enables an explanation of the processes of the relationship between original and transposed schemas, as situated in what Emirbayer and Mische term "the structural contexts of action." These operate in "temporal as well as relational fields—multiple, overlapping *ways of ordering time,* toward which … actors can assume *different simultaneous* agentic orientations" (Emirbayer and Mische 1998, 963–4, emphasis added). These contexts thus involve multiple temporalities within which actors can find themselves oriented toward the past, the future, and the present at any one time, but also within which they themselves can choose which of these will predominate in guiding their actions.

Thus where Sewell (op. cit., 18) defines agency as "entailing the capacity to transpose and extend schemas to new contexts," Emirbayer and Mische (op. cit., 964) explain this "capacity to transpose" in terms of "different simultaneous agentic orientations:" "as actors move within and among [the] different unfolding contexts, they switch between (or "recompose") their temporal orientations—as constructed within and by means of those contexts—and thus are capable of changing their relationship to structure.

From these notions of agency, it is possible to conceptualize the relationship between original and transposed schemas as agency, or the process through which agency occurs (see Figure 7.2).

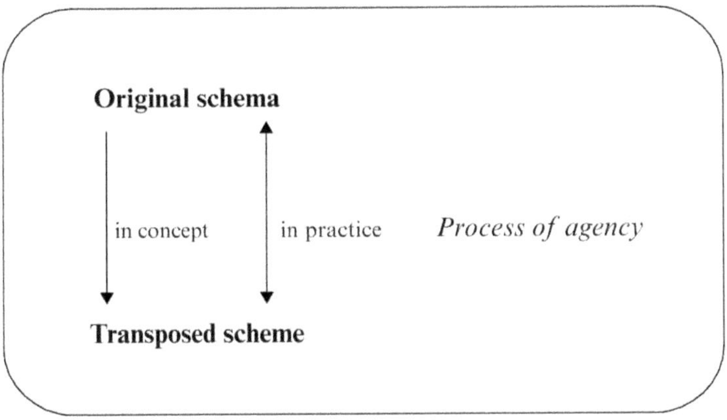

Figure 7.2 The process of agency

Emirbayer and Mische's temporal paradigm of agency allows exploration into what constitutes this process. Where Giddens characterizes the agent with the ability to reflexively monitor, rationalize and have motivation of action, Emirbayer and Mische (ibid., 971, original emphasis) frame these to correspond, respectively, to the iterational, projective and practical evaluative functions of agents' actions.

The iterational element which corresponds to agentic orientations towards the past, "refers to *the selective reactivation by actors of past patterns of thought and action, as routinely incorporated in practical activity, thereby giving stability and order to social universe and helping to sustain identities interactions, and institutions overtime.*" As such, Emirbayer and Mische synonymously refer to iteration as "habitual."

The projective element, which corresponds to agentic orientations toward the future, refers to "*the imaginative generation of actors of possible future trajectories of action, in which received structures of thought and action may be creatively reconfigured in relation to actors' hopes, fears and desires for the future.*"

The practical-evaluative element, which corresponds to agentic orientations in the present, refers to "*the capacity of actors to make practical and normative judgments among alternative possible trajectories of action, in response to the emerging demands, dilemmas, and ambiguities of presently evolving situations.*"

Again, consistent with structuration theory, these elements of agency are possible to conceive of as analytically separate components, but in practice, they actively interrelate as a kind of "chordal triad" (ibid., 970). It is thus that Emirbayer and Mische define agency as

> the temporally constructed engagement by actors of different structural environments—the temporal-relational contexts of action—which, through the interplay of habit, imagination and judgment, both reproduces and transforms those structures in interactive response to the problems posed by changing historical situations.

Woven through the FODW context, this process-oriented perspective on agency completes the theoretical framework from which to explain the experience of agency by the individual FODW. Extending from the transposition of the original schema, it shows how, through her structure, the FODW temporally constructs engagement of the different structural environment of overseas domestic work through the interplay of habit, imagination, and judgment, to reproduce and transform her structure in interactive response to the problems posed by the "changing historical situation" of an impoverished Philippine economy and its impact on her resource-access. For a diagrammatic explanation of this, see Figure 7.3.

It is through this process of agency that we can conceptualize *agency in*, and importantly how it incorporates, rather than is incorporated by, *the agency of* the FODW. Figure 7.3 shows how *agency in* the FODW is situated in her own structure—the FODW structure (Figure 7.3a) while *agency of* is situated within her structural set or institution—the FODW Institution (Figure 7.3b). It becomes evident here, that the change in the FODW structure is about empowering the FODWs themselves, while the participation in the overseas

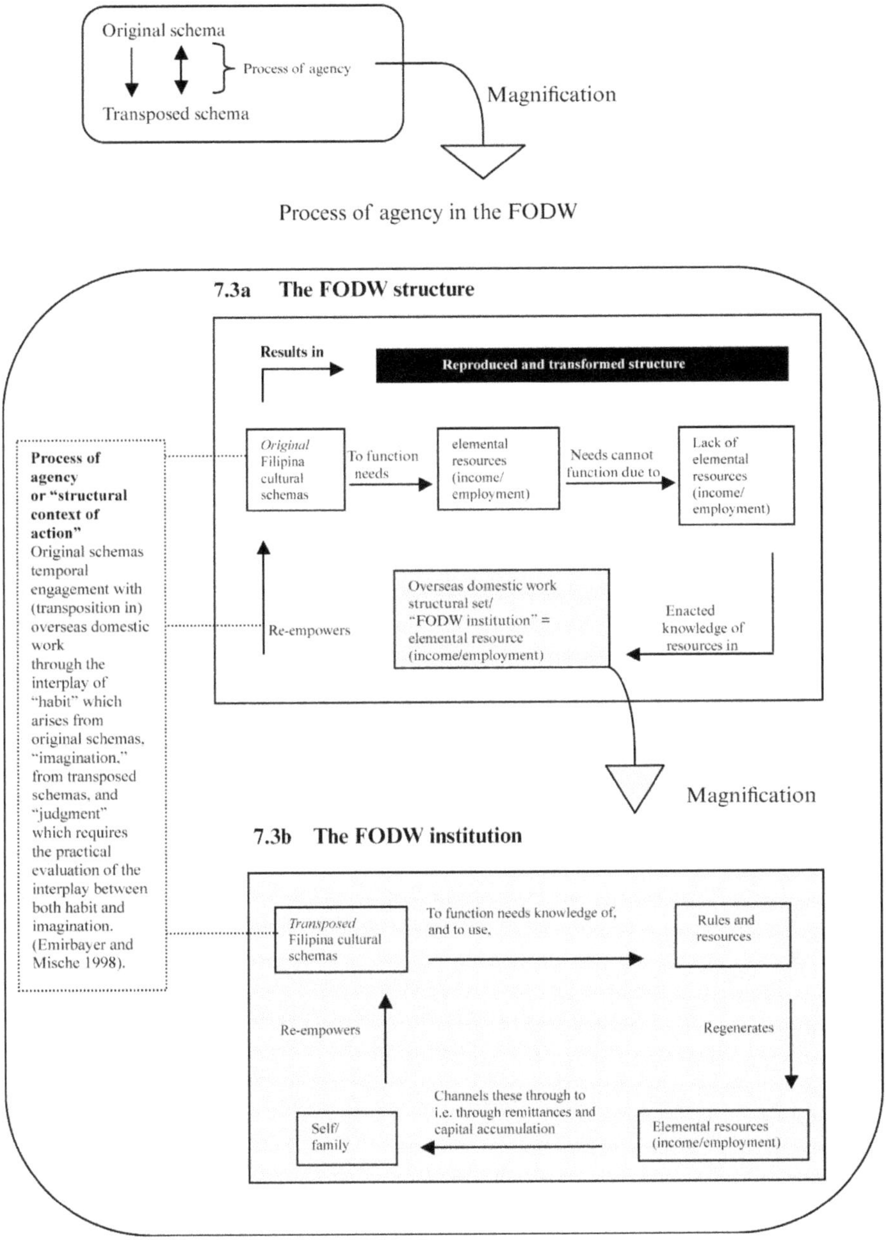

Figure 7.3 Agency in the FODW context

domestic work structural set/institution is about ensuring the supply of resources for such empowerment. (How the FODW institution is conceptualized as a "capability set" is discussed in Chapter 8). Referring to Figure 7.3, this point becomes clearer when empowerment of the FODW herself is shown to rest on her access to the elemental resources of gainful employment, and not just to generic resources, which although they re-empower her elemental resources, are not in themselves sufficient to empower the FODW herself.

This framework reveals that the FODW Structure transcends or encompasses the FODW Institution, and thus understanding her agency must also, as this section has demonstrated, go beyond understanding the agency she exerts in overseas domestic work to that in understanding her experience of agency in her own terms—in her own structure—the FODW structure. Here, experience itself goes beyond the act of exertion, conceived of "in its vital form [as] experimental, an effort to change the given; [and] is characterized by projection, by reaching forward into the unknown …" (Dewey, 1981, in Emirbayer and Mische 1998, 988).

The FODW Structure

Melanie's response to why, in her opinion, so many Filipinas migrate overseas as domestic workers provides a FODW's version of this experience:

> Life is hard back home … [F]or me, dealing with [being a domestic worker here in Paris] is a practical matter. If I was in the Philippines, what would I do there? … There's no money. There's no life … Whereas if you are here, you … can make … your dreams come true … I can give … [everything to my children] ….
>
> … they endure hardship here … [and] why so many sell and leave everything they have, and borrow large amounts of money, because in the Philippines, there is really nothing. Nothing …
>
> People who have reached some level of education in the Philippines, like me, come here to become a *ménage* [domestic worker]. They are willing to stoop lower because … of the wage differentials; professionals earn next to nothing in the Philippines. [So] I am willing to sacrifice my education for the sake of my family. Once you have a family, you replace dreaming for yourself with dreaming for … your children … [T]his is enough to give you the strength to go on. (Melanie, Paris)

This experience is both confirmed and shared by Bernie in Hong Kong:

> … you have to leave your pride behind and nurture strength within yourself to be able to play the role of domestic worker. At least, until you have saved enough and can go home again. … All I want is to be able to support my children … I don't plan to be here forever. I just came here to save some capital … [I]f I stayed in the Philippines, we would just stay the way we are—with nothing. Our economy is so bad and I don't see it recovering any time soon … I can't do for my children what they

> want ... Now, if you are here, you can give this to them. You see, most important of all, is to be able to provide for them financially. (Bernie, Hong Kong)

Thus for both Melanie and Bernie, transposing their schema from the Philippines to "here," where there is the elemental resource of gainful employment, enables them to regenerate their schemas by providing for their families, and in effect, their own needs. The interplay between habit (sustaining their identities as self-sacrificing mothers), imagination (their dreams and plans) and judgment (their practical evaluation of their situation) is a salient feature of their narrative, thus implicating the process of agency within their experiences. Because this process arises as a response to the problems of economic hardship faced in the Philippines, their imagination or projective orientation to a future void of such hardship, predominates in guiding their action within their temporal engagement of the FODW institution.[8]

Through this process, it becomes evident that the experience of agency by the FODW is dependent upon her access to the elemental resource of overseas domestic work employment that provides the "money," the "capital" to enable a "life." Indeed, to enable the very experience of agency. Without this access, there is no transposition of schemas, hence no process of agency, and therefore no experience of agency. Put another way, using Melanie's and Bernie's context, their agency is "nothing" without resources.[9] This illustrates the role of resources as integral to the very existence of the FODW, rather than as simply quantifiable inputs.

The difference between the *exertion* of agency and the *experience* of agency is particularly crucial to grasp here if the fuller understanding of FODW agency is to be gained. Exertion suggests that agency already exists—a product to exert. Hence, one can speak of the *agency of* the FODW. But it is the experience of agency, which suggests an ongoing, temporal process involving agentic orientations; a producing and reproducing of agency itself—of its very existence, that elucidates *agency in* the FODW. In this way, it enables analysis to gain understanding of her capability to mediate an array of structuring contexts within which her actions, or indeed, exertion of agency, unfolds. The exertion of agency is thus a mere part of the bigger experience of agency itself. The remaining sections of this chapter explore how the capability of agency to go on unfolding via its intrinsic use of resources may be conceptualized. First,

---

8 Refer for instance to McKay's (2004a, 11) observation that FODWs endure exploitative working conditions because they anticipate a future reversal in their status once they return home. On this point see also McKay (2004b, 11; Parreñas 2001, 173; Ebron 2002). For a theoretical observation of this "projectivity," see Aguilar (1999).

9 Or "value-less." Again, as McKay's (2004b, 17) research on "performing identities" illustrates, "the local [such as, in a sending community in the Philippines] ... cannot generate either value or support the performance of the kinds of identities to which women aspire. This local is deficient in providing the 'nice things' and the 'respect' that underpin performances of Filipina femininity at home".

it is important to note the limits of agency and the implications of these for understanding capability.

Limits of Agency and the Issue of Capability

Along with other theorists dealing with agency, Sewell and Emirbayer and Mische take as a given that the capacity for agency is inherent in all humans.[10] What they fail to explore is the significance of this capacity in determining the extent or capability for individuals to practice agency at all. In other words, they fail to explore the distinction between being capable of action and the capability of action to produce intended outcomes.

It was established earlier that resources play a central role in making agents' actions capable; agency is the capability to use power, via access to resources, for its intended purposes. Supporting this is the discussion above on the process of agency, which shows the use of resources as the source of power that enables the agent and her structure to reproduce and to transform. In this sense, it can be said that FODW agency cannot occur without the particular array of elemental and generic resources that contribute in enabling the existence of her structure, and therefore her experience of agency.

It was also discussed earlier how the "unpredictable accumulation of resources" and the "intersection of structures" provide a threat to the intended outcome of actions. Because the accumulation of resources depends on the agent's schematic use of them, where the agent's social knowledge is limited to the conditions and consequences of their own actions, and because the intersection of structures suggests impacts of simultaneous actions by others, the reproduction/transformation of the agent's structure (Figure 7.3a), although intended to re-empower the agent, does not necessarily materialize. Thus, although embarking on domestic work for the intended purpose of gainful employment, the FODW may find herself enslaved, with her access to resources obstructed by unscrupulous employers and/or recruitment agencies and/or constraining state apparatus.

These limits of agency can therefore be said to lie in the absence of resources and/or the blocked access to them. The previous section has already shown how the experience of agency is entirely dependent on the presence of resources. The next section provides insight into how the "blocked access" to resources occurs, by exploring the extent or capability of the respondents' agency within the varying degrees of constraints in their work situations.

10 For other theorists, including Giddens, see Emirbayer and Mische's (1998, 963) review of these other approaches; for Sewell's (1992, 21) specific discussion on this topic.

Capability and Filipina Experiences of Domestic Work in Paris and Hong Kong

Building on the respondents' classifications of their work situations presented in the previous chapter, this section explores the degree of capability in the respondents' agency to achieve their intended purposes of gainful employment in the FODW institution.

The earlier discussion of agency in the FODW shows her intended access of the elemental resource of paid overseas domestic work, which in turn provides access to generic resources that can facilitate capability in agency; that can allow her actions to go on as intended. These generic resources include other agents and institutions such as migrant NGOs, recruitments agents, employers and so on, as discussed in Chapter 5. Using this framework for analysis, in-depth discussions with the respondents on their experiences of constraints, and their exertion of agency to challenge and triumph over them, revealed three different processes of agentic functions. The first involved that of respondents "continuing as intended," the second that of "desiring to continue as intended," and the third, "persisting to continue as intended (that is, despite obstacles)." To aid the following discussion on the elaboration of these functions it is useful here to refer to Table 7.1 below.

Table 7.1 Agentic functions of respondents

1 Continuing as intended	
Wageworker	Gudilia, Indiana, JB, Nene, Lilia, Michelle
Slave-wageworker	Ellen
Slave	Gemini
2 Desiring to continue as intended	
Slave	Ana, Lani
Oppressed/abused wageworker	Amity
3 Persisting to continue as intended	
Wageworker	Delia, Felise, Mila, Virgo, Red Loveley, Bernie
Former slave now wageworker	Melanie, Minda, Sally
Former slave now abused wageworker	Helena
Abused wageworker	Jinky
Oppressed/abused wageworker	Alili

Those "continuing as intended" consist mainly of respondents who classified their experience of their work situations as wageworkers. They are those whose access to the elemental resource of overseas domestic work employment, and the generic resources this entails, remain intact. This means that the exertion of agency in overseas domestic work goes on uninterrupted, as intended. Indiana's narrative on the gains she has made after 18 years of domestic work employment in Paris, and of Michelle, after 23 years of overseas domestic work, 19 of which was in Hong Kong, illustrate this:

> Step by step, I was able to help my children finish their schooling … Also, I am able to help my sisters and aunties and mother … They have someone they can borrow money from in emergency situations … [I've lost] nothing really, just my time with the children but this hasn't been such a problem because I am in regular contact with them anyway. I always think that this is a small price to pay for a good future for us all than living in the squatters in the Philippines. I always tell them, if I hadn't left to work here, you wouldn't know what it's like to have cell-phones, to have your own ATM accounts with deposit amounts that [professionals] there earn! (Indiana, wageworker, Paris)

> I was able to help my family. I helped my sibling who has nine children. I then helped one of her children to come here and work so she can help her family. Between us, we were able to help the rest of her siblings finish college … I suppose you can say that we are happier now because we now enjoy a better standard of living. I think if we had stayed in the Philippines, we … would have been [just able to survive. Instead,] … I was able to … buy land, build a house. So you could say I'm happy now. (Michelle, wageworker, Hong Kong)

Particularly important to note for those "continuing as intended," is that their intact access to gainful employment supersedes self-classifications that seem to contradict gainful employment. This is evident in the cases of Ellen and Gemini, who, despite classifying their work situation as "slave-wageworker" and "slave," continue as intended. In other words, their agency, even when they have classified their situation as gravely constrained, can be said to have the "capability to function." Thus, Ellen's evaluation of her 12 years of slave-like work, includes a reflection of the gains she had made: "It seems that it was a huge help with me coming here … of course I'm happy with my pay [and that] I could help my family." Gemini's affirmation of the financial gains of the work too, despite classifying her situation as a "slave," illustrates how she nevertheless sees herself as continuing as intended: "I was already in my forties when I decided to go abroad, and now I keep telling myself, gee, if only I had started when I was younger, I'd be rich by now!"

In contrast, it is when this slavery results in the unintended consequence of losing access to the elemental resource of gainful employment that a FODW can be said to lose capability in her agency. Among the respondents, these include those who have more recently experienced abuse from their employers. Although classifying their situations as slavery or as laden with abuse and oppression, these respondents nevertheless remained tenacious in their desire to continue as intended. Ana, who classified herself as a slave, had nevertheless resigned herself to securing a second contract to achieve a savings plan that would cover her future application expenses for work in Canada. However, after three months in the second contract, she was charged with child abuse. Finding herself both in prison, and without employment, she recalls that:

> It was cold and horrible. I feared for my plans to go to Canada. And to be with my boyfriend of 12 years eventually. And my mother who depends on my monthly remittance.

But her "desire to continue as intended" required enacting her knowledgeability to access the generic resources in her social networks, which in this case, included another FODW and a Filipino-based NGO, to enable her to regenerate her elemental resource:

> The next day I was allowed out on bail … I called up a [FODW friend] … but she said she herself couldn't help. Instead, she gave me [a domestic workers' NGO's] number. Fortunately, they came and bailed me out and brought me here to the [shelter]. They helped me to win my case. (Ana, slave, Hong Kong)

Amity, too, had resorted to the help of an NGO to fight her case to stay in Hong Kong, and to regain access to employment. She had received slave-like treatment for over one year. Amity had endured the treatment because she had entered into a secret and illegal contract agreement with her employer who promised to provide her with the opportunity to earn above the minimum wage, and to allow her to practice her educational qualifications as a teacher. But after constant abusive treatment which culminated in the employer pushing her out of a moving car, she decided to terminate her own contract. With the help of the NGO, Amity was able to take her case to court but her access to the elemental resource of employment became uncertain. As she recounts the situation:

> With my first employer, I had no real problems. Just extreme hard work with two toddlers and a … baby. I finished the contract with them. But with this current one, I [had] to initiate the termination of my contract …
>
> With this particular contract, I agreed to help her with her professional teaching on top of domestic work duties … Before we signed the contract, she said that she would give me above the minimum wage for this extra work … I took this on because I [also] saw it as a rare opportunity to get out of domestic work eventually. I also wanted to put my education into practice. It was fine in the beginning … But within a week, her true, scary colours came out! She was hot tempered, abusive …
>
> … I would sleep around 2 or 3am because I was helping [her] with half of her teaching load, on top of my domestic duties. At the same time, I couldn't let the authorities know because I had gotten myself into this even though I knew it was illegal …
>
> But when all is said and done, after all the hardship and the hard feelings, I still have to be thankful for the employment opportunity and the pay I received from them …

....I would be happy with one more two-year contract, but it depends on the result of my current court case. I may or may not be able to stay. (Amity, oppressed/abused wageworker, Hong Kong)

Like Ana and Amity's situations, Lani's case in Paris provides another example of how her limited knowledge of the consequences of her actions, led to the unintended result of her enslavement:

I wanted to go to Manila because I had studied to be a midwife and I wanted to apply in a hospital so that I could save enough money to pay for the placement fee to go [and work] abroad. But I could not save enough for the ... fee. It so happened that I had a friend who was working for a travel agency and I knew that with this agency, one could get into a salary-deduction program. ... she was kind enough to take me through the application process without fees. In return, I would volunteer from time to time at the recruitment agency ...

Then came the day when [I was told that the agency had] found me a Prince in Saudi to work for. I was very happy to hear this—a Prince! ...

[But] When I got to Saudi [Arabia], I found that I ... would not be working directly for him. I was to work for one of his wife's sisters. I was very unlucky because she was the meanest of all the sisters. (Lani, slave, Paris)

As her situation eventuated, the employer underpaid, overworked and hit her, as well as confiscated her passport and bankbooks. So when she was brought along on her employer's family holiday in Paris to look after a child, she took the opportunity to escape. However, the capability of her agency was dispossessed in her three failed attempts to escape. Her employer had employed guards to ensure that she did not escape again. Nevertheless, one of those attempts had alerted an unidentified person who worked at the hotel at which she was staying with her employer. This opened up access to the generic resources of the CCEM, and from there, importantly for the regeneration of her elemental resources, to the Filipino domestic workers network in Paris. After the CCEM had rescued her, she was given a few months to recover in a shelter before repatriation to the Philippines. In the meantime, the CCEM had organized a meeting between Lani and a member of a local Filipino-based NGO to raise some donations for her return. As another form of generic resource, this "established" NGO member, well aware of the hardship back in the Philippines, suggested instead that Lani disappear into the undocumented world in Paris: "you are already here, and there are so many others who are earning well even though they are undocumented," she advised (Diary PRC 18/09/03). It was at this meeting that Lani resolved, despite what she had been through, to continue on as intended:

I would really rather take the legal way as much as possible. But in my situation, I cannot go home with just the E1000 the CCEM and Filipino community has kindly raised for me. If I do, this money will only last me and my four children two months

... and then what? So, I have to stay here and look for work ... even though I will be without papers. I know that there are many Filipinas who are in this position here and they seem to be doing ok, so I don't see any reason why I shouldn't give it my best shot. (Lani, slave, Paris)

What these cases show is how access to elemental resources and generic resources can be blocked by employer-inflicted deprivation in a number of ways including being framed (as Ana's case showed), being blackmailed or through an outright abuse of contractual entitlements (as in Amity's case), as well as being "locked up" (as in Lani's case). They also show, however, the importance of the generic resources in enabling the possibility of regenerating the elemental resources, as expressed through the "desire to go on as intended" (see also Figure 7.3b). That, however, their continued access to overseas domestic work employment depends on volatile factors such as court cases or on "illegal" status, which could result in their deportation and thus discontinued access to elemental resources, highlights the high level of precariousness of capability in FODW agency.

Nevertheless, the possibilities that the "desire to continue" generates, has been proven to materialize. This is demonstrated by those who have managed to mitigate or challenge the unintended consequences of abuse and/or enslavement, and who are thus "persisting to continue as intended." The persistent respondents consists of those who see their situations as essentially that of wageworkers, but who have triumphed over various degrees of abuse, including enslavement, or who are surviving abuse and/or oppression that is nevertheless acceptable to them, since in effect, it does not obstruct their access to resources, and thus allows them to go on as intended.

Sally's case is an example of a FODW who has succeeded in challenging enslavement, and who now sees her situation as that of a wageworker:

I can say that my life is a little better now because we are not so poor ... Now I can buy my children new clothes and things that they need for school ...

There's more that I have gained by being here ... I can speak French well now and I've received the most important education I could ever have wished for in my life; my experience here with my three-year case ... has taught me so much about the situation of domestic workers here, and most important, about ... our rights ...

[I now] work here with a labour union ... we have to protect our profession because even though we are seen as just a "katulong ["helper"]," this is in fact a true profession ... (Sally, former slave now wageworker, Paris)

Sally persists to continue as intended because as she explains: "I have to be practical. [The children] still haven't finished their college and I still have to build my own house."

Helena's case shows that she, too, persists to continue as intended because of financial commitments to herself and her family:

> [I will work here] until I can … because my family still needs my help and especially now, I cannot stop because life is even harder in the Philippines. So even though I am very tired and I endure a lot of trials, I will keep working ….even though sometimes I am treated … like a slave … I have to accept. (Helena, former slave now abused wageworker, Paris)

What makes Helena's situation different from Sally's, however, is that Helena sees being "treated a little like a slave" as acceptable, especially when she compares this to her previous experience working for Saudi Arabian employers:

> I'm in Paris because I escaped from my abusive Saudi employer when they came here for a holiday. I would sleep at 1am because they would make me work the whole day and night … the pay was very low … we had no days off … If it wasn't for their baby-sitter [who was also a Filipina] who pushed me to escape with her, I would still be with them. I remember … she was intent on escaping … I had a phone number of a Filipina here who apparently helped "escapees," which I got from a Filipina acquaintance in Saudi [Arabia], "just in case" she had said. So we called this contact and she encouraged us to escape. …
>
> I want to leave my current employment but … I'm scared that I will not find a better one … It's not ideal, but I suppose my employment situation could be worse. At least I do get paid and my employer is more or less nice to me. She is also looking into my papers, so even though she [pays less than the minimum wage and] gives me so much work, I won't leave her. It's a very unusual opportunity to get one's papers if one has only been here for three years so it's worth putting up with some abuse from time to time …

Note here also how Helena's ability to access contacts in Paris reveals a transnational characteristic of generic resources, which correlates with the transnational character of the FODW institution, identified in Chapter 5.

Similarly, Alili, who classified her situation as oppressed/abused wageworker, and who, when I met her, had just been newly elected as president of a prominent NGO in Hong Kong, has worked there for 17 years. Despite displaying extensive knowledge of oppressive working conditions, however, she can also claim that:

> … I've left most of my employers when they had changed in the course of my employment with them; when they start developing an attitude which makes me feel disrespected … [like] shouting at me for no reason. I just don't tolerate this kind of attitude … [and] abuse.

What Alili leaves implicit here is that the "kind of person" she is, is one that has the skill, experience and knowledge to reach the high ranks of a major NGO. This suggests that Alili possesses a significant level of knowledgeability of the rules and resources in overseas domestic work that can assist in informing her actions to go on as intended. Indeed, despite oppressive working conditions, her jobs in Hong Kong still enabled her to continue as intended, allowing her to reflect on the gains she had made over her years of persistence:

> My status in my family; I've gained respect from my family … I could help my family through the years when their financial situation worsened because of the Philippine's poor economy … It's really nice to think … that after all the hardship my mother had endured … she could … taste a nicer life before she died. And to think that she could die in peace, without having to worry about her children's and grandchildren's welfare. I feel … good, that somehow, I was able to serve her as a daughter. I've also managed to renovate our house. We don't have to put up with a leaky roof anymore! And my mother got to experience this, so I'm happy when I think about this. (Alili, oppressed/abused wageworker, Hong Kong)

It is evident in these examples that, through access to generic resources, the FODWs have been able to reinforce the capability in their agency to successfully redirect unintended consequences to those originally intended. Thus Sally, having been enslaved, was able to use the generic resources of local community and receiving-state apparatuses; Helena, through the use of her transnational Filipino network, found better working conditions; and Alili, through her active participation in a migrant-rights NGO, was able to confidently negotiate her oppression by leaving abusive employment situations for better ones.

In doing so, these FODWs have increased their knowledge and experience. They have become more knowledgeable of the possibilities in the "rules and resources" of the FODW institution, thus serving in effect to lessen the likelihood of unnecessary endurance of abuse. This is not to say that such improved knowledgeability guarantees that their future actions will never again result in unintended consequences. However, when compared to the situations of those "continuing" and "desiring to continue as intended," the agency of those "persisting to continue as intended" can be said to be the most capable. This is because the new knowledge and experience translates into new or reinforced resources that add to her capability. Drawing from the earlier discussion on schemas and resources, and referring back to the conceptualization of agency in Figure 7.3a, the new knowledge, particularly of the positive experience, can be said to add to the schema which then re-enacts resources in the type of human resources. These produced human resources are crucial to strengthening FODW capability as they serve to "enhance or maintain power, including knowledge of the means of gaining, retaining, controlling and propagating [both] human and nonhuman resources" (Sewell 1992, 9).

Having thus established the nature and degree of capability in the respondents' exertion of agency within varying degrees of constraints, it becomes evident how it is that resources make agents' actions capable. That all the FODWs in this study, continue, and despite experiences of enslavement still desire and persist to continue as intended, underscores the primacy of access to the elemental resource of overseas domestic work employment. Integral to this is the access to generic resources in the FODW institution to "unblock" and regenerate the capability of their agency to continue (intended) access to the elemental resource. Put simply, the capability of agency is thus the capability to "continue as intended." Although I have simplified the goals of FODWs here to financial gain through income—where income as a generic resource is understood to directly affect capability by strengthening it, it must be remembered that capability goals presume "combined capabilities" (Chapters 1 and 6). Thus, income capability cannot be understood apart from other agency goals that enable the agency success or achievement of that income. Of interest here is not so much that a FODW has income, but that she has the capability of converting that income into constitutive elements of her well-being.

Conclusion

So what does it mean for FODW agency to be capable? This chapter showed how the FODWs in the study can be said to be capable agents because they exert agency even when abused/oppressed/enslaved. However, it also showed that the capability in their agency is vulnerable not only to the violent and/or physically constraining forces inherent in enslavement, but also to the threat of a "de"-transposition of their schemas back to the Philippines, where the elemental resource of gainful employment is absent for them. This concurs with the previous chapter's finding that internal as well as external constraints present a threat to FODW capability, and therefore agency.

Due to the FODW's experience of agency that embeds her within a larger structure, as well as with and against other structures or agents/institutions/sub-structures, it is impossible, and indeed, not in her interest, to disengage with them, even when their constraining elements threaten to annihilate the capability in her agency. On the surface, this contradictory position seems problematic. However, consistent with the duality of structure, constraints entail counter-constraints. Thus, while for most of the respondents in the study, agency doesn't necessarily prove powerful enough to alter the structural elements conducive to her enslavement, it can prove powerful enough to challenge them, and even triumph over them. It is, however, when FODWs find themselves in a form of enslavement that either prevents them from acting within their (FODW) structure (say, through employer-inflicted imprisonment and similar abuses) or forces them out of their structure (such as through deportation/de-transposition), that agency can lose its power or capability to challenge structural constraints. In this case, being "out of" the FODW structure, and therefore the FODW institution (Figure 7.3), is a FODW agency without capability. As I have attempted to show, it is through capability in FODW agency in terms of going on, or being able to continue, as intended, that she transforms her structures.

This chapter importantly found that it is possible to re-inject capability into agency by firstly ensuring that it is reconnected to a resource base of elemental resources, and then by providing continued access to generic resources, thus ultimately enabling the FODW to continue as intended. This finding reinforces the need to retain and strengthen the capability of the agent by securing the existence of her resources as well as her access to them. A final observation to make here is with the particular agentic function of "persisting to continue as intended." Because it encompasses all the array of experiences in the work situations from wageworkers to slaves, and because it is evident that the desire to go on as intended can in fact materialize, it illuminates a path along which intervention may perhaps be most effective. This agentic function in other words, shows how capability can be reinforced, so as to enable the agents to continue as intended.

The theorization of agency in this chapter demonstrates the limitations and context of agency in the FODW at a micro or individual level. It has also shown that an approach based on a notion of "capable agency" in the FODW, where the capability of agency can thus be defined as *the capability to go on or continue as intended*, is an important tool to enable understanding, and therefore effective intervention in the infinite variation of experiences in overseas domestic work. The implications of these conclusions for identifying the value and possibilities of capability in FODW agency for policy and research action are discussed in the final chapter.

PART IV
Conclusion

Chapter 8
A Capable Agency Approach: Livelihood, Resources and Human Rights

This chapter brings together the main findings of the study and discusses their implications for policy action and further research on the situation of FODWs. I firstly outline the study's framework for conceptualizing and evaluating capability in FODW agency. I term this framework a "capable agency approach (CAA)." I then show how this approach is useful in policy implementation at three related levels: the FODW institution level, the level of the individual FODW in the FODW institution, and the level of the individual out of the FODW institution. I discuss these policy implications within the other main institutional components of the FODW structural complex: immigration policies, host country domestic work labour policies and development policies. The discussion then turns to looking at how the present study's contributions can provide some key directions for future research. Finally, I conclude that a CAA is important in unsettling the current polarized views and policy actions on migrant domestic workers' oppression, which has been unsuccessful in meeting their needs not only for empowerment but also for sustainable livelihoods. In particular, I show how the CAA can advance these current views by discussing the reconciliation of rights with livelihoods through an assertion of capability as not only the theoretical but also the political goal for migrant domestic worker empowerment.

A Capable Agency Approach (CAA)

Chapters 1 and 2 provided an introduction of how the study conceives agency and capability. Building on the discussion of FODW agency in Chapter 4, Chapters 5 and 6 provided a discussion on how capability in agency may be understood. To complete the explanation of the agency-capability relationship or as I term it, "capable agency," this section demonstrates how agency is conceived in capability. As a starting point, it is possible to simply understand the CAA in terms of the CA itself, but with a theory of, rather than just an evaluative framework for, agency processes within a capability set.[1] In foregrounding agency within the CA, the CAA conceives of the body not just in how it works (agency through structuration) or what it requires to work, and why (resistance, capability and capabilities), but in terms of what it is actually working on to be able to do and be (capable agency). More specifically, articulating a theory of agency within the CA allows a focus on the agent and on her particular structural context, which in turn allows a more specific conceptualization of capability/ies specific to the agent and her relevant structural environment. A more tacit view of the agent within the CA allows us to see that while capability describes the limitations and possibilities in, and of, agency, it is the agent that enacts capability.

Drawing upon the comprehensive discussion on agency and capability in the preceding three chapters, I firstly provide here, an overview of the relationship between agency and capability that defines the concept of capable agency. I then take the major component-clusters of this definition[2] and explain them in light of the lessons thus far learned from FODW experiences. I am then able to demonstrate how the articulation of "agency in capability" completes the definition of a capable agency approach. It may be useful to refer to the Glossary (xiii) for the following discussion.

The Capable Agency Concept

Agency is the capability to do, but not necessarily to be. Capability is the freedom to make agency capable to do *and* be. Capability cannot occur without agency. Although agency can occur without capability,[3] for the purposes of intended valued-ends (such as that of a quality of life) pursued in a capability set, agency cannot occur without capabilit*ies*, which in turn provides it with capability. This interdependence between agency and capability in a capability set, forms the concept of "capable agency."

1 For critiques on the insufficient theorization of agency within the CA, see Gasper (2002, 20–21).

2 Think analogically here, for instance, of the separate component of an automobile's engine that work together in groups or clusters (the transmission system with the motor system, with the cooling system and so on) to put the engine in operation.

3 As for instance, in the discussion in Chapter 6 of Giddens' (1984a) example of someone pointing a gun at another's head. Giddens was here demonstrating how agency is practised through valued choices albeit for the purpose of allowing the end of one's life in such a way. In this sense then, agency doesn't require "capability to function."

Major Component Clusters: Capability, Capabilities and Capability Sets

In Chapter 5, the concept of a FODW institution was introduced. This institution enables a FODW to pursue her own interests through the access and use of its resources. Chapter 6 then showed how such an institution could be understood in terms of a structural set that serves as the elementary resource of overseas domestic work (or gainful employment). This structural set was shown to compose of generic resources that enable a FODW continued access to the elemental resource. Chapter 6 further showed how it is through a FODW's retained access to resources that she is able to transform her structure and empower herself—in the language of structuration theory, "to go on as intended" and of the CA, "to achieve her valued-ends."

Because these resources serve to give the FODW the capability to empower herself, I assert here that they be understood as synonymous with capability and capabilities; more specifically, elemental resources as capability and generic resources as capabilities.[4] This distinction provides a tacit illustration of the distinction between Sen's use of capability as synonymous to a capability set and Nussbaum's use of capabilities as synonymous to resources and opportunities. For the present study, this distinction allows analysis to "embody" the FODW institution as a structural set by identifying it as a capability set.

As discussed in Chapter 6, a capability set can be understood as a person's chosen array of feasible functionings (or "doings and beings") to achieve valued goals in her life. For FODWs, this "chosen set" can more specifically be understood in terms of the transposition of their cultural schemas into the FODW institution. It is the elementary resource of overseas domestic work that enables the FODW's access to, and hence, achievement of her valued functionings (Chapter 7). This process, in short, constitutes her capability. Her capability is, in turn, enabled by the expansion of feasible alternative functionings and opportunities through the generic resources and functionings available in the FODW institution. As distinct from the process of capability, this process constitutes her capabilities. Through both these processes, the FODW institution provides a resource-filled environment in which the FODW can both do and be. It is in this sense, therefore, that a FODW institution can be conceived of in terms of a capability set. Note that "capabilities" here takes a slightly different context from Sen and Nussbaum's use of capabilities. That is, here, capabilities are specified in terms of a particular capability set (the FODW institution), whereas Sen and Nussbaum employ it more generally to apply to

4 It is important to be reminded here of how the capability approach adopts the use of resources as intrinsic to the capability to function: that is, the functionings and capabilities of a person as produced through the use of resources as opposed to the possession and accumulation of resources as mere commodities. See here for instance Sen (2003, 48). For further clarification, see footnote no. 5 below. As demonstrated in the previous chapter, the current study adheres to this view of resources.

issues of poverty and disadvantage. However, in both usages, the essential role of capabilities as enabling and supporting the existence of capability is retained. Put another way, while capabilities, in the form of resources, functionings, opportunities and the like constitute a capability set, it is the capability set that constitutes a person's overall capability (or her freedom to achieve valued ends).

Having thus outlined how a capability set might be more tangibly conceived of in terms of a FODW institution, what requires further clarification is the corresponding meaning and usage of capability and capabilities with functioning and freedom, and functionings and freedoms, respectively. These components will then enable the theorization of capability with agency or "capable agency."

Capability, Functioning, and Freedom through Capabilities, Functionings, and Freedoms

To distinguish between capability and functioning, I use Sen's rebuttal of Cohen's criticism of the failure of the term "capability" to fully account for the "two distinct aspects of a person's condition" (Sen 2003, 42–6). Cohen identifies the first aspect as "a person being able to do certain basic things." The second, as the *midfare* or the "constituted states of the person produced by goods, states in virtue of which utility levels take the values they do." Cohen argues that the states of the person produced by goods, which in turn, generates utility, is better understood as *midfare*, not capability. Thus, for example, food supply and the utility which a person gets out of eating food produces a person's *midfare* condition, not capability, since goods and utility do not necessarily determine a person's nutrition level (Cohen in Sen 2003, 42–3). Respectively taking these aspects to mean an achieved state of being; and the process of achieving that state of (well-)being through commodities and utilities, Sen attempts to resolve the confusion by pointing out that capability must be seen as related to, but different from, functionings: functionings as a set of valuable doings and beings, constitutes but presupposes capability (Sen 2003 38, 42–4). Functionings thus, Sen argues, can account for Cohen's *midfare* condition of a person, while capability can be more clearly seen as that first aspect in which a person is able to do certain things.

Taking capability to constitute a set of functionings synonymous to capabilities,[5] the study differentiates but also relates functionings and capabilities by simply assigning the two concepts either under the category of elemental resource, or of generic resources. By grouping capabilities and functionings, and other nonhuman resources such as utilities and commodities, under generic

5 For further clarity on this synonymity here, perhaps it could be thought of as functionings, as Sen has explained it, not explaining the function of functionings itself.

resources on the one hand, and by identifying capability as the elemental resource on the other, it becomes possible to see how these resources (or functionings) relate to capability or the capability set. That is, generic resources presuppose and constitute the freedom to ensure continued *functioning* of capability, the elementary resource.

Sen (2003, 34) contextualizes freedom in the CA in both its negative and positive forms. In the negative context, he understands freedom as a state—as the "range of choice a person has." In its positive context, Sen understands freedom in terms of "freedoms'—how that person values the elements in that range or what she chooses from it."[6] The study adopts "freedom" to constitute the elemental resource, and "freedoms" to constitute the generic resources in a capability set. Thus, where capability can be understood as the freedom to achieve valuable functionings/capabilities (elemental), functionings/capabilities can be understood as valuable freedoms (generic resources).

Keeping with this elemental-generic resource distinction, it is possible to see the relationship of capability, functioning and freedom with capabilities, functionings and freedoms. However, it is important to remember that these distinctions arise out of those "two aspects of a person's condition": an acknowledged state of being (to do and be), and the process of achieving that state of being (to do in order to be). In this sense, the CA necessarily requires the notion of agency to explain the dynamics of the relationship between doings, (that is, functionings/capabilities/freedoms) and beings (that is, functioning/capability/freedom). To reiterate here: functionings/capabilities enable functioning/capability. Highlighting these distinctions reveals what can be conceived of as the operating system that dynamically constitute capability; and it is dynamic because it is used by agents according to their own configurations or sets of functionings which can expand or contract, in their lifetime pursuits or projects (as was evident in the FODWs' narratives discussed in Chapter 6). How then does the relationship between agency and capability actually operate?

Sen's concepts of *agency freedom* and *agency achievement* are useful in explaining the capability of agency within a capability set (Chapter 6). It is, however, Giddens' structuration theory that allows the study to provide a theorization of agency with capability. As discussed below, herein lies the basic reason for the need to theorize agency *in* capability, and expand on the capability approach to that of a "capable agency approach."

6 Drawing from the "Two Concepts of Liberty" (Berlin 1969) as negative; as having the space to choose ("not being prevented from choosing as I do by other[s]"), and positive; as being one's own master in doing the choosing, Sen bases the capability approach on the notion of positive freedom (see especially, Sen 1997, 307). He ensures a more complete treatment of freedom, however, by asserting that the evaluation of a person's well-being requires simultaneous valuation of both the positive and negative aspects of freedom (Sen 2002, 12). As will become apparent in the course of the discussion, the present study's theorization of agency with capability shares the same understanding of freedom.

Agency in Capability

As demonstrated in the discussion of structuration theory in chapters 5 and 6, agency is the capability to do—but not to be. In the context of a chosen or a capability set, agency engages in the achievement of valued-ends. This engagement involves the use of capabilities and other generic resources, thus forming two purposes: on the one hand, maintaining the operation of the capability set, and on the other, adding the capability to be, to the capability to do.

The first purpose necessitates the theorization of agency with capability (or well-doing with well-being in the language of the CA) given its constitutive role with capability in a capability set. In light of the detailed discussions on agency and capability thus far, a theorization of agency with capability simply involves identifying capability as an inanimate concept without agency to power it—to act it out, or in the case of a capability set, to use it. In other words, capability requires agency not only to pursue or achieve, or to "continue as intended," but also to articulate valued goals or ends—through knowledgeability and action—the goals *to be*. Theorizing agency in capability therefore foregrounds the importance of pairing agency with capability. One cannot talk of capability without the agent. Capability is what makes the agent, within a set, able to do in order to be. Thus, without the user of a capability set, it is no more than a theory; capability and capabilities only come into practical existence through a *capable agent*. In this sense, therefore, talk of agency freedom and agency achievement makes sense only as articulations of agency-capability, or the capability of agency to retain chosen functionings within a capability set. In short, agency is necessary for the actual enactment of capability.

The second purpose shows how agency understood in the context of capability gains a characteristic different from that of agency as understood in structuration theory. That is, from agency that exists outside of a capability set, to that of an agency that can operate only within a capability set. Agency in a capability set becomes a form of agency that articulates "continuing as intended" (through agency) *along with* "valued-ends" (through capability). This way of understanding agency with capability provides a refined and more complete understanding of capability in agency as "intended valued ends." However, valued ends do not always result as intended. In light of the purpose of the *capable agent* to maintain a capability set and achieve intended valued ends despite unintended consequences, agency in a capability set can appropriately be called capable agency.

Characteristically, "capable agency" thus arises from the meeting of capability in agency (intended actions) with capability (valued-ends) in a capability set. Put another way, it is the articulation of an agent's valued freedoms within a set that bridges agency with capability. Valued freedoms refer to the value of freedom to a person in terms of her capability to do and be, on the one hand, and freedoms in enabling doings and beings that are deemed valuable by that person, on the other. This is why Sen asserts that "the freedom to lead different types of life is reflected in the person's capability set" (Sen 2003, 33). An agent's exercise of valued freedoms involves both constraints (that is, the extent of her capable agency) and possibilities in terms of resources usage. As thus a product of an agent's intended orientation towards her valued freedoms, capability fuses with agency. This fusion constitutes a *chosen* capability set. This in turn, provides important information on what type of agency and capabilities are of focus in analysis, since it is the agent, through her valued freedoms, who chooses that set.

This account of an agency-capability relationship brings the discussion back to understanding capable agency as "the interdependence between agency and capability, in a capability set." It also allows us to identify how an approach that begins from the viewpoint of the "capable agent" can be useful for policy implementation and further research on FODWs.

A CAA on Policy Implementation

To theoretically capture the relationship of agency with capability in the FODW context, the study needed to go beyond the current analytical paradigms of structure, agency and structuration, which it showed as inadequate not only for fully theorizing FODW agency, but for theorizing FODW capability at all. The study refined these current paradigms in a structural-structurationist approach to consolidate the micro, meso and macro contexts of FODW agency and capability, thus providing the analytical paradigm for the CAA. The structural-structurationist approach retains the focus on the agent, while recontextualizing and embodying agency within both the limits and possibilities of structural constraints. In this way, it allows a conceptualization of FODWs in terms of a transnationally coherent group in the form of a FODW institution of survival, but also of how it is an institution that needs to survive.

Through the lens of the CAA, the FODW institution can be more specifically understood as a FODW's capability set of feasible functionings. It is for this reason that FODWs tenaciously reproduce, and remain in the institution (as discussed in chapters 5 and 6). The institution is where the functioning of earning a livelihood is feasible. For policymakers, this highlights three distinct and directly related levels at which capability protection must be simultaneously implemented. The first is at the FODW institution level; protection of the FODW institution means protection of FODW livelihoods. The second level involves that of individual FODWs within the FODW institution; protection of FODW agency means protection of their continued participation in the institution, unabused and unenslaved. The final level involves individuals outside of the FODW institution. These individuals include those who plan to participate in the institution or those who are out of the institution through repatriation/deportation but who want to resume participation in the institution.

Protection of such individuals leads to protection of sustainable livelihoods, even outside of the FODW institution. The following discussion details how protection can be more tangibly achieved in the context of other more powerful and often oppressive institutions in the structural vicinity of the FODW.

A CAA on Immigration Policy

As a close relation of the "migrant institution," the FODW institution essentially consists of mostly unskilled migrant workers from developing countries who are specifically involved in the domestic work sector of the destination locale. Because immigration regulations determine who become migrants and in which sectors, it is the protection of the FODW institution that is most relevant in the area of immigration controls.

In light of increasing immigration controls in receiving countries (Chapter 2), it might seem unrealistic to expect receiving states to protect the FODW institution. In this case, protection must come from the wider area of development policies, discussed below. There are, however, currently two avenues of possibility in the area of immigration policy. The first is the dynamic and complex relationships among state institutions within the receiving states which show that immigration policies can be superseded by other policies such as the need to import or allow certain types of migrant labour in receiving economies (Chapter 2). A manifestation of this is currently occurring in western Europe, where the rights of immigrants are increasingly determined by residence rather than by citizenship, with immigrant associations and citizens' organizations providing support to immigrant populations through formal and informal services (Jacobson 1996; Piper 1998; Sosyal 1994; also, Yamanaka and Piper 2003). Thus, in France, as the present study has shown, even undocumented workers are able to use the justice and health systems, while receiving support from local organizations like the CCEM. Moreover, even in the case of Hong Kong, where eventual attainment of citizenship is almost impossible, migrant workers' rights to organize have yielded some success, for example, in protecting their wages, as well as in challenging unfair contract termination in the Hong Kong labour courts. In addition, overseas domestic workers in Hong Kong are entitled to the same medical benefits as residents (Bell and Piper 2005, 199). That there remains uncertainty about the continuity of these provisions, however, and that on the whole, state provisions of rights and welfare for migrant workers remain inadequate, points to the necessity of expanding and protecting these generic resources. This necessity becomes even more crucial when "less" generous receiving governments, such as those of other European states, of authoritarian states in Asia and the Middle East, and the USA (Chapter 3) are taken into consideration.

The second avenue of possibility is the growth of transnational activism within the FODW institution. In light of the inaction and/or incapacity of sending governments to protect their nationals who migrate for overseas domestic work, NGO transnational activism has been identified as the most likely form of feasible protection (Yamanaka and Piper 2003). In the present study, we have seen examples of this activism in the RESPECT network in Europe and in UNIFIL in Hong Kong. However, while some political influence has been achieved through these activities, and while membership grows in strength, the very capability of these networks to challenge the power of states and capital interests, has in itself been found to be relatively weak (Piper 2004; Uhlin 2001, 2002, 2003). This therefore points to the need to encourage, support and further develop this generic resource in the FODW institution. In addition, it is important to take into account the transnational property of the FODW institution, that is, its global characteristic as not specific to any one place, whether Manila, Paris, or Hong Kong, so that policy actions do not concentrate on one locale only. These locales, it must be remembered, are intrinsically connected for the purposes of retaining access to the elemental resource of paid domestic work.

A CAA on Host Country Domestic Work Regulation

As the elemental resource, paid domestic work within the FODW institution necessarily refers to the individual migrant's capability. As demonstrated in Chapter 7, it is the elementary resource of overseas domestic work that enables the FODW's access, and hence, achievement of her valued functionings. Host country regulation of the work, therefore, is the major policy area in which protection is most immediately important. Since it is abuse, enslavement and other similar forms of oppression that are experienced by workers as a direct result of inadequate provisions in this area (e.g. in employer and recruitment-inflicted abuse controls), it is the capability of the individual FODWs to challenge and/or leave these conditions for better ones that must be protected.

Thus far, calls for improvements in this area have focused on the visibility of the workers and society-wide respect for the work. While this is important, there must be equal concern on protecting and developing generic resources that allow FODWs to continue as intended, even after experiences of abuse and enslavement, so that they can leave abusive situations to find better employment. Policy discussions in this area should therefore foreground the need to develop and increase access to resources such as accommodation for interim periods of unemployment, counseling, health cover, as well as social security access. In this regard, the fight for rights must also include an articulation of rights to access these and other useful resources, where resources are thus necessarily looked at from an allocative or capabilities sense, not just authoritatively or as a struggle against the powerful (Chapter 5). Indeed as Pietilä (2006, 181) has so importantly observed of feminist struggles, it is simply not enough to know what to struggle against. To truly benefit from empowerment also means to know what to struggle *for*. Importantly, these resources should be made available to users in such a way that it is independent of, as well as protected from, immigration rules (for an important beginning here, see Rodríguez 2004, 155–6). These forms of assistance that allow the FODW to remain in the FODW institution underscore the importance of ensuring that involuntary repatriation in both immigration and emigration policies should be abolished.[7]

A CAA on Development Policies

Given the more likely scenario that host governments will resist such protective strategies, however, what then can be done? One way could be to build on the current transnational approach to protect and develop these resources. This must be undertaken *in the particular context of development policies*. The structural-structurationist approach of the present study has been particularly useful in highlighting the intrinsic connection between FODW migration for work, and economic-centred development policy outcomes that cause them to migrate in the first place. In foregrounding a capability evaluation of the FODW situation, the study has also been careful to retain the use of the CA in a global human development program that treats the individual not only as the means to, but also the end of, development.

Using development as the main framework of a transnational approach to protection of resource broadens the issue of FODWs protection beyond that of migration policies to development-based policies. This is of practical importance because the bureaucracy and delivery of assistance is not only more developed in development-based policies in terms of an overseas development assistance industry, but also where direct financial assistance could be made more readily available to secure much needed funding for migrant-based NGOs. With uncertainty surrounding the bare necessities currently provided by a few states like France and Hong Kong mentioned earlier, this is all the more crucial to offset receiving states' reluctance, and sending states' impotence, in making migration-based policies more responsive. Currently, emergency shelters, counseling, legal assistance, hotline and other services that assist the migrant worker to "persist as intended," are for the most part shouldered by local religious and civic groups (Luan 2005, 39).

Despite sending states' incapacity in influencing immigration policies, a development-based framework also highlights both the culpability and responsibility of sending governments. This points to another way in which reliance on host states may be curbed. The present study's focus on the "capable agency" of the workers has highlighted the central importance of how poverty and corruption in the Philippines is structurally and primarily responsible for making these women's agency incapable, hence their "forced

7 The Indian and Indonesian governments, for instance, immediately repatriates migrant domestic workers who leave their contracts in Hong Kong (see Swider 2006, 120).

migration." Questioning the capability of agency in an impoverished woman's situation in Philippine society, in this way, has been particularly helpful in highlighting the responsibility of the sending country to provide a capability set, as it reveals capability as only possible outside of the Philippines. Sending country development policies will therefore need to more seriously pursue a human development agenda that provides resource accessibility for the individual in terms of livelihood creation and security. But it must be stressed here that the success of such an agenda heavily depends on the support for a human development-centred approach by the major international development institutions of not only the UN, but also the IMF, the World Bank and the WTO. A sending country–international development institutions coalition should provide enough pressure on bilateral approaches from receiving countries to base immigration policies on a human, rather than border, security approach (see also here, Piper 2005). This coalition however must be wary of dominant debates on a migration-development nexus (Chapter 1) that focus more on how remittances can aid development in the sending country than on how development can aid the migrant worker. An immediate change in this area is particularly crucial as the lack of livelihoods access in the country of origin has been a major cause of both risks and endurance of abuse and enslavement in host locales, as the present study has shown.

It is important to conclude here with a reiteration of the simultaneous implementation of these policy recommendations. The policy areas outlined here are "structurally" integrated, and so the plan of action and protection must also be coordinated. While admittedly "idealistic," a simultaneously applied and coordinated approach would benefit not only those in the FODW institution, thus ensuring an institution of revival, it would, most importantly, secure sustainable livelihoods, even out of the FODW institution.

A CAA to Further Research

The present study is a response to approaches by feminist migration researchers and migration theorists on overseas domestic work. Feminist migration researchers have been strong in arguing for the visibility and identity of migrant domestic workers. Where they are weak, however, has been in their focus on oppression and victimization within the borders of receiving country settings (for an important exception see Eviota 1992, 2004). Likewise, those works deviating from the victim-centred approach, and oriented instead towards an agency-based or cost-benefit analysis approach, do not sufficiently incorporate constraints within host settings, let alone beyond them. This has resulted in a feminist migration research agenda separate from that of feminist development researchers. Feminist development researchers are important allies in the analysis of the plight of migrant domestic workers for two main reasons. The first is that they engage with development processes that cause and perpetuate migration for overseas domestic work, at local, national and global levels. The second is that they include postcolonial or third world feminists who provide more accurate insights into the needs and concerns of non-western, low-income women in a western or high income setting.

Underscoring the centrality of (under)development in Filipina experiences of migration for domestic work in high-income settings, a CAA can provide the bridge between feminist migration research and feminist development research. In particular, a CAA's focus on capability and capabilities puts into context "the victim" and "the agent" as a problem not of oppression as a result of migration, nor liberation through migration. Rather, it foregrounds the concept of a "capable agent" to overcome victimization at the same time as she is able to practice her agency as intended, not only in migration but also in development. Analytically, a closer engagement with development research would thus allow feminist migration research to advance analysis beyond the victim/slave—agent/worker dichotomy to more fully engage with approaches that can make a migrant worker "capable" through human development and human security (see here especially, Gasper and Truong 2004).

Given that on the one hand, the CA occupies a significant position in the current international development policy agenda, and on the other, the issue of migration is likely to remain at the top of the political agenda of governments, it will be both practically and politically strategic to frame overseas domestic work migration as intrinsically connected to development. This could have the effect of simultaneously securing and making more pronounced the issue of migrant domestic workers' oppression as both a migration and development issue in policy and political agendas. In this way, analysis can move the issue of livelihoods away from border controls, focusing less on the right to protect borders and more on the right to development for the purposes of livelihood and human security.

The other main research area in which migration for domestic work has received attention is in migration theory. This is also an area in which the present study can contribute. There is much support for examining migrant workers' experiences in migration through an inclusive framework of individual, structural and institutional interrelations (or structuration) (Hugo 1994; Lee 1996; Phizacklea 1998; Tyner 1995). However, as a significant amount of labour migrants find themselves in the unskilled sector, and in "illegal" and precarious forms of not only migration passages but also daily working conditions, there is a need to put this structuration approach into the context of constraints. The present study has shown that a structurationist approach to migration requires an account of its embodiment or constraints, so as to see the full extent of both its possibilities and pitfalls for the migrant's intended valued ends. The study thus outlined a structural-structurationist approach, arguing that the "structuralist" in this approach needs to go beyond current structuralist feminist migration theorizing, by expanding and more fully articulating structural constraints beyond migration experiences to that of livelihood constraints as a direct result of underdevelopment in the country of origin.

While the study is not primarily a response to the undertheorization of agency in the CA, it has contributed to a more complete theorization of agency through its structural-structurationist analysis. It has done so in two particular ways. First, it allows a definition of exactly what type of agency is at issue when talking of capability conceptualization and evaluation. In the present study for instance, the type of agency looked at was that used by FODWs for the purposes of livelihoods (or FODW agency). Whenever we talk of capability/ies we cannot know what this means for the individual if we do not know the type of agency at issue. Thus a more nuanced theorization of agency illuminates for what particular purpose and towards what valued-ends the individual's agency is "working." Second, the study's focus on the specific type of FODW agency also enabled the conceptualization of its collective manifestation in the form of an institution. In this way perhaps, the FODW institution can provide that "social framework" for "Sen's highly abstracted individualism" (Gasper 2002, 21; see here also Stewart 2005). A concept like the FODW institution could also circumvent concerns on the over-generalities of the social indicators in the Human Development Reports. Apthorpe (1997, in Gasper 2002, 13), for example, argues that "the social indicators used are demographic, sectoral, never about social institutions, social structures or group's own social categories." Thus, the FODW institution might just be one of the ways in which the rather "thick toothed comb" of the capability approach (Gasper 2002, 29) may be refined.

Conclusion: Reconciling Rights and Livelihoods through Capability

Although current approaches polarize understanding of the migrant domestic worker situation in terms of the question "slavery or work?," the narratives in the study point to no conclusive evidence to support one or the other. What the narratives show is that the issue of gainful work is of central importance to these women and their livelihoods—so much so that they would endure slave-like conditions to keep open the possibility of gainful employment, which, due to the combination of a "push" effect caused by their structural impoverishment in the sending country, and a "pull" by the global economic demand for domestic service, has become available only in overseas domestic work. A main conclusion of the study, therefore, is that slavery and work are intrinsic to each other in the FODW context.

Given such a situation, however, as "slaves of their hopes to work, must they choose between work and human rights?" (Bals 1999, 190).[8] Rather than

8 My translation: "... esclaves de l'espoir de travailler, les travailleurs devront... choisir entre le travail ou les droits humains?"

frame the FODW situation in these polarized terms, the present study sought to foreground the central issue of capability in FODW agency to determine the extent of the applicability of this choice to FODW experiences. Drawing closely from FODW experiences in Paris and Hong Kong, the study found that the choice between work and human rights is more accurately understood as a choice between work and no work. Indeed, the study found that this more immediate choice was not only why a FODW could find herself in enslavement, but also why she would endure enslavement and other similar abuses. "No work" means no livelihood and therefore no resources to nourish the body to fight for human rights. So, it is not that human rights is not of central importance, it is that having work is the more immediate issue.

Taking into consideration the highly constraining environment of overseas domestic work to FODW agency, the study underscored the importance of a "capable agent" to retain such work. By showing that the "capable agent" is both means and ends to understanding FODW experiences, it makes the issue of protection clearer for both researchers and policymakers: protecting FODW human rights doesn't guarantee livelihoods, but protecting their access to resources for a livelihood creates the opportunity or capability for securing rights. A CAA approach crucially underscores the significance of looking at the capability of FODW agency—what the FODW is actually able to do and be—to define what type of rights are at issue. Through a CAA, FODW agency is theorized in terms of her capability or freedom to achieve valued functionings, which in turn allows seeing her *capability as her right or freedom to access resources in overseas domestic work for the function of sustaining livelihoods*. Through a CAA, therefore, it becomes possible to more accurately identify the issue of rights for the FODW as most primarily an issue of capability.

While we must remain careful to maintain the strong fight for rights, this points to the need in current policy action to define the fight in terms of capability. Doing so provides two major benefits. First, fighting for capabilities instead of rights can avoid the inherent difficulties in the lack of political will by some states to implement, let alone consider, migrant workers' rights. As I emphasize again, here, Nussbaum has convincingly argued that capability transcends the traditional distinction between state action and state inaction in implementing human rights, since securing capability in a person will necessarily require state action to provide the economic and material resources necessary to secure that capability. Second, and most important, framing rights in the context of capability can allow the FODW herself to reclaim her right for her intended and valued end of a quality of life. So far, it is mostly researchers and state-oriented NGOs and policymakers that have dominated both the discourse and actions on the reclaiming of this right. It has hopefully been made clear through a CAA, that it is the agent herself that transforms her structure. Other agents can contribute and support that transformation, but only in terms of serving as generic resources to the migrant herself.

A clear example of why the fight for rights must be undertaken in the context of capability is the support given to Sally by the CCEM, discussed in Chapter 5. Although an anti-slavery organization that fights for the rights of migrant domestic workers, its longer-term policy is associated with anti-trafficking policy protocols of rescue and repatriate (see for instance the case of Lani in Chapter 7). This means that while the CCEM helped Sally to defend her human rights in court, Sally had to turn elsewhere to secure rights of residency in France. Due to her illness, she could apply for documented status through the health care system in France. Had she not been granted residency due to her illness, however, Sally would have remained working in France, undocumented ("the children still haven't finished their college and I still have to build my own house"). So, securing her residency must not be understood in the context of securing citizenship per se, but securing the right to stay in the FODW institution; or more specifically and more sustainably, the right to secure her capability to earn a livelihood. The CCEM's support highlights that while absolutely essential, human rights in themselves are not enough to protect Sally, her family and her livelihood. The practical feasibility of a CAA will require exploration. However, to end here for the moment, in recollection of Sally's and the other respondents' struggles to secure a livelihood, is to hopefully mark the beginning of a research and policy agenda that centralizes the issue of capability along with rights for migrant domestic workers' empowerment.

APPENDICES

Appendix 1
Respondents' Profiles

Name	Self-classification of work status	Work location + time	Current mode of employment	Mode of recruitment	Member of NGO/ assoc.?	Age	Educational level	Province	Current marital/family status	Current concerns
Alili	Oppressed wageworker	HK, 17 yrs	Live-in	Agency	Yes	Mid 40s	Some college	Manila	Single: siblings in the Philippines.	Planning to go home for good after 1 or 2 more contracts.
Amity	Oppressed/abused wageworker	HK, 4 yrs	Part-time*	Agency	Yes	Mid 30s	College	Nueva Vizcaya	Married: husband and children in the Philippines.	Awaiting court case outcome against her ex-employer which will determine if she can stay and work in Hong Kong or go back to the Philippines.
Ana	Slave	HK, 2 yrs	Live-in	Agency	No	Early 30s	Some college	Sorsogon, now Manila-based	Single: 4 siblings and mother (1 sister in Canada).	Saving to join her sister in Canada.
Bernie	Wageworker	HK, 11 mths	Part-time	Agency	No	Early 30s	Some college	Antique, Visaya	Remarried: 3 children with first husband, 1 child with second partner in the Philippines.	Currently fighting theft case made against her by employer. If successful, she will work one more full contract and then return home. If found guilty, she will ask a friend to help her get into Canada.
Delia	Wageworker	Paris, 2 yrs	Live-by^	smugglers/ traffickers~	Yes	Early 40s	Primary	Baguio	Married: husband and 3 children in the Philippines.	Working on obtaining her papers. Still paying off recruitment agency fees loaned from family members.

Name	Self-classification of work status	Work location + time	Current mode of employment	Mode of recruitment	Member of NGO/ assoc.?	Age	Educational level	Province	Current marital/family status	Current concerns
Ellen	Slave wageworker	HK, 12 yrs	Live-in	Direct hire	No	Mid 40s	College	Visaya	Single: supporting family in the Philippines.	Waiting to retire in 2005. Provides funds for her nephews and nieces' schooling in the Philippines.
Felise	Wageworker	Paris, 8 yrs	Live-by	"Left," in her own words, Kuwaiti employers while in Paris	No	Early 40s	Vocational	Manila	Single parent: 15 yr old son in the Philippines. Kuwaiti husband in Bahrain.	Waiting for her 10th yr to apply for her papers. She expects that her long-time employer will help her.
Gemini	Slave	HK, 1 yr	Live-in	Agency	Yes	Late 40s	Vocational	Mindoro, now Manila-based	Single parent: 2 children in the Philippines.	Earning and saving as much capital before making the final return home to retire.
Gudilia	Wageworker	Paris, 14 yrs	Live-by	Direct hire	Yes	Late 40s	Primary	Tanawan, Leyte	Single parent: 3 children and 2 grandchildren.	Earning and saving as much capital before making the final return home to retire.
Helena	Former slave now abused wageworker	Paris, 3 yrs	Live-by	Escaped from Saudi employer while in Paris	Yes	Early 40s	Primary	Cavite	Widow: 2 children and 2 grandchildren, and 5 unemployed brothers in the Philippines.	Employer is helping her to obtain legal papers so that she can go home for Christmas at the end of the year.
Indiana	Wageworker	Paris, 18 yrs	Live-by + part-time	Agency + smugglers/ traffickers	No	Early 50s	Vocational	Quezon Province	Single parent: 4 children in the Philippines; sister with papers (married to a French man).	Has papers. Working until all her children have finished schooling and have their own jobs. Expresses interest in staying in Paris for as long as possible.

Name	Self-classification of work status	Work location + time	Current mode of employment	Mode of recruitment	Member of NGO/ assoc.?	Age	Educational level	Province	Current marital/family status	Current concerns
JB	Wageworker	Paris, 5 yrs	Live-by + part-time	Agency (overstayed tourist visa)	Yes	Mid 20s	College	Dulag, Leyte	Single (lesbian); siblings in the Philippines.	To help her girlfriend migrate to Paris to work and live with her.
Jinky	Abused wageworker	HK, 7 mths	Part-time	Agency	Yes	Late 30s	Secondary	Quezon Province	Single: mother in the Philippines; 6 other siblings, eldest is also in Hong Kong.	Waiting for the Immigration Department to approve new contract with a new employer by by-passing the 2-week rule.
Lani	Slave	Paris, 3 wks	Recovering in a shelter; no work yet	Escaped from Saudi employer while in Paris	Yes	Late 20s	Vocational	Cotabato, Mindanao	Married: 4 children and mother and younger sister in the Philippines. Father in Saudi Arabia.	Plans to stay in Paris to find work.
Lilia	Wageworker	HK, 2 yrs	Live-in	Direct hire	Yes	Mid 40s	College	Las Pinas, Manila	Married: husband and children in the Philippines.	Waiting another 6-8 mths before she joins her husband and sister to work in Dubai.
Loveley	Wage Worker	HK, 4 yrs	Live-in	Direct hire	Yes	Late 20s	Some college	Isabela	Single: 1 father and 1 brother in the Philippines.	Currently in a shelter as she has overstayed her visa in Hong Kong. Scheduled to return to the Philippines in a few months, but plans to find work in other countries.
Melanie	Former slave now wageworker	Paris, 1.5 yrs	Live-by	Agency (overstayed tourist visa)	No	Mid 20s	Vocational	Laguna	Single parent: 3 children in the Philippines; 1 in the USA.	Plans to eventually get papers, bring over her children and stay in France indefinitely.

Name	Self-classification of work status	Work location + time	Current mode of employment	Mode of recruitment	Member of NGO/ assoc.?	Age	Educational level	Province	Current marital/family status	Current concerns
Michelle	Wageworker	HK, 19 yrs	Live-in	Agency	Yes	Late 40s	Vocational	Nueva Vizcaya	Single parent: 1 child in the Philippines.	Likely to stay in Hong Kong for as long as possibe, and to continue working to improve migrant workers' rights.
Mila	Wageworker	Paris, 3 yrs (France 19 yrs)	Live-in (own floor in the basement)	The first time: agency (overstayed tourist visa). The second time: smugglers/ traffickers	No	Mid 50s	Vocational	Quezon City, Manila	Single parent: children grown up. 1 in Canada. 1 in Indonesia. 2 in the Philippines.	Waiting to retire in 4 yrs time when she will receive her pension and can then go back to live in the Philippines with her children and grandchildren. Has her papers.
Minda	Former slave now wageworker	Paris, 21 yrs	n/a	Escaped from Lebanese employer while in Paris	No	Late 40s	Some college	Laguna	Single: siblings in the Philippines.	Currently unemployed but has her papers. Currently doing volunteer work at a Filipino hairdressing salon. Will stay in Paris as long as possible before retiring to the Philippines.
Nene	Wageworker	Paris, 4 yrs	Live-by	Agency (overstayed tourist visa)	No	Late 40s	Vocational	Manila	Single: mother and siblings in the Philippines.	Saving up to get her brother who is currently working in Singapore, to Paris. Will work in Paris until she retires and goes back to the Philippines.
Red	Wageworker	HK, 10 mths	Live-in	Agency	No	Late 20s	College	Manila	Single parent: 2 children.	Will continue to work in Hong Kong but eventually plans to find work in Europe or America.

Name	Self-classification of work status	Work location + time	Current mode of employment	Mode of recruitment	Member of NGO/ assoc.?	Age	Educational level	Province	Current marital/family status	Current concerns
Sally	Former slave now wageworker	Paris, 10 yrs	Live-by	Smugglers/ traffickers	Yes	Early 40s	Primary	Pangasinan	Single parent: 2 children in the Philippines.	Has papers. Will work in Paris until retirement. Currently unsure whether she will then retire in the Philippines or bring her children to France.
Virgo	Wageworker	HK, 4 mths	Part-time	Agency	No	Late 30s	College	Pangasinan, originally Mindanao	Single parent: 2 children; father in the Philippines; all siblings in USA.	To obtain a visa to work in Canada and then bring over children.

* Part-time: As observed by other researchers in Hong Kong (e.g. Constable 1997), "Part-time" or "aerobics" work involves undocumented work. The FDH employment contract in Hong Kong specifically requires that a FDH works full time and for one employer for the duration of the contract. However, some workers choose to undertake additional work outside of these regulations to increase their earnings. FODWs in Paris also use the term "Part-time" but with a slight variation. For those who are documented in Paris and working full time for an employer, this involves additional work for other employers on a casual basis. Those who are undocumented usually take more than one "Part-time" position to match or exceed the earning capacity of a full time position.

^ Live-by: In Hong Kong, all contract workers ""live in"" their employer's house. If not given their own rooms, they either have to share a room with a child/children or are made to sleep in a communal part of the house e.g. the kitchen or laundry. This does not apply to FODWs who undertake "part-time" work and have pre-negotiated work hours for an employer or for several employers in which case the FODWs retire to a boarding house after their work hours. In Paris, live-ins are more likely to have their own quarters to which they retire after work. FODWs who do not live with their employers have their own place to which they retire after work. These places are either rented apartments (most team up with each other to be able to rent apartments in the more affordable areas on the outskirts of Paris) or they are chambres de bonne (maid's quarters). These are around $10m^2$ service apartments in a less-kept, 7/8-storey building without elevators, situated right next to their employers' apartment building. These very small apartments are usually found in the wealthier areas of Paris like the XV1th arrondissement. I have termed those FODWs who retire to these *chambres de bonne* after work, as "Live-bys."

~ Smuggled/trafficked: As I explain in Chapter 2, despite recent efforts to distinguish between traffickers and smugglers (see e.g. in ILO 2001), there is still insufficient explanation of how, and when during the process of recruitment, they can be distinguished. This vague definition is also reflected in the experience of those respondents who used smugglers. Smugglers seem to have connections with traffickers, or their business involved elements of trafficking. For example, Indiana's sister had hired smugglers for Indiana's passage to Paris. When, at the time of "delivery", Indiana's sister was late in picking Indiana up from the "drop-off point," and had yet to pay the full amount for the smugglers' services, Indiana tells of how the smugglers warned her that should her debt remain unpaid, she would not be allowed to leave and would have to work for them. The smugglers had explicitly suggested that sex work would be one way that she could pay the debt. Fortunately for Indiana, her sister came to pay and pick her up.

Appendix 2
Profiles of NGOs and Associations Contacted during Fieldwork

	Location	Profile	Type of support given to the present study
CCEM	Paris	The CCEM or Comité Contre l'Esclavage Moderne (Committee Against Modern Slavery) is an NGO founded by journalist Dominique Torrès in 1994. Composed of lawyers, social workers, journalists and other interested parties, the Comité works to combat domestic slavery through research and lobbying, as well as through practical assistance. Assistance involves shelter and counselling provision, outright rescue, and judicial action against perpetrators. The CCEM was a partner to the EU funded RESPECT network project (1997–2002). For more information see http://www.esclavagemoderne.org/index.php.	* Provision of research materials. * Provided access to respondents and other informants.
Euro-Pinoy Association	Paris	The Euro-Pinoy Association was established in Paris in 2002. A major project of the association is the MadPinoy online journal magazine which comprehensively covers social and political affairs relevant to Filipinos living and working in France. For more information see http://www.madpinoy.com/perm_pages/about.html.	* Provided access to respondents and other informants. * Provision of research material. * Conversations with Nina Tuazon, president of the Association. * Provided access to social and political gatherings.
Babaylan	Paris	Babaylan is a small organization founded by Maya Jezewski, a long-term residence in France. The organization offers advice and support to FODWs in France. Babaylan was a partner to the EU-funded RESPECT network project (1997–2002).	* Provision of research materials. * Provided access to respondents and other informants. * Conversations with Maya.

	Location	Profile	Type of support given to the present study
Mission for Migrant Workers (MFMW)	Hong Kong	The Mission is an ecumenical organization established in Hong Kong in 1981. It provides legal and shelter assistance (Bethune House) to migrant workers in distress. The Mission also undertakes research and advocacy work. It retains close network with UNIFIL and other Asia Migrants Coordinating Body member organizations, as well as with the Asia Pacific Mission for Migrant Workers, all in Hong Kong. For more information, see http://www.migrants.net.	* Provision of research materials. * Provision of access to respondents and other informants. * Provision of quantitative data. * Voluntary work for the office in Garden Street, Central. * Provided open access to social and political gatherings.
Asian Migrant Centre (AMC)	Hong Kong	A regional NGO, established in Hong Kong in 1989. AMC focuses on the concerns of Asian migrant workers. It is a monitoring, research, information, publishing, training, support and action centre advocating for the human rights and empowerment of migrant workers and their families in Asia. For more information see http://www.asian-migrants.org.	* Provision of research materials.

Appendix 3
Typical Migration Cycle of a Migrant Worker

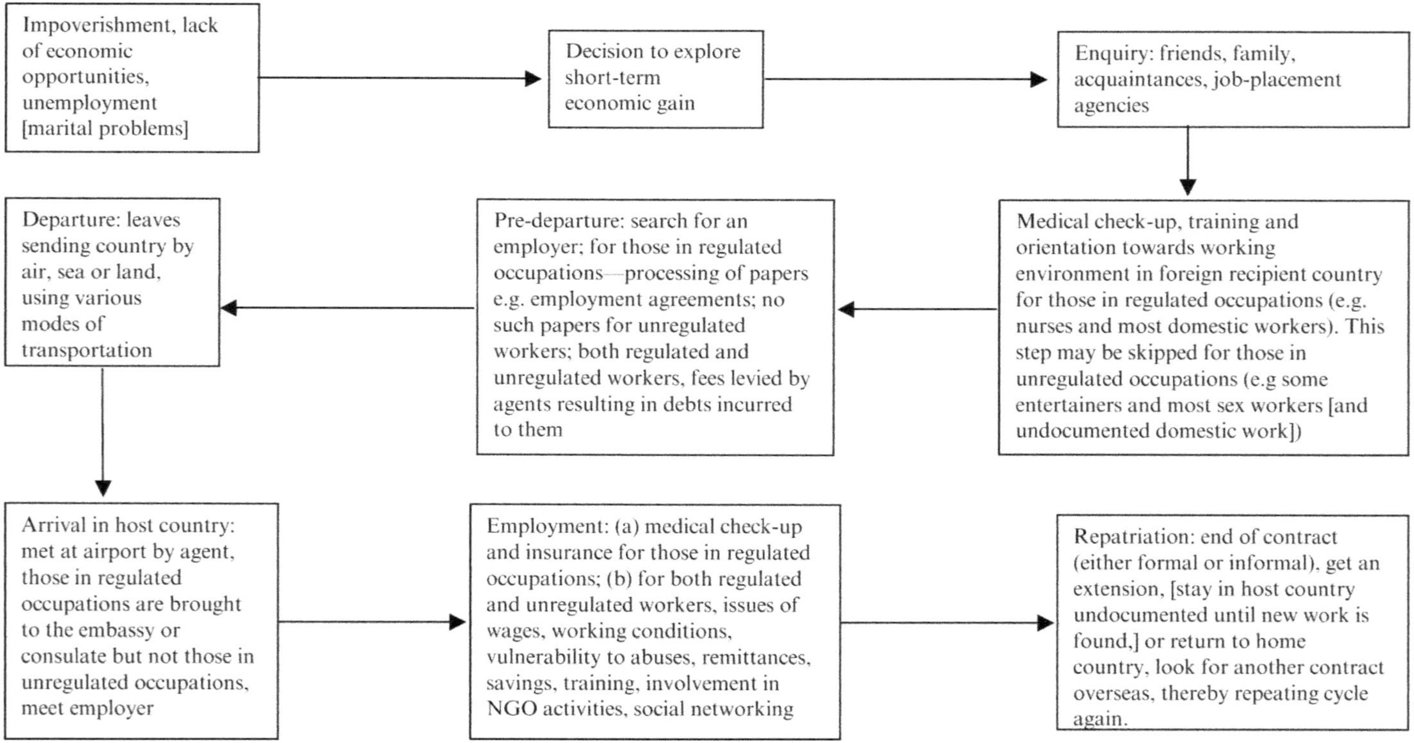

Source: Adapted from: Sim (2001), "Organising Discontent: NGOs for Southeast Asian migrant workers in Hong Kong," SEARC working papers, City University Hong Kong.

Appendix 4 RESPECT—Migrant Domestic Workers Charter of Rights: Rights, Equality, Solidarity, Power, Europe, Cooperation, Today

Domestic work in private households is important to European family life, to European economies and to European support systems. It is demanding work which requires a variety of skills and is often done by women who have migrated to Europe. Many have left their families and children in an attempt to find a way out of poverty.

Migrant domestic workers are part of the fabric of European society. Their dignity and their rights as people and workers must be protected.

We call for justice and equity for all migrant domestic workers; whether they are documented or undocumented; whether they are live-in or live-out; whether first or second generation; whether they are born in Africa, Asia, South America or Europe. Member states of the European Union must recognise the intrinsic dignity and crucial importance of domestic work and seek to educate their citizens accordingly. Relevant organisations in the EU have a duty to ensure that migrant domestic workers have information and the means to access the following rights:

- THE RIGHT to an immigration status which recognises that domestic work in private households is proper work.
- THE RIGHT to an immigration status for the worker independent of any employer.
- THE RIGHT to travel both within the host country and between all countries of the European Union.
- THE RIGHT to full and non-discriminatory employment rights and social protection, including minimum wage, sickness and maternity pay, and pension rights.
- THE RIGHT to change employer.
- THE RIGHT to a legally enforceable contract of employment setting out minimum wages, maximum hours and responsibilities.
- THE RIGHT to work free from fear of physical, sexual or psychological abuse.

- THE RIGHT to join a trade union.
- THE RIGHT to live and work free from racism.
- THE RIGHT to family life, including health, education and social rights for the children of migrant domestic workers.
- THE RIGHT to recognition of qualifications, training and experience obtained in the home country.
- THE RIGHT to personal and leisure time.

THE RESPECT NETWORK UNDERTAKES:

- To transform policy and practice at all levels, from the European Commission to the households of the European Union, to reflect this charter of rights.
- To ensure that migrant domestic workers are informed of their rights and have the means to access these rights.
- To work for the implementation of the charter of rights with migrants and refugees, trades unions, parliamentarians, human rights activists, and other relevant sectors.

Source: Solidar: http://www.solidar.org/Document.asp?DocID=162&tod=52441 (2 December 2005).

Appendix 5
Interview Schedule (English Version)

1 Preliminaries

Q1 How old are you, approximately? e.g. late teens, 20s, 30s, 40s etc?
Q2 How long have you been working as an overseas domestic worker?
Q2a How long have you been working as a domestic worker in this city?
Q2b How long do you plan to stay on the job?
Q3 Which region in the Philippines do you come from?

2 "Filipina"ness

Q4 What would you say are the main features of Filipino culture?
Q4a Is it in the culture to treat working overseas as a journey of achievement?
Q4b How central is the Catholic Religion in the culture?
Q4c How central is it to being a Filipina?
Q5 What does being a "Filipina" mean to you?
Q6 How have you experienced "being a Filipina" in this country?
Q7 How different do you think being a Filipina is compared to domestic workers of other nationalities?
Q8 Are you married?
Q8a If yes, is your husband here with you or in the Philippines?
Q8b Any children? If yes, who is caring for them back home? Do you visit them? Why/not? How often?
Q9 How do you think "Filipina" women fare in their personal relationships with the male family members of their family such as the husband, the father, or the older brother etc? Are the men more dominant?
Q9a How different do you think are the roles of men to women in Filipino families?
Q9b How do you think being a "Filipina" differs from being a "Filipino?"
Q10 Would you say you were disproportionately income-poor compared to the men in your family? Vice versa? Or is it more or less equal?
Q11 Anything else on Filipinaness?

3 On Going Overseas

- Q12 If you have worked in other places and in other roles, please describe your thoughts on this experience.
- Q13 Why do you think so many Filipinas migrate overseas as domestic workers?
- Q14 To what extent do you think your decision to work overseas was influenced by other Filipinas/Filipinos who were already working here or in other countries, or who have gone as far as obtaining citizenship in those countries?
- Q15 What does going overseas mean to you?
- Q15a Do you think it has helped you grow personally?
- Q15b What role, if any, does modernity play in your experience overseas? Do you think host societies are more modern?
- Q15c What does modernity mean to you?
- Q16 If you were paid as much working as a domestic worker in the Philippines, would you still prefer to work overseas as a domestic worker? Why/Why not?
- Q.17 Do your future plans in life include more travelling? Would you say "definitely," "maybe," or "not at all?"
- Q.18 Would you have used unofficial ways to get here i.e. used community and other familial/social networks, if say the host government rejected your formal application Yes or No will do here.
- Q.19 Just very broadly, how did you get here? i.e. straight from the Philippines or through other countries?
- Q20 Do you think you are somehow different from other Filipinos who have not gone overseas to work? If yes, how?
- Q21 Would you go to Paris [HK] to work? How do you think it would differ from Hong Kong [Paris]?
- Q22 What does "home" mean to you?
- Q22a If it is a particular place, where is it?
- Q22b If it's in the Philippines, how do you feel about going "home?"
- Q23 Anything else on going overseas?

4 On Domestic Work(er)

- Q24 What does "domestic work" mean to you?
- Q24a Is there a difference between just domestic work and overseas domestic work in your opinion?
- Q25 What does being a domestic worker mean to you?
- Q25a Would you agree that Filipino culture sees being a domestic worker as shameful? If yes, why do you think this is so? If no, why not?

Q26 Do you employ a domestic worker for your family in the Philippines?
Q26a If yes, how different and/or the same would you say your situation as a domestic worker here compared to that of your employed domestic worker?
Q26b What kinds of responsibilities does your domestic worker have at your home in the Philippines?
Q26c How do you think you benefit from this kind of help?
Q27 Did you work in the Philippines?
Q27a If yes, what kind of job?
Q27b How does it compare to your work now? Better, same or worse?
Q28 Would you recommend overseas domestic work to others back in the Philippines? Why? Why not?
Q29 Would you consider doing this job again after your contract is finished? Why? Why not?
Q30 Because your work entails both professional and personal relationships, what are your thoughts on this, and how do you manage the crossing of boundaries in this situation?
Q31 Anything else on domestic work(er)?

5 On Domestic Work Employment

Q32 What would you say are the things you like and the things you hate about being employed as an overseas domestic worker?
Q32a Do you think that becoming an overseas domestic worker has elevated your status in an unusual kind of way? If yes, how? If no, why not?
Q33 Would you say that being an overseas domestic worker is an easy or difficult job? Why is it easy or why is it difficult?
Q34 Do [Did]* you have a clear idea of your work content? "Yes" or "No" will do here. If yes, what are [were]* they e.g cooking, cleaning, aged-care, child-care, all of the above, others?
Q35 Do [Did] you receive time-off? "Yes" or "No" will do hereI f yes, what kind e.g. holidays, weekends, sick days, others?
Q.36 Are [were] you satisfied with your pay? "Yes" or "No" here will do. How did it compare to your pay in your last job that you had in the Philippines? "Better," "the same," "worse."
Q37 Please tell me about your employers and employment situation?
Q37a How important is it to have a good employer for you? Very important, Important or Not important? Why? Why not?
Q37b In your opinion, what characteristics and attributes should a "good" employer have?

Q37c Do you practice any form of resistance e.g. in times when you may have been unhappy with an employer's request of or from you? "Yes" or "No" will do here. Why? Why not?

Q38 Do you think recruitment agencies are helpful to those FODWs who need to find work? Why? Why not?

Q39 Do you know anything about smuggling/trafficking? If yes, what are your thoughts on its costs and benefits to the FODW?

Q40 Anything else on domestic work employment?

6 On Your Choices

Q41 Do you feel that you are able to leave an employment situation in which you are not happy? [Did you feel that you were able to leave the unhappy employment situation you were in]? "Yes" or "No" will do here.

Q42 Did you, yourself choose to undertake overseas domestic work, or did someone else make the choice for you? "Yes" or "No" will do here. If yes, do you think, in retrospect, that you've made the right decision—yes, no or not sure?

Q42a If yes, do you think, in retrospect, that you've made the right decision—yes, no or not sure?

Q43 Do you send money back home. If yes, why? What does this mean for you—an obligation or a choice? If no, why not?

Q44 How would you compare your life here now, and your life back home—would you say you have more, or less choices (or freedom to choose) here than back home? Why?

Q45 If you had a choice, would you stay here or overseas permanently or would you return home? Why? Why not?

Q46 Would you say you took a risk or gamble by undertaking overseas domestic work?

Q46a What steps, if any did you take, to minimize the risks of overseas domestic work?

Q47 What do you think you have gained in undertaking overseas domestic work?

Q47a What do you think you have lost in undertaking overseas domestic work?

Q47b Do you have any regrets?

Q48 Why did you decide to work overseas as a domestic worker?

Q48a Would you say that you decided to undertake overseas work for economic reasons more so than personal/social ones—or the other way around?

Q49 If you were earning enough i.e. rich in the Philippines, do you think you would still consider migrating? Why? Why not?

Q50 What is your definition of "rich/wealthy?"
Q51 What are your plans and dreams for the future?
Q52 If you had the choice to work in any country in the world, where would it be and why?
Q53 From what you know, is there much difference between the earning power of FODW who those who are illegally and legally here?
Q54 As a rough guess, how many, in percentage, FODWs around the world are working illegally? Legally?
Q55 As a rough guess, how many FODWs are here in this country illegally? Legally?
Q55a What are the chances of getting caught if one is here illegally?
Q55b What do you think is the worst that can happen if one is caught?
Q56 If all the foreigners in this country were all suddenly sent back home (as with La Peine and the Asian Financial Crisis), what would you do?
Q57 Anything else on "your choices?"

7 On Your Social Life here

Q58 Please tell me a little about your social life here, including church and other social gatherings attendance, hobbies, social relations with employers and the host community etc.
Q59 Would you say you are happy with your social life here? Why? Why not?

8 On Abuse and Slavery

Q60 What do you understand "abuse" of overseas domestic workers to involve?
Q61 What do you think constitutes "enslavement" of overseas domestic workers?
Q61a How, if at all, do you think this differs from "abuse?"
Q62 Were you aware of the risks of abuse and enslavement before you decided to undertake domestic work here? If yes, did you take them seriously or not? If yes to this, why did you still decide to come? If not, why not?
Q63 Do you feel that you have experienced some form of abuse as an overseas domestic worker now and at other times in other countries? "Yes" or "no" will do here.
Q64 If you see "abuse" and "enslavement" as different, do you feel also that you have experienced some form of "enslavement" as an overseas

domestic worker now and at other times in other countries? "Yes" or "no" will do here.

Q65 Who or what do you think enslaves/abuses?

Q66 How do you think abuse of (Filipina) overseas domestic workers differs from or similar to abuse of domestic workers in the Philippines?

Q67 I have a list here of the types of abuse that some overseas domestic workers have been reported, especially by NGOs, to have experienced. Please let me know if you are aware of other types of abuse which I may have forgotten to include here: Physical, mental, emotional, sexual, wage-withholding, passport-withholding, and "enslavement." Please let me know if you have any comments about this list.

Q68 As a "guess," how many Filipina overseas domestic workers do you think suffer or have suffered from some form of abuse in this country; around the world?

Q69 Do you think that the abuse and/or enslavement of Filipina Overseas domestic workers is a problem?

Q69a If yes, in what ways do you think we can go about solving the problem?

Q70 If you have been abused, or if you were to be abused, are you (now) aware of the help you can get in this city? If yes, what are they, to who would you go and how would you go about it?

Q71 How do you think an "employed" Filipina overseas domestic worker differs from an "enslaved" Filipina overseas domestic worker? If you think they differ, which category would you put yourself in?

Q72 Out of the following three categories, in which would you say your situation fits most appropriately: "enslaved worker;" oppressed worker; not enslaved or oppressed worker i.e. ordinary wageworker?"

Q72a If none of the above, how would you describe your situation?

Q73 Anything else on "abuse and enslavement?"

9 Your Political Views

Q74 How do you understand "oppression?"

Q74a How do you think "abuse" and "enslavement" differs from "oppression?"

Q75 What are your thoughts on Filipino and overseas domestic workers non-government organizations?

Q75a Do you think NGOs do a fair job of representing your thoughts and experiences in public such as abused, servants/slaves etc? Do you think this has repercussions for your situation? If yes, how?

Q76 Do you think the Philippine government does a fair job of representing you as "heroines" of your country? Why? Why not?

Q77 In 1988, then President Corazon Aquino banned Filipinos from undertaking domestic work in Hong Kong as a move to protect them from abuse. There was a massive protest against this. Just recently, the Philippine government again issued a ban on entering Hong Kong as a result of the SARS outbreak. But it has been reported that a large number of Filipinos proceeded with their contracts for Hong Kong. What can you say about this? If for example, you had planned to leave the Philippines to go overseas and undertake domestic work, would these issues of abuse and grave health risks stop you from proceeding with your own contract?

Q78 What is your opinion about research on FODWs oppression? Do you think it is useful, not useful, other? Why, why not?

Q78a How do you think I, as a researcher, should be representing you? If you were the researcher, and you had to choose either to protect FODWs from abuse but not from losing their jobs, how would you suggest your situation be handled?

Q79 Are you happy with being called a "Filipina Overseas Domestic Worker?" If not, what term do you think is more appropriate? Why?

Q80 What do you understand "human rights" to be about?

Q81 Are you part of any labour/trade union here? Why? Why not?

Q82 Anything else on your political views?

Bibliography

Abdul Rahman, N. (2003), "Negotiating Power: A Case Study of Indonesian Foreign Domestic Workers in Sigapore," unpublished PhD dissertation, Department of Social Sciences, Perth: Curtin University of Technology.

Abdul Rahman, N. (2005), "Shaping the Migrant Institution: The Agency of Indonesian Domestic Workers in Singapore," in L. Parker (ed.) *The Agency of Women in Asia* (Singapore: Marshall Cavendish), pp. 182–226.

Adams, K. and Dickey, S. (eds) (2000), *Home and Hegemony: Domestic Service and Identity Politics in South and Southeast Asia* (Ann Arbor, MI: University of Michigan Press).

Aguilar, D. (2002), "Imperialism, Female Diaspora, and Feminism," *The Red Critique* 6, September/October. Accessed at www.redcritique.org.

Aguilar, D. and Lacsamana, A. (eds) (2004), *Women and Globalization* (New York: Humanity Books).

Aguilar, F. (1999), "Ritual Passage and the Reconstruction of Selfhood in International Labour Migration," *Sojourn: Journal of Social Issues in Southeast Asia* 14:1, 98–139.

Agustìn, L. (2005), "Migrants in the Mistress's House: Other Voices in the 'Trafficking' Debate," *Social Politics* 12:1, 96–117.

Agustìn, L. (2006), *Sex at the Margins: Migration, Labour Markets and the Rescue Industry* (London and New York: Zed Books).

Alegado, D. and Finin, G. (2000), "Exporting People: The Philippines and Contract Labor in Palau," *The Contemporary Pacific* 12:2, 359–70.

Alkire, S. (2002), *Valuing Freedoms: Sen's Capability Approach and Poverty Reduction* (Oxford: Oxford University Press).

Altink, S. (1995), *Stolen Lives: Trading Women into Sex and Slavery* (London: Scarlett Press).

AMC (1995a), *Living and Working with Migrants in Asia: Report of the Conference on Migrant Labour Issues, 15–19 May 1994, Hsinchu, Taiwan* (Hong Kong: Asian Migrant Centre).

AMC (1995b), *Ratifying the UN Convention Protecting Migrant Workers: Migrant Women's Quest for Justice* (Hong Kong: Asian Migrant Centre).

AMC (1995c), *Unlad Kabayan: A Primer on Migrant Worker Re-entry Programs; Migrant Savings for Alternative Investments* (Hong Kong: Asian Migrant Centre).

AMC (2000), *Asian Migrant Yearbook* (Hong Kong: Asian Migrant Centre).

AMC, ASPBAE and MFA (2001), *Clearing a Hurried Path: Study on Education Programs for Migrant Workers in Six Asian Countries* (Hong Kong: Asian

Migrant Centre (Hong Kong), Asian South Pacific Bureau of Adult Education (India) and Migrant Forum in Asia (Philippines)).

AMC and CMW (2001), *Baseline Research on Racial and Gender Discrimination Towards Foreign Domestic Helpers in Hong Kong* (Hong Kong: Asian Migrant Centre and Coalition for Migrant Workers).

AMCB (1999), "We Strongly Denounce the Decision of the Hong Kong Government to Lower the Minimum Wage of Foreign Domestic Workers!," Hong Kong: Asian Migrants Coordinating Body. Retrieved April 8, 2003. Accessed at www.hk.super.net/migrant.

Anderson, B. (1993), *Britain's Secret Slaves: An Investigation into the Plight of Overseas Domestic Workers in the UK* (London: Anti-Slavery International and Kalayaan, No. 5, Anti-Slavery International's Human Rights Series, Whistable and Litho).

Anderson, B. (1996), *Overseas Domestic Workers in the European Union* (Utrecht: Report for Stichting Tegen Vrouwenhandel).

Anderson, B. (1997), "Servants and Slaves: Europe's Domestic Workers," *Race and Class* 39:1, 37–49.

Anderson, B. (2000), *Doing the Dirty Work? The Global Politics of Domestic Labour* (New York: Zed Books).

Anderson, B. (2001a), "Different Roots in Common Ground: Transnationalism and Migrant Domestic Workers in London," *Journal of Ethnic and Migration Studies* 27:4, 673–84.

Anderson, B. (2001b), "Just Another Job? Paying for Domestic Work," in C. Sweetman (ed.), *Gender, Development and Money* (Oxford: Oxfam GB), pp. 25–33.

Anderson, B. (2001c), "Why Madam Has so Many Bathrobes? Demand for Migrant Workers in the EU," *Economic and Social Geography* 92:1, 18–26.

Anderson, B. (2002), "Just Another Job? The Commodification of Domestic Labour," in B. Ehrenreich and A.R. Hochschild (eds), *Global Woman: Nannies, Maids and Sex Workers in the New Economy* (New York: Henry Holt and Company), pp. 104–14.

Anderson, B. (2004a), "The Devil is in the Detail: Lessons to be Drawn from the UK's Recent Exercise in Regularising Undocumented Workers," in M. le Voy, N. Verbruggen and J. Wets (eds), *Undocumented Migrant Workers in Europe* (Brussels: Platform for International Cooperation on Undocumented Migrants (PICUM) and the Higher Institute for Labour Studies (HIVA), K.U. Leuven), pp. 89–101.

Anderson, B. (2004b), "Migrant Domestic Workers and Slavery," in C. van den Anker (ed.), *Political Economy of New Slavery* (New York: Palgrave Macmillan), pp. 107–17.

Anderson, B. (2004c), "Who Needs Yehudi Menuhin? Costs and Impact of Migration," in D.D. Aguilar and A. Lacsamana (eds), *Women and Globalization* (New York: Humanity Books), pp. 262–77.

Anderson, B. and O'Connell Davidson, J. (2003), *Trafficking—a Demand-led Problem? A Multi-country Pilot Study* (Sweden: Save the Children).

Anti-Slavery International (2003), *Forced Labour and Exploitation of Indonesian Migrant Workers: Submission to the United Nations Commission on Human Rights by the Working Group on Contemporary Forms of Slavery on behalf of the Asian Migrant Centre and the Indonesian Migrant Workers Union* (London: Antislavery International). Retrieved May 2, 2003. Accessed at www.antislavery.org/archive/submission/submission2003–Indonesia.htm.

Appadurai, A. (2000), "Grassroots Globalization and the Research Imagination," *Public Culture* 12:1, 1–19.

Appleyard, R. (2001), "International Migration Policies: 1950–2000," *International Migration* 39:6, 7–20.

APWLD (2002), *The New Conditions of Stay or "Two Week Rule"*, Asia Pacific Forum on Women, Law and Development. Retrieved May 18, 2004. Accessed at www.apwld.org/pdf/Two_week_rule_Timeline.pdf.

Arnold, F. and Abad, R. (1985), "Linkages between Internal and International Migration: The Illocos Norte Experience," *Philippine Populations Journal* 1:2, 1–17.

Asia Pacific Mission for Migrants (APMM) (2003a), "Development Aid and Forced Migration," *Migrant Monitor* 1:2, 20–24.

Asia Pacific Mission for Migrants (APMM) (2003b), *Evaluation Report: Asian Migrants Coordinating Body (AMCB)* (Hong Kong: APMM).

Asis, M. (1995), "Family Ties in a World without Borders," *Philippine Sociological Review* 42, 16–26.

Asis, M. (2002), "From the Life Stories of Filipino Women: Personal and Family Agendas in Migration," *Asian and Pacific Migration Journal* 1:11, 67–93.

Baber, Z. (1991), "Beyond the Structure/Agency Dualism: An Evaluation of Giddens' Theory of Structuration," *Sociological Inquiry* 61:2, 219–30.

Bakan, A.B. and Stasiulis, D.K. (1995), "Making the Match: Domestic Placement Agencies and the Racialisation of Women's Household Work," *Signs: Journal of Women in Culture and Society* 20:21, 303–35.

Bakan, A.B. and Stasiulis, D.K. (1997a), "Introduction," in A.B. Bakan and D. Stasiulis (eds), *Not One of the Family: Foreign Domestic Workers in Canada* (Toronto: University of Toronto Press), pp. 3–28.

Bakan, A.B. and Stasiulis, D.K. (eds) (1997b), *Not One of the Family: Foreign Domestic Workers in Canada* (Toronto: University of Toronto Press).

Ball, R. and Piper, N. (2002), "Globalisation and Regulation of Citizenship—Filipino Migrant Workers in Japan," *Political Geography* 21, 1013–34.

Bals, M. (1999), *Les domestiques étrangères au Canada: Esclaves de l'espoir* (Paris: Logiques sociales éditions de l'Harmattan).

Barber, P.G. (2000), "Agency in Philippine Women's Labour Migration and Provisional Diaspora," *Women's Studies International Forum* 23:4, 399–411.

Battistella, G. (1995), "Philippine Overseas Labour: From Export to Management," *ASEAN Economic Bulletin* 12, 257–74.

Battistella, G. (2002), "International Migration in Asia vis-à-vis Europe: An Introduction," *Asian and Pacific Migration Journal* 11:4, 405–14.

Behar, R. and Gordon, D. (eds) (1995), *Women Writing Culture* (Berkeley, CA: University of California Press).

Bell, D.A. and Piper, N. (2005), "Justice for Migrant Workers? The Case of Foreign Domestic Workers in East Asia," in W. Kymlicka and H. Baogang (eds), *Multiculturalism in Asia* (Oxford: Oxford University Press), pp. 196–222.

Berlin, I. (1969), *Four Essays on Liberty* (Oxford: Oxford University Press).

Bernard, H.R. (1994), *Research Methods in Anthropology: Qualitative and Quantitative Approaches* (Thousand Oaks, CA: Sage).

Bhabha, H. (ed.) (1994), *The Location of Culture* (London and New York: Routledge).

Blackett, A. (1998), *Making Domestic Work Visible: The Case for Specific Regulation* (Geneva: ILO Infocus Programme on Social Dialogue, Labour Law and Labour Administration, International Labour Organisation).

Blackmore, J. (2005), "Feminist Strategic Rethinking of Human Rights Discourses in Education," in W.S. Hesford and W. Kozol (eds), *Just Advocacy? Women's Human Rights, Transnational Feminisms, and the Politics of Representation* (New Brunswick, NJ and London: Rutgers University Press), pp. 243–65.

Boyce, J. (1990), *The Political Economy of External Indebtedness: A Case Study of the Philippines* (Makati, Manila: Philippine Institute for Development Studies, Monograph Series No. 12).

Boyce, J. (1993), *The Philippines: The Political Economy of Growth and Impoverishment in the Marcos Era* (London, Honolulu and Quezon City: Macmillan, University of Hawaii Press, Ateneo de Manila University Press. Published in conjunction with the OECD Development Centre's Research Programme on Alternative Development Strategies).

Briones, L. (2001), "The Making of 21st Century Global Slavery: '3D' International Pilipino Labour Migration as a Case Study," Honours thesis, Flinders University of South Australia.

Butler, J. (1990), *Gender Troubles: Feminism and the Subversions of Identity* (London: Routledge).

Butler, J. (1993), *Bodies that Matter: On the Discursive Limits of Sex* (London: Routledge).

Butler, J. (1997), *Excitable Speech: A Politics of the Performative* (New York: Routledge).

Bynum, C. (1995), "Why All the Fuss about the Body? A Medievalist's Perspective," *Critical Inquiry* 22, 1–33.

Campani, G. (1993), "Labour Markets and Family Networks: Filipino Women in Italy," in M. Morokvasic and R. Hedwig (eds), *Bridging States and Markets: International Migration in the Early 1990s* (Berlin: Sigma), pp. 191–205.

Carroué, L. (2003), "La Grand Braderie de Main—d'oeuvre," *Alternatives Economiques* 215, 62–5.

Castells, M. (1996), *The Information Age: The Rise of the Network Society* (Cambridge, MA and Oxford: Blackwell).

Castles, S. (1999), "International Migration and the Global Agenda: Reflections on the 1998 UN Technical Symposium," *International Migration* 37:1, 5–20.

Castles, S. and Miller, M. (2003), *The Age of Migration* (Basingstoke and New York: Macmillan).

Chang, G. (2000), *Disposable Domestics: Immigrant Women Workers in the Global Economy* (Cambridge, MA: Southend Press).

Chang, G. (2004), "Globalization in Living Color," in D.D. Aguilar and A. Lacsamana (eds), *Women and Globalization* (New York: Humanity Press), pp. 230–61.

Chang, K. (2000), "Globalization and its Intimate Others: Filipina Domestic Workers in Hong Kong," in M.H. Marchand and A.S. Runyan (eds), *Gender and Global Restructuring: Sightings, Sites and Resistances* (London, New York: Routledge), pp. 27–43.

Chant, S. (1996), "Women's Roles in Recessions and Economic Restructuring in Mexico and the Philippines," *GenEros* 5:17, 25–38.

Chant, S. (1997), "Marginal (M)others: Lone Parents and Female Householdship in the Philippines," *European Journal of Development Research* 9:2, 1–34.

Chant, S. and McIlwaine, C. (1995), *Women of a Lesser Cost: Female Labour, Foreign Exchange and Philippine Development* (London: Pluto Press).

Chell-Robinson, V. (2000), "Female Migrants in Italy: Coping in a Country of New Immigration," in F. Anthias and G. Lazaridis (eds), *Gender and Migration in Southern Europe* (Oxford: Berg), pp. 103–23.

Cheng, S.A. (1996), "Migrant Women Domestic Workers in Hong Kong, Singapore and Taiwan: A Comparative Analysis," *Asian and Pacific Migration Journal* 5:1, 139–52.

Cheng, S.A. (2001), "Serving the Household and the Nation: Filipino Domestics and the Development of Nationhood in Taiwan," PhD thesis, University of Texas.

Cheng, S.A. (2004), "Contextual Politics of Difference in Transnational Care: The Rhetoric of Filipina Domestics' Employers in Taiwan," *Feminist Review* 77:1, 46–64.

Chin, C.B.N. (1997), "Walls of Silence in Late Twentieth Century Representations of Foreign Female Domestic Workers: The Case of Filipina and Indonesian Female Servants in Malaysia," *International Migration Review* 31:2, 353–85.

Chin, C.B.N. (1998), *In Service and Servitude: Foreign Female Domestic Workers and the Malaysian "Modernity" Project* (New York: Columbia University Press).

Chin, C.B.N. (2003), "Visible Bodies, Invisible Work: State Practices Toward Migrant Women Domestic Worker in Malaysia," *Asian and Pacific Migration Journal* 12:1–2, 49–76.

Clegg, S. (1989), *Frameworks of Power* (London: Sage).

Clifford, J. and Marcus, G.E. (eds) (1986), *Writing Culture: The Poetics and Politics of Ethnography* (Berkeley, CA: University of California Press).

Close, P. and Askew, D. (2004), *Asia Pacific and Human Rights* (Aldershot and Burlington, VA: Ashgate).

Cock, J. (1980), *Maids and Madams: A Study in the Politics of Exploitation* (Johannesburg: Ravan Press).

Constable, N. (1997), *Maid to Order in Hong Kong : Stories of Filipina Workers* (New York: Cornell University Press).

Corbridge, S. (2002), "Development as Freedom: The Spaces of Amartya Sen," *Progress in Development Studies* 2:3, 183–217.

Cornelius, W.A. (1998), "The Structural Embeddedness of Demand for Mexican Immigrant Labour," in M. Suárez-Orozco (ed.), *Crossings: Mexican Immigration in Comparative Perspectives* (Cambridge, MA: Harvard University Press/David Rockefeller Center for Latin American Studies), pp. 115–55.

Cornelius, W.A. and Tsuda, T. (2004), "Controlling Immigration: The Limits of Government Intervention," in W.A. Cornelius, T. Tsuda, P.L. Martin and J.F. Hollifield (eds), *Controlling Immigration: A Global Perspective* (Palo Alto, CA: Stanford University Press), pp. 3–50.

Council of Europe (2001), *Domestic Slavery: Report to the Parliamentary Assembly* (Strasbourg: Committee on Equal Opportunities for Women and Men).

Council of Europe (2004), *Domestic Slavery: Servitude, Au Pairs and "Mail-order Brides"* (Strasbourg: Parliamentary Assembly).

Cowen, M.P. and Shenton, R.W. (1996), *Doctrines of Development* (London and New York: Routledge).

Cox, D. (1997), "The Vulnerability of Asian Migrant Workers to a Lack of Protection and Violence," *Asian and Pacific Migration Journal* 6:1, 59–75.

Cox, R. and Narula, R. (2003), "Playing Happy Families: Rules and Relationships in Au Pair Employing Households in London, England," *Gender, Place and Culture* 10:4, 333–44.

Crocker, D. (2004), "Deliberating Global Development: Ethics, Capability and Democracy," unpublished manuscript, University of Maryland.

Cruz, V. and Paganoni, A. (1989), *Filipinas in Migration: Big Bills, Small Change* (Quezon City: Scalabrini Migration Center).

Dales, L. (2005), "Lifestyles of the Rich and Single: Reading Agency in the 'Parasite Single' Issue," in L. Parker (ed.), *The Agency of Women in Asia* (Singapore: Marshall Cavendish), pp. 133–57.

de Dios, A.J. (1992), "Japayukisan: Filipinas at Risk," in P. Beltran and A.J. de Dios (eds), *Filipino Women Overseas Contract Workers: At What Cost?* (Manila: Goodwill Trading Co.).

de Laine, M. (2000), *Fieldwork, Participation and Practice: Ethics and Dilemmas in Qualitative Research* (London: Sage).

de Vries, P. (1992), "A Research Journey: On Actors, Concepts and Texts," in N. Long and A. Long (eds), *Battlefields of Knowledge* (London and New York: Routledge), pp. 47–84.

Department of International Development (2007), *Moving Out of Poverty: Making Migration Work Better for Poor People* (London: DFID).

Devereux, S. (2001), "Sen's Entitlement Approach: Critiques and Counter-critiques," *Oxford Development Studies* 29:3, 245–63.

Doezema, J. (1998), "Forced to Choose: Beyond the Voluntary v. Forced Prostitution Dichotomy," J. Doezema and K. Kempadoo (eds), in *Global Sex Workers: Rights, Resistance and Redefinition* (New York and London: Routledge).

Doezema, J. (2000), "Loose Women or Lost Women? The Reemergence of the Myth of White Slavery in Contemporary Discourses of Trafficking in Women," *Gender Issues* 18:1, 13–54.

Doezema, J. (2002), "Who Gets to Choose? Coercion, Consent, and the UN Trafficking Protocol," in R. Masika (ed.), *Gender, Trafficking and Slavery* (Oxford: Oxfam GB), pp. 20–27.

Drèze, J. and Sen, A. (2002), *India: Development and Participation* (Oxford: Oxford University Press).

Ebron, G. (2002), "Not Just the Maid: Negotiating Filipina Identity in Italy," *Intersections: Gender, History and Culture in the Asian Context* 8. Retrieved November 5, 2003. Accessed at www.sshe.murdoch.edu.au/intersections/issue8/ebron.html.

Ehrenreich, B. and Hochschild, A.R. (eds) (2002), *Global Woman: Nannies, Maids and Sex Workers in the New Economy* (New York: Henry Holt and Company).

Elson, D. (1991), "Male Bias in Macro-economics: The Case of Structural Adjustment," in D. Elson (ed.), *Male Bias in the Development Process* (Manchester: Manchester University Press).

Emirbayer, M. and Mische, A. (1998), "What is Agency?," *American Sociological Review* 103, 962–1002.

England, K. and Stiell, B. (1997), "'They Think you're as Stupid as your English Is:' Constructing Foreign Domestic Workers in Toronto," *Environment and Planning* A:29, 192–215.

Escobar, A. (1995), *Encountering Development: The Making and Unmaking of the Third World* (Princeton, NJ: Princeton University Press).

Eviota, E.U. (1992), *The Political Economy of Gender: Women and the Sexual Division of Labor in the Philippines* (London: Zed Books Ltd).

Eviota, E.U. (2004), "The Context of Gender and Globalization in the Philippines," in D.D. Aguilar and A. Lacsamana (eds), *Women and Globalization* (New York: Humanity Books), pp. 52–67.

Falk, R. (1999), *Predatory Globalization—A Critique* (Cambridge: Polity Press).

Faux, J. (2002), "Rethinking the Global Political Economy," Economic Policy Institute. Retrieved December 20, 2005. Accessed at www.epinet.org/content.cfm/webfeatures_viewpoints_global_polit_econ.

Ferguson, A. (1998), "Resisting the Veil of Privilege: Building Bridge Identities as an Ethico-politics of Global Feminisms," *Hypatia* 13:13, 95–14.

Ford, M. (2001), "Indonesian Women as Export Commodity: Notes from Tanjung Pinang," *Labour and Management in Development Journal* 2:5, 2–9.

Gamburd, M.R. (2000), *The Kitchen Spoon's Handle: Transnationalism and Sri Lanka's Migrant Housemaids* (Ithaca, NY: Cornell University Press).

Gasper, D. (2002), "Is Sen's Capability Approach an Adequate Basis for Considering Human Development?," *Institute of Social Studies Working Paper Series No. 360*, The Hague.

Gasper, D. (2004), *The Ethics of Development* (Edinburgh: Edinburgh University Press).

Gasper, D. and Truong, T.D. (2004), "Deepening Development Ethics Through the Lenses of Human Security: Care, Migration and Women's Lives," European Standing Group on International Relations (SGIR). Retrieved November 15, 2005. Accessed at www.sgir.org/conference2004/papers/Gasper%20Truong%20–%20Deepening%20development%20ethics.pdf.

Gatmaytan, D. (1997), "Death and the Maid: Work, Violence and the Filipina in the International Labour Market," *Harvard Women's Law Journal* 20 (Spring), 229–61.

Gibson, K., Law, L. and McKay, D. (2001), "Beyond Heroes and Victims: Filipina Contract Migrants, Economic Activism and Class Transformations," *International Feminist Journal of Politics* 3:3, 365–86.

Giddens, A. (1979), *Central Problems in Social Theory* (London: University of California Press).

Giddens, A. (1982), *Profiles and Critique in Social Theory* (London: Macmillan).

Giddens, A. (1984a), *The Constitution of Society: Outline of the Theory of Structuration* (Cambridge: Polity Press).

Giddens, A. (1984b), "Space, Time and Politics in Social Theory: An Interview with Anthony Giddens, by Derek Gregory," *Environment and Planning D: Society and Space* 2, 123–32.

Giddens, A. (1990), "Structuration Theory and Sociological Analysis," in J. Clark, C. Modgil and S. Modgil (eds), *Anthony Giddens: Consensus and Controversy* (New York and London: Falmer Press), pp. 297–315.

Giddens, A., Bryant, C.G.A. and Jary, D. (2001), "The Reflexive Giddens: Christopher G.A. Bryant and David Jary in Dialogue with Anthony Giddens," in C.G.A. Bryant and D. Jary (eds), *The Contemporary Giddens: Social Theory in a Globalizing Age* (Basingstoke and New York: Palgrave), pp. 229–70.

Giddens, A. and Pierson, C. (1998), *Conversations with Anthony Giddens: Making Sense of Modernity* (Cambridge: Polity Press).

Giri, A.K. (2000), "Rethinking Human Well-being: A Dialogue with Amartya Sen," *Journal of International Development* 12:7, 1003–18.

Glenn, E.N. (1992), "From Servitude to Service Work: Historical Continuities in the Racial Division of Paid Reproductive Labour," *Signs: Journal of Women in Culture and Society* 18:1, 1–43.

Gonzalez, J.L. II (1998), *Philippine Labour Migration: Critical Dimensions of Public Policy* (Singapore: Institute of Southeast Asian Studies).

Gore, C. (1997), "Irreducible Social Goods and the Informational Basis of Amartya Sen's Capability Approach," *Journal of International Development* 9:2, 235–50.

Goss, J. and Lindquist, B. (1995), "Conceptualising International Labour Migration: A Structuration Perspective," *International Migration Review* 29:2, 317–51.

Grandea, N. and Kerr, J. (1998), "'Frustrated and Displaced:' Filipina Domestic Workers in Canada," in C. Sweetman (ed.), *Gender and Migration* (Oxford: Oxfam), pp. 7–12.

Guest, P. (1989), *Labour Allocation and Rural Development: Migration in Four Javanese Villages* (Boulder, CO: Westview Press).

Hammar, T. (2001), "Politics of Immigration Control and Politicisation of International Migration," in M.A.B. Siddiqe (ed.), *International Migration into the 21st Century: Essays in Honour of Reginald Appleyard* (Cheltenham and Northampton, MA: Edward Elgar), pp. 15–28.

Hart, G. (2001), "Development Critiques in the 1990s: Culs de Sac and Promising Paths," *Progress in Human Geography* 25:4, 649–58.

Hart, G. (2002), "Geography and Development: Development/s beyond Neoliberalism? Power, Culture and Political Economy," *Progress in Human Geography* 26:6, 812–22.

Hatton, T.J. and Williamson, J.G. (2005), *Global Migration and the World Economy: Two Centuries of Policy and Performance* (Cambridge, MA and London: MIT Press).

Hesford, W.S. (2005), "Kairos and the Geopolitical Rhetorics of Global Sex Work and Video Advocacy," in W.S. Hesford and W. Kozol (eds), *Just Advocacy? Women's Human Rights, Transnational Feminisms, and the Politics of Representation* (New Brunswick, NJ and London: Rutgers University Press), pp. 146–72.

Hesford, W.S. and Kozol, W. (eds) (2005), *Just Advocacy? Women's Human Rights, Transnational Feminisms, and the Politics of Representation* (New Brunswick, NJ and London: Rutgers University Press).

Heyzer, N., Nijeholt, G.L. and Weerakoon, N. (eds) (1994), *The Trade in Domestic Workers: Causes, Mechanisms and Consequences of International Migration* (London: Zed Books).

Hill, M.T. (2003), "Development as Empowerment," *Feminist Economics* 9:2,3, 117–35.

HKID (2005), Hong Kong Immigration Department, monthly statistics for August 2005, ref: IL/INT/E42561/2005, Hong Kong.

HKLD (1992), *Report on Labour and Employment in Hong Kong* (Hong Kong: Hong Kong Labour Department).

HKSAR (2004) *Hong Kong: The Facts—Immigration*, Hong Kong Special Administration of China. Retrieved April 19, 2005. Accessed at www.info.gov.hk/hkfacts/immi.pdf.

Hollifield, J.F. (2004), "France: Republicanism and the Limits of Immigration Control," in W.A. Cornelius, T. Tsuda, P.L. Martin and J.F. Hollifield (eds), *Controlling Immigration: A Global Perspective* (Palo Alto, CA: Stanford University Press), pp. 183–214.

Hondagneu-Sotelo, P. (1994), *Gendered Transitions: Mexican Experiences of Immigration* (Berkeley, CA: University of California Press).

Huang, S. and Yeoh, B. (2003), "The Difference Gender Makes: State Policy and Contract Migrant Workers in Singapore," *Asian and Pacific Migration Journal* 12:1–2, 75–98.

Hugo, C. (1994), "Introduction," in M. Wooden, R. Holton, H.G. and J. Sloan (eds), *Australian Immigration: A Survey of the Issues* (2nd edn) (Canberra: AGPS).

Hugo, G. (1995), "Illegal International Migration in Asia," in G.A. Cohen (ed.), *The Cambridge Survey of World Migration* (Cambridge: Cambridge University Press), pp. 397–402.

Hugo, G. (2004), "International Migration in the Asia-Pacific Region: Emerging Trends and Issues," in D. Massey and J. Taylor (eds), *International Migration: Prospects and Policies in a Global Market* (Oxford: Oxford University Press), pp. 77–103.

Human Rights Watch (2006), "Swept under the Rugs: Abuses against Domestic Workers around the World," Human Rights Watch Report, 18, 7. (C). Retrieved February 20, 2008. Accessed at www.hrw.org/reports/2006/wrd0706/.

ILO (2001), *Stopping Forced Labour: Global Report under the Follow-up to the ILO Declaration of Fundamental Principles and Rights at Work* (Geneva: International Labour Conference, 89th Session).

ILO (2004a), *The Report: A Fair Globalization—Creating Opportunities for All* (Geneva: World Commission on the Social Dimensions of Globalization).

ILO (2004b), *Towards a Fair Deal for Migrant Workers in the Global Economy* (Geneva: International Labour Conference, 92nd Session).

IOM (2003), *World Migration 2003: Managing Migration: Challenges and Responses for People on the Move* (Geneva: International Organisation for Migration).

IOM (2005), *World Migration 2005: Costs and Benefits of International Migration* (Geneva: International Organisation for Migration).

Jacobson, D. (1996), *Rights across Borders: Immigration and the Decline of Citizenship* (Baltimore, MD: The John Hopkins University Press).

Jordan, B. and Düvell, F. (2002), *Irregular Migration: The Dilemmas of Transnational Mobility* (Cheltenham: Edward Elgar).

Kearney, M. (1986), "From the Invisible Hand to Visible Feet: Anthropological Studies of Migration and Development," *Annual Review of Anthropology* 15, 331–61.

Kempadoo, K. (1999), "Slavery or Work? Reconceptualizing Third World Prostitution," *Positions* 7:1, 225–37.

Kiely, R. (1998), "Transnational Companies, Global Capital and the Third World," in R. Kiely and P. Marfleet (eds), *Globalisation and the Third World* (London and New York: Routledge), pp. 45–66.

Kofman, E. (2004), "Gendered Migration and Entitlements in the European Union," unpublished background paper (Geneva: United Nations Research Institute for Social Development).

Koser, K. and Lutz, H. (1998), "The New Migration in Europe: Contexts, Constructions and Realities," in K. Koser and H. Lutz (eds), *The New Migration in Europe: Social Constructions and Social Realities* (London: Macmillan), pp. 1–17.

Lan, P.C. (2000), "Global Divisions, Local Identities: Filipina Domestic Workers and Taiwanese Employers," PhD thesis, Northwestern University, Evanston.

Lan, P.C. (2001), "Among Women: Migrant Domestics and their Taiwanese Employers across Generations," *Center for Working Families Working Paper 30*, University of California.

Lan, P.C. (2006), *Global Cinderellas: Migrant Domestics and Newly Rich Employers in Taiwan* (Durham and London: Duke University Press).

Landry, D. and MacLean, G. (eds) (1996), *The Spivak Reader* (New York and London: Routledge).

Lauby, J. and Stark, O. (1988), "Individual Migration as a Family Strategy: Young Women in the Philippines," *Population Studies* 42, 473–86.

Law, L. (2002a), "Defying Disappearance: Filipino Labour Migrants and Public Space in Hong Kong," *Urban Studies* 39:9, 1625–45.

Law, L. (2002b), "Sites of Transnational Activism: Filipino NGOs in Hong Kong," in B. Yeoh, P. Teo and S. Huang (eds), *Gender Politics in the Asia Pacific Region* (London and New York: Routledge), pp. 205–22.

Layder, D. (1997), "Power, Structure and Agency," in C.G.A. Bryant and D. Jary (eds), *Anthony Giddens: Critical Assessments* (London and New York: Routledge), pp. 104–22.

Lee, S.M. (1996), "Issues in Research on Women, International Migration and Labor," *Asian and Pacific Migration Journal* 5:1, 5–26.

Lerner, G. (1983), "Women and Slavery," *Slavery and Abolition* 4:3, 173–98.

Li, F.L.N., Findlay, A.M. and Jones, H. (1998), "A Cultural Economy Perspective on Service Sector Migration in the Global City: The Case of Hong Kong," *International Migration* 36:2, 131–58.

Lightfoot, P., Fuller, T. and Kamnuansilpa, P. (1983), "Circulation and Interpersonal Networks Linking Rural and Urban Areas: The Case of Roi-et, Northeastern Thailand," *Papers of the East-West Population Institute No. 84* (Honolulu, HI: East-West Center).

Limanowska, B. (2004), *Trafficking in Human Beings in Southeastern Europe* (Geneva: joint UNICEF, OSCE-ODIHR and UNOHCHR report).

Lindio-McGovern, L. (2003), "Labour Export in the Context of Globalisation: The Experience of Filipino Domestic Workers in Rome," *International Sociology* 18:3, 513–34.

Lloyd, C. (2003), "Women Migrants and Political Activism in France," in J. Andall (ed.), *Gender and Ethnicity in Contemporary Europe* (Bath: Oxford), pp. 97–116.

Long, N. (1992), "From Paradigm Lost to Paradigm Regained," in N. Long and A. Long (eds), *Battlefields of Knowledge: The Interlocking of Theory and Practice in Social Research and Development* (London and New York: Routledge), pp. 16–43.

Long, N. and Long, A. (eds) (1992), *Battlefields of Knowledge: The Interlocking of Theory and Practice in Social Research and Development* (London and New York: Routledge).

Lowe, C.T. (2000), "The Outsider's Voice: Discourse and Identity among Filipina Domestic Workers in Hong Kong," PhD thesis, City University of Hong Kong.

Luan, B. (2005) "Migration and Development," *Asian Migrant Yearbook 2005*, Asia Migrant Centre, 31–49.

Lucas, R.E.J. (1993), "Making a Miracle," *Econometrica*, 251–72.

Mahmood, S. (2001), "Feminist Theory, Embodiment and Docile Agent: Some Reflections of the Egyptian Islamic Revival," *Cultural Anthropology* 16:2, 202–36.

Marigold, J.A. (1995), "Narratives of Masculinity and Transnational Migration: Filipino Workers in the Middle East," in A. Ong and M.G. Peletz (eds), *Bewitching Women, Pious Men: Gender and Body Politics in Southeast Asia* (Berkeley, CA, Los Angeles, CA and London: University of California Press), pp. 274–94.

Martin, P. (1993), "The Migration Issue," in R. King (ed.), *The New Geography of European Migrations* (London: Belhaven Press), pp. 1–15.

Massey, D. (1988), "International Migration and Economic Development in Comparative Perspective," *Population and Development Review* 14, 383–414.

Massey, D. (1990), "Social Structure, Household Strategies, and the Cumulative Causation of Migration," *Population Index* 56:1, 3–26.

Massey, D. (1999), "International Migration at the Dawn of the Twenty First Century: The Role of the State," *Population and Development Review* 25:2, 303–22.

Massey, D., Alarcon, R., Durand, J. and González, H. (1987), *Return to Azlan: The Social Process of International Migration from Western Mexico* (Berkeley, CA: University of California Press).

Massey, D., Arango, J., Hugo, G., Kouaouci, A., Pellgrino, A. and Taylor, E.J. (1993), "Theories of International Migration: A Review and Appraisal," *Population and Development Review* 19:3, 431–66.

Massey, D. and Espinosa, K.E. (1997), "What's Driving Mexican Migration to the United States," *American Journal of Sociology* 102:4, 939–99.

Massey, D., Gross, A.B. and Shibuya, K. (1994), "Migration, Segregation, and the Geographic Concentration of Poverty," *American Sociological Review* 59, 424–45.

Mattingly, D.J. (1999), "Making Maids: United States Immigration Policy and Immigrant Domestic Workers," in J. Henshall Momsen (ed.), *Gender, Migration, and Domestic Service* (New York: Routledge), pp. 62–79.

Mattingly, D.J. (2001), "The Home and the World: Domestic Service and the International Networks of Caring Labour," *Annals of the Association of American Geographers* 91:2, 370–86.

McClintock, A. (1995), *Imperial Leather: Race, Gender and Sexuality in the Colonial Conquest* (New York: Routledge).

McCulloch, L. and Stancich, L. (1998), "Women and (In)Security: The Case of the Philippines," *Pacific Review* 11:3, 16–43.

McKay, D. (2004a), "Everyday Places—Philippine Place-Making and the Translocal Quotidian," *Everyday Transformations, The Twenty-First Century Quotidian: Proceedings of the Cultural Studies Association of Australasia* (CSAA), Conference, Murdoch University.

McKay, D. (2004b), *Performing Identities, Creating Cultures of Circulation: Filipina Migrants between Home and Abroad*, 15th Biennial Conference of the Asian Studies Association of Australia, Canberra.

Medina, B.T.G. (1991), *The Filipino Family* (Manila: University of the Philippines).

Medina, B.T.G. and Natividad, J. (1985), "Filipino Chain Migration to the United States," *Philippine Populations Journal* 1:4, 67–94.

Menon, N. (2002), "Universalism without Foundations?," *Economy and Society* 31:1, 152–69.

Meyers, E. (2004), *International Immigration Policy: A Theoretical and Comparative Analysis* (New York: Palgrave Macmillan).

MFMW (2000a), *Migrant Focus Magazine: The Lucrative Business that is Labor Export* (Hong Kong: Mission for Migrant Workers, Vol. 1).

MFMW (2000b), *Migrant Focus Magazine: When the Only Option is Migration* (Hong Kong: Mission for Migrant Workers, Vol. 1).

MFMW (2001a), *Migrant Focus Magazine: Breaking the Cycle of Forced Migration* (Hong Kong: Mission for Migrant Workers, Vol. 1).

MFMW (2001b), *Migrant Focus Magazine: There's More to Migration than Money Problems* (Hong Kong: Mission for Migrant Workers, Vol. 1).

Mies, M. (1998), *Patriarchy and Accumulation on a World Scale: Women in the International Division of Labour* (London: Zed Books).

Minh-ha, T.T. (1989), *Woman, Native, Other: Writing Postcoloniality and Feminism* (Bloomington, IN: University of Indiana Press).

Misra, J., Woodring, J. and Merz, S. (2005), "The Globalization of Carework: Immigration, Economic Restructuring, and the World System," paper presented at the International Conference on *Migration and Domestic Work in Global Perspective*, Wassenar, Amsterdam, May 26–29.

Momsen, J.H. (ed.) (1999a), *Gender, Migration and Domestic Service* (London and New York: Routledge).

Momsen, J.H. (1999b), "Victim or Victor?," in J. Henshall Momsen (ed.), *Gender, Migration and Domestic Service* (London and New York: Routledge), pp. 1–20.

Moors, A. (2003), "Migrant Domestic Workers: Debating Transnationalism, Identity Politics and Family Relations. A Review Essay," *Comparative Studies in Society and History* 45:2, 386–92.

Morokvasic, M. (1984), *Migrant Women in Europe: A Comparative Perspective* (Paris: UNESCO).

Mouzelis, N. (1989), "Restructuring Structuration Theory," *Sociological Review* 37, 613–35.

Mozère, L. (1999), "Travail au noir et informalité. Liberté ou sujétion?," *Logiques Sociales*.

Mozère, L. (2001), "La philippine ou la 'Mercédès Benz' des domestiques. Entre archaïsme et mondialisation. Carrières de femmes dans l'informalité," *Sextant*:15–16, 297–317.

Mozère, L. and Maury, H. (2002), "Les Domestiques Philippines "entrepreneures d'elles-memes": le marche mondial de la domesticité," Working Paper: Mission du Patrimoine Ethnologique: "formes contemporaines de l'economie informelle: activites, echanges et reseaux de relations," Université de Metz, France.

Mozère, L., Maury, H., Fijalkow, Y., Dahan, V. and Lenhart, C. (2001), "Petites métiers urbains au féminin ou comment échapper à la précarisation," *Migration et Etudes* 101 (September–October), 1–6.

Mulder, N. (1997), *Inside Philippine Society: Interpretations of Everyday Life* (Quezon City, Philippines: New Day Publishers).

Narula, R. (1999), "Cinderella Need not Apply: A Study of Paid Domestic Work in Paris," in J. Henshall Momsen (ed.), *Gender, Migration and Domestic Service* (London: Routledge), pp. 148–63.
Nast, H. and Pile, S. (1998), *Places Through the Body* (London and New York: Routledge).
Nolin, C. (2006), *Transnational Ruptures: Gender and Forced Migration* (Aldershot and Burlington, VA: Ashgate).
NSCB (2003), "Higher Unemployment Rates for Women than Men," Philippine National Statistical Coordination Board (NCSB). Retrieved April 6, 2003. Accessed at www.nscb.gov.ph/factsheet/pdf03/fs3_01.asp.
Nussbaum, M. (1988), "Nature, Functioning and Capability: Aristotle on Political Distribution," *Oxford Studies in Ancient Philosophy Supplementary Volume*, 145–84.
Nussbaum, M. (1992), "Human Functioning and Social Justice: In Defense of Aristotelian Essentialism," *Political Theory* 20:2, 202–46.
Nussbaum, M. (1995), "Human Capabilities, Female Human Beings," in M. Nussbaum and J. Glover (eds), *Women, Culture and Development: A Study of Human Capabilities* (Oxford: Clarendon Press), pp. 61–115.
Nussbaum, M. (1998), "Public Philosophy and International Feminism," *Ethics* 108, 762–96.
Nussbaum, M. (1999), "Women and Equality: The Capabilities Approach," *International Labour Review* 138:3, 227–45.
Nussbaum, M. (2000), *Women and Human Development: The Capabilities Approach* (Cambridge: Cambridge University Press).
Nussbaum, M. (2002), "Capabilities and Human Rights," in P. de Grieff and C. Ciaran (eds), *Global Justice: Transnational Politics* (London and Cambridge, MA: MIT Press), pp. 117–50.
Nussbaum, M. (2003), "Capabilities as Fundamental Entitlements: Sen and Social Justice," *Feminist Economics* 9:2,3, 33–59.
Nussbaum, M. (2004), "Beyond the Social Contract: Capabilities and Global Justice," *Oxford Development Studies* 32:1, 3–18.
Nussbaum, M. (2006), *Frontiers of Justice: Disability, Nationality, Species, Membership* (Cambridge, MA: Harvard University Press).
Nussbaum, M. and Sen, A. (1993), *The Quality of Life* (Oxford: Clarendon Press).
O'dy, S. (2001), *Esclaves En France* (Paris: Albin Michel).
Oakley, A. (1988), *The Sociology of Housework* (Oxford: Basil Blackwell).
OECD (2006), *International Migration Outlook: Annual Report 2006 Edition* (Paris: Organisation for Economic Co-operation and Development).
Ogaya, C. (2004a), "Filipino Domestic Workers and the Creation of New Subjectivities," *Asian and Pacific Migration Journal* 13:3, 381–404.
Ogaya, C. (2004b), "Social Discourses on Filipino Women Migrants," *Feminist Review* 77:1, 180–82.

Olwig, K.F. and Sørensen, N.N. (2002), "Mobile Livelihoods: Making a Living in the World," in K.F. Olwig and N.N. Sørensen (eds), *Work and Migration: Life and Livelihoods in a Globalizing World* (London and New York: Routledge), pp. 1–20.

Ong, P., Bonacich, E. and Cheng, L. (eds) (1994), *The New Asian Migration in Los Angeles and Global Restructuring* (Philadelphia, PA: Temple University Press).

Outhwaite, W. (1990), "Agency and Structure," in J. Clark, C. Modgil and S. Modgil (eds), *Anthony Giddens: Consensus and Controversy* (New York and London: Falmer Press), pp. 63–72.

Parker, L (ed.) (2005a), *The Agency of Women in Asia* (Singapore: Marshall Cavendish).

Parker, L. (2005b), "Conclusion," in L. Parker (ed.), *The Agency of Women in Asia* (Singapore: Marshall Cavendish), pp. 227–39.

Parker, L. (2005c), "Introduction," in L. Parker (ed.), *The Agency of Women in Asia* (Singapore: Marshall Cavendish), pp. 1–25.

Parker, L. (2005d), "Resisting Resistance and Finding Agency: Women and Medicalized Birth in Bali," in L. Parker (ed.), *The Agency of Women in Asia* (Singapore: Marshall Cavendish), pp. 62–97.

Parreñas, R.S. (2000), "Migrant Filipina Workers and the International Division of Reproductive Labour," *Gender and Society* 14:4, 560–80.

Parreñas, R.S. (2001), *Servants of Globalisation: Women, Migration and Domestic Work* (Palo Alto, CA: Stanford University Press).

Pécoud, A. and de Guchteneire, P. (2004), "Migration, Human Rights and the United Nations: An Investigation into the Low Ratification Record of the UN Migrant Workers Convention," *Global Migration Perspectives No. 3*, Global Commission on International Migration, Geneva.

Pécoud, A. and de Guchteneire, P. (2005), "Migration without Borders: An Investigation into the Free Movement of People," *Global Migration Perspectives No. 27*, Global Commission on International Migration, Geneva.

Phizacklea, A. (1998), "Migration and Globalization: A Feminist Perspective," in K. Koser and H. Lutz (eds), *The New Migration in Europe* (London: Macmillan), pp. 21–38.

Phizacklea, A. and Anderson, B. (2001), *Impact of Legal Status and Children of Transnational Household Strategies of Migrant Domestics* (UK: Research Programme for the Economic and Social Research Council (ESRC) under the Transnational Communities Programme, Research Briefing No. 3).

Pietilä, H. (2006), "Women as Agents for Development: Learning from the Experiences of Women in Finland?", in M.M. Ferree and A.M. Tripp (eds), *Global Feminism: Transnational Women's Activism, Organizing, and Human Rights* (New York: New York University Press), pp. 166–86.

Piper, N. (1998), *Racism, Nationalism and Citizenship* (Ashgate: Avebury).

Piper, N. (2003), "Bridging Gender, Migration and Governance," *Asian and Pacific Migration Journal* 12:1–2, 21–48.

Piper, N. (2004), "Rights of Foreign Workers and the Politics of Migration in South-East and East Asia," *International Migration* 42:5, 71–97.

Piper, N. (2005), "A Problem by a Different Name? A Review of Research on Trafficking in Southeast Asia and Oceania," *International Migration* 43:1/2, 203–33.

Piper, N. and Uhlin, A. (eds) (2004), *Transnational Activism in Asia: Problems of Power and Democracy* (London: Routledge).

POEA (1995), *Migrant Workers and Overseas Filipinos Act*, Philippine Overseas Employment Agency. Retrieved October 11 2005. Accessed at www.poea.gov.ph/html/ra8042.html.

POEA (2004), *Tips to OFWs: How to Avoid Illegal Recruitment Fees*, Philippine Overseas Employment Administration. Retrieved May 30 2004. Accessed at www.poea.gov.ph/html/tips.htm.

Portes, A. (1998), "Globalization from Below: The Rise of Transnational Communities," in W.P. Smith and R.P. Korczenwicz (eds), *Latin America in the World Economy* (Westport, CT: Greenwood Press), pp. 157–68.

Portes, A., Haller, W. and Guarzino, L.E. (2001), "Transnational Entrepreneurs: An Alternative Form of Immigrant Economic Adaptation," *American Sociological Review* 67, 278–98.

Powers, M. (1998), "The Dissemination of Development," *Environment and Planning D: Society and Space* 16, 577–98.

Pratt, G. (1997), "From Registered Nurse to Registered Nanny: Discursive Geographies of Filipina Domestic Workers in Vancouver, BC," *Economic Geography* 75:3, 215–36.

Pratt, G. (2004), *Working Feminism* (Edinburgh and Philadelphia, PA: Edinburgh University Press and Temple University Press).

Pratt G. and The Philippine Women Center (1998), "Inscribing Domestic Work on Filipina Bodies," in H. Nast and S. Pile (eds), *Places through the Body* (London: Routledge), pp. 283–304.

Pratt G. and The Philippine Women Center (1999), "Is this Canada? Domestic Workers' Experiences in Vancouver, BC," in J. Henshall Momsen (ed.), *Gender, Migration and Domestic Service* (New York: Routledge), pp. 23–42.

Pries, B. (2002), "Human Rights as Cultural Practice: An Anthropological Critique," in S. Schech and J. Haggis (eds), *Development: A Cultural Studies Reader* (Oxford: Blackwell), pp. 132–43.

Qizilbash, M. (1997), "A Weakness of the Capability Approach with Reference to Gender Justice," *Journal of International Development* 9:2, 251–62.

Raijman, R., Schammah-Gesser, S. and Kemp, A. (2003), "International Migration, Domestic Work, and Care Work: Undocumented Latina Migrants in Israel," *Gender and Society* 17:5, 727–49.

Ramamurthy, B. (2003), *International Labour Migrants: Unsung Heroes of Globalisation* (Stockholm: SIDA Studies).

Ramirez-Machado, J.M. (2003), "Domestic Work, Conditions of Work and Employment: A Legal Perspective," *ILO Conditions of Work and Employment Series*, No. 7, ILO, Geneva.

Ravenhill, J. (2005), "The Study of Global Political Economy," in J. Ravenhill (ed.), *Global Political Economy* (Oxford: Oxford University Press), pp. 3–27.

Reich, R. (1993), *The Work of Nations* (New York: Simon and Schuster).

RESPECT (2000), *Migrant Domestic Workers in Europe: A Case for Action*, Solidar and the RESPECT Network of Migrant Domestic Workers. Retrieved March 17, 2005. Accessed at www.solidar.org/English/pdf/Briefing10.doc.

Rigg, J. (1989), "International Contract Labor Migration and the Village Economy: The Case of Tambon Don Han, Northeastern Thailand," *Papers of the East-West Population Institute No. 112* (Honolulu, HI: East West Center).

Robeyns, I. (2005), "The Capability Approach: A Theoretical Survey," *Journal of Human Development* 6:1, 93–117.

Rodríguez, E.G. (2004), "'We Need your Support but the Struggle is Primarily Ours:' On Representation, Migration and the Sans Papier Movement, ESF, Paris, 12th–15th November 2003," *Feminist Review* 777:1, 152–56.

Rodrìguez, N. (1996), "The Battle for the Border: Notes on Autonomous Migration, Transnational Communities and the State," *Social Justice* 23:3, 21–37.

Romero, M. (1992), *Maid in the USA* (New York: Routledge).

Root, B.D. and Dejong, G.F. (1991), "Family Migration in a Developing Country," *Population Studies* 45, 221–33.

Salt, J. (1992), "The Future of International Labour Migration," *International Migration Review* 26:4, 1077–111.

Santo Tomas, P. (1999), "Enhancing the Capabilities of Emigration Countries to Protect Men and Women Destined for Low-Skilled Employment: The Case of the Philippines," *International Migration* 37:1, 319–38.

Santo Tomas, P. (2005), "Filipinos Working Overseas: Opportunity and Challenge," in International Organisation for Migration (ed.), *World Migration Report 2005: Costs and Benefits of International Migration* (Geneva: IOM), pp. 239–52.

Sassen, S. (1984), "Notes on the Incorporation of Third World Women into Wage Labor through Immigration and Offshore Production," *International Migration Review* 18:4, 1144–67.

Sassen, S. (1988), *The Mobility of Labor and Capital: A Study in International Investment and Labor Flow* (Cambridge: Cambridge University Press).

Sassen, S. (1998), *Globalization and its Discontents: Essays on the Mobility of People and Money* (New York: The New York Press).

Sassen, S. (2002a), "Global Cities and Survival Circuits," in B. Ehrenreich and A.R. Hochschild (eds), *Global Woman: Nannies, Maids and Sex Workers* (New York: Henry Holt and Company), pp. 254–74.

Sassen, S. (2002b), "Women's Burden: Countergeographies of Globalization and the Feminization of Survival," *Nordic Journal of International Law* 7:2, 231–62.

Schech, S. and Haggis, J. (2000), *Culture and Development: A Critical Introduction* (Oxford: Blackwell Publishing).

Schech, S. and Haggis, J. (eds) (2002), *Development: A Cultural Studies Reader* (Oxford: Blackwell Publishing).

Schmink, M. (1984), "Household Economic Strategies: A Review and Research Agenda," *Latin American Research Review* 19:3, 87–101.

Schwenken, H. (2003), "RESPECT for All: The Political Self-Organization of Female Migrant Domestic Workers in the European Union," *Refuge: Canada's Periodical on Refugees* 21:3, 45–52.

Schwenken, H. (2005), "'Domestic Slavery' versus 'Workers Rights:' Political Mobilizations of Migrant Domestic Workers in the European Union," *Working Paper 116*, Center for Comparative Immigration Studies, University of California, San Diego.

Scipes, K. (1999), "Global Economic Crisis, Neoliberal Solutions, and the Philippines," *Monthly Review* 51:7. Retrieved December 21, 2005. Available at www.monthlyreview.org/1299scip.htm.

Scott, J. (1990a), *Domination and the Arts of Resistance: Hidden Transcripts* (New Haven, CT: Yale University Press).

Scott, J. (1990b), *Weapons of the Weak* (Delhi: Oxford University Press).

Sen, A. (1980), "Equality of What?," in S. McMurrin (ed.), *The Tanner Lectures on Human Values* (Salt Lake City, UT: University of Utah Press).

Sen, A. (1983), "Poor, Relatively Speaking," *Oxford Economic Papers* 35, 153–69.

Sen, A. (1984), *Resources, Values and Development* (Cambridge, MA: Harvard University Press).

Sen, A. (1985a), *Commodities and Capabilities* (Amsterdam: North-Holland).

Sen, A. (1985b), "Well-being, Agency and Freedom: The Dewey Lectures 1984," *Journal of Philosophy* 82:4, 169–221.

Sen, A. (1987), "The Standard of Living," in G. Hawthorn (ed.), *The Standard of Living* (Cambridge: Cambridge University Press), pp. 1–39.

Sen, A. (1990), "Justice: Means versus Freedoms," *Philosophy and Public Affairs* 19, 111–21.

Sen, A. (1992), *Inequality Reexamined* (Oxford: Clarendon Press).

Sen, A. (1993), "Capability and Well-being," in M. Nussbaum and A. Sen (eds), *The Quality of Life* (Oxford: Clarendon Press), pp. 30–53.

Sen, A. (1995), "Gender Inequality and Theories of Justice," in M. Nussbaum and J. Glover (eds), *Women, Culture and Development* (Oxford: Clarendon Press), pp. 259–76.

Sen, A. (1997), *Resources, Values and Development* (Cambridge, MA: Harvard University Press).

Sen, A. (1999), *Development as Freedom* (New York: Alfred A. Knopf).

Sen, A (ed.). (2002), *Rationality and Freedom* (Cambridge, MA: The Belknap Press of Harvard University Press).

Sen, A. (2003), Capability and Well-Being," in M. Nussbaum and A. Sen (eds), *The Quality of Life* (Oxford: Clarendon Press), pp. 30–53.

Sen, A. (2004), "Elements of a Theory of Human Rights," *Philosophy and Public Affairs* 32:4, 315–56.

Sewell, W. (1992), "A Theory of Structure: Duality, Agency and Transformation," *American Journal of Sociology* 98, 1–29.

Shadid, W.A., Spaan, E.J.A.M. and Speckman, J.D. (1992), "Labour Migration and the Policy of the Gulf States," in F. Eelans, T. Schampers and J.D. Speckman (eds), *Labour Migration to the Middle East: From Sri Lanka to the Gulf* (London and New York: Kegan Paul), pp. 63–86.

Shaw, T.M., MacLean, S.J. and Black, D.R. (2006), "Introduction: A Decade of Human Security: What Prospects for Global Governance and New Multilateralisms," in T.M. Shaw, S.J. MacLean and D.R. Black (eds), *A Decade of Human Security: Global Governance and New Multilateralisms* (Aldershot and Burlington, VA: Ashgate), pp. 3–18.

Shilling, C. and Mellor, P.A. (2001), "Embodiment, Structuration Theory and Modernity: Mind/Body Dualism and the Repression of Sensuality," in C.G.A. Bryant and D. Jary (eds), *The Contemporary Giddens* (Basingstoke and New York: Palgrave), pp. 140–46.

Shuto, M. (2006), "Labour Migration and Human Security in East and Southeast Asia," in H. Kleinschmidt (ed.), *Migration, Regional Integration and Human Security* (Aldershot and Burlington, VA: Ashgate), pp. 205–24.

Silvey, R. (2004a), "Power, Difference and Mobility: Feminist Advances in Migration Studies," *Progress in Human Geography* 28:4, 1–17.

Silvey, R. (2004b), "Transnational Domestication: State Power and Indonesian Migrant Women in Saudi Arabia," *Political Geography* 23, 245–64.

Sim, A. (2002), "Organising Discontent: NGOs for Southeast Asian Migrant Workers in Hong Kong," *Working Paper Series No. 18, Southeast Asia Research Centre*, City University of Hong Kong.

Singhanetra-Renard, A. (1992), "The Mobilization of Labour Migrants in Thailand: Personal Links and Facilitating Networks," in M. Kritz, L. Lim and H. Zlotnik (eds), *International Migration Systems: A Global Approach* (Oxford: Clarendon Press), pp. 150–76.

Skeldon, R. (1997), *Migration and Development: A Global Perspective* (Harlow: Addison Wesley Longman).

Smet, M. (2000), *Rapport sur la normalisation du travail domestique dans l'économie informelle* (Brussels: Commission des droits de la femme et de l'egalite des chances, Parlement Européen).

Smith, M.P. and Guarnizo, L.E. (eds) (1998), *Transnationalism from Below* (New Brunswick, NJ: Transaction).

Social Alert (2000), *Invisible Servitude: An In-depth Study on Domestic Workers in the World—Description and Recommendations for Global Action* (Brussels: Research on Human Rights Series).

Sørensen, N.N. (2004), "The Development Dimension of Migrant Remittances," *International Organisation for Migration Working Papers Series, Migration Policy Research*, No.1.

Sørensen, N.N., van Hear, N. and Engberg-Pedersen, P. (2002a), "The Migration-Development Nexus: Evidence and Policy Options," *International Migration* 40:5, 49–74.

Sørensen, N.N., van Hear, N. and Engberg-Pedersen, P. (2002b), "The Migration-Development Nexus: Evidence and Policy Options State-of-the-Art Overview," *International Migration* 40:5, 3–48.

Sosyal, Y. (1994), *Limits of Citizenship: Migrants and Postnational Membership in Europe* (Chicago, IL: University of Chicago Press).

Spivak, G.C. (1988), "Can the Subaltern Speak?," in C. Nelson and L. Greenberg (eds), *Marxism and the Interpretation of Culture* (Urbana, IL: University of Illinois Press), pp. 271–313.

Spivak, G.C. (1993), *Outside in the Teaching Machine* (New York: Routledge).

Spivak, G.C. (1996), "Diasporas Old and New: Women in the Transnational World," *Textual Practice* 10, 245–69.

Spradley, J.P. (1979), *The Ethnographic Interview* (New York: Holt, Rinehart and Winston).

Spradley, J.P. (1980), *Participant Observation* (New York: Holt, Rinehart and Winston).

Stalker, P. (2000), *Workers Without Frontiers: The Impact of Globalization on International Migration* (Boulder, CO: Lynne Rienner).

Stark, O. and Levhari, D. (1982), "On Migration and Risk in LDCs," *Economic Development and Cultural Change* 31, 191–6.

Stasiulis, D. and Bakan, A.B. (1994), "Foreign Domestic Worker Policy in Canada and the Social Boundaries of Modern Citizenship," *Science and Society* 58:1, 7–33.

Stasiulis, D. and Bakan, A.B. (1996), "Structural Adjustment, Citizenship and Foreign Domestic Labour: The Canadian Case," in I. Bakker (ed.), *Rethinking Restructuring: Gender and Change in Canada* (Toronto: University of Toronto Press), pp. 112–39.

Stasiulis, D. and Bakan, A.B. (1997), "Regulation and Resistance: Strategies of Migrant Domestic Workers in Canada and Internationally," *Asian and Pacific Migration Journal* 6:1, 31–57.

Stasiulis, D. and Bakan, A.B. (2000), "Negotiating Citizenship: The Case of Foreign Domestic Workers in Canada (West Indians and Filipinos)," in K. Willis and B. Yeoh (eds), *Gender and Migration* (Cheltenham: Edward Elgar), pp. 383–410.

Stasiulis, D. and Yuval-Davis, N. (1995), *Unsettling Settler Societies: Articulation of Gender, Race, Ethnicity and Class* (London: Sage).

Stewart, F. (2005), "Groups and Capabilities," *Journal of Human Development* 6:2, 185–204.

Swider, S. (2006), "Working Women of the World Unite? Labor Organization and Transnational Gender Solidarity among Domestic Workers in Hong Kong," in M.M. Ferree and A.M. Tripp (eds), *Global Feminism: Transnational Women's Activism, Organizing, and Human Rights* (New York and London: New York University Press), pp. 110–40.

Tacoli, C. (1996a), "Gender, Life Course and International Migration: The Case of Filipino Labour Migrants in Rome," PhD thesis, University of London.

Tacoli, C. (1996b), "Migrating 'for the Sake of the Family'?: Gender, Lifecourse and Intrahousehold Relations among Filipino Migrants in Rome," *Philippine Sociological Review* 44:1–4, 12–32.

Tacoli, C. (1999), "International Migration and the Restructuring of Gender Asymmetries: Continuity and Change Among Filipino Labor Migrants in Rome," *International Migration Review* 33:3, 658–82.

Tadiar, N.X. (1997), "Domestic Bodies of the Philippines," *Sojourn: Journal of Social Issues in Southeast Asia* 12:2, 153–91.

Tam, V.C.W. (1999), Foreign Domestic Helpers in Hong Kong and their Role in Childcare Provision," in J. Henshall Momsen (ed.), *Gender, Migration and Domestic Service* (London: Routledge), pp. 263–76.

Taylor, J. (2004), "Remittances, Savings, and Development in Migrant-Sending Areas," in D. Massey and J. Taylor (eds), *International Migration: Prospects and Policies in a Global Market* (Oxford: Oxford University Press), pp. 157–73.

The Sun (2003), 'Filipina Maid Petitions Court for Right of Abode," *The Sun*, Hong Kong: 3.

Thomas, C. (2000), *Global Governance, Development and Human Security* (London: Pluto Press).

Thomas, C. (2005), "Globalization and Development in the South," in J. Ravenhill (ed.), *Global Political Economy* (Oxford: Oxford University Press), pp. 317– 43.

Torrés, D. (1996), *Esclaves* (Paris: Phebus).

Trager, L. (1984), "Family Strategies and the Migration of Women: Migrants to Dagupan City," *International Migration Review* 18:4, 1264–77.

Trager, L. (1988), *The City Connection: Migration and Family Interdependence in the Philippines* (Ann Arbor, MI: The University of Michigan Press).

Tsuda, T. (1999), "The Permanence of 'Temporary' Migration: The Structural Embeddedness of Japanese-Brazilian Migrant Workers in Japan," *Journal of Asian Studies* 58:3, 687–722.

Turley, D. (2000), *Slavery* (Oxford: Blackwell).

Tyner, J. (1995), "Individuals, Institutions, and Structure: The Decision-Making Process of Philippine International Migrants," in W.L. Ng, S.Y. Chin, J.S. Moy and G. Okihiro (eds), *Reviewing Asian America: Locating Diversity* (Pullman, WA: Washington State University Press).

Tyner, J. (1999), "The Global Context of Gendered Labour Migration from the Philippines to the United States," *American Behavioural Scientist* 42:4, 671–89.

UC-CIIP (2004), "International Migration and Terrorism: Prevention, Prosecution and Protection," University of California—Davis Seminar (UC-CIIP), March 5–6. Retrieved December 21, 2005.

Uhlin, A. (2001), "The Transnational Dimension of Civil Society: Migration and Independence Movements in Southeast Asia," in E. Beckman, E. Hansson and A. Sjögren (eds), *Civil Society and Authoritarianism in the Third World* (Stockholm: PODSU/Stockholm University).

Uhlin, A. (2002), "Globalization, Democratization and Civil Society in Southeast Asia: Observations from Malaysia and Thailand," in C. Kinnvall and K. Jõnsson (eds), *Globalization and Democratization in Asia* (London: Routledge).

Uhlin, A. (2003), "Regionalism from Below: Transnational Civil Society Links in Southeast Asia," in E. Palmujoki (ed.), *Southeast Asian Regionalism from Above and from Below*, Tampere: TAPRI Occasional Paper No. 90.

UNDP (2004), *Human Development Report 2004: Cultural Liberty in Today's Diverse World* (New York: United Nations Development Programme).

United Nations Trafficking Protocol (2000), *Protocol to Prevent, Suppress and Punish Trafficking in Persons, Especially Women and Children, Supplementing the United Nations Convention Against Transnational Organized Crime.* Retrieved December 8, 2005. Accessed at www.uncjin.org/Documents/Conventions/dcatoc/final_documents_2/convention_%20traff_eng.pdf.

van den Anker, C. (2004), "Introduction: Combating Contemporary Slavery," in C. van den Anker (ed.), *The Political Economy of New Slavery* (New York: Palgrave Macmillan) , pp. 1–14.

Vaz Cabral, G. (2001), *Les Formes Contemporaines d'Esclavage dans six pays de l'Union Europèene: Autriche, Belgique, Espagne, France, Grande-Bretagne, Italie* (Paris: Comité Contre L'Esclavage Modern CCEM).

Visweswaran, K. (1988), "Defining Feminist Ethnography," *Inscriptions* 3:4, 27–57.

Visweswaran, K. (1994), *Fictions of Feminist Ethnography*. (Minneapolis, MN: University of Minnesota Press).

Weekley, K. (2003), "Saving Pennies for the State: A New Role for Filipino Migrant Workers?," *Southeast Asia Research Centre Working Paper Series*: 57.

Weinert, P. (1991), *International Migration for Employment: Foreign Female Domestic Workers: Help Wanted!* (Geneva: ILO World Employment Programme Working Paper).

Widgren, J. and Martin, P. (2002), "Managing Migration: The Role of Economics Instruments," *International Migration* 40:5, 213–30.

Wilks, R. (1995), "Learning to be Local in Belize: Global Systems of Common Difference," in S. Schech and J. Haggis (eds), *Development: A Cultural Studies Reader* (Oxford: Blackwell), pp. 194–208.

Wood, C.H. (1982), "Equilibrium and Historical-Structural Perspectives on Migration," *International Migration Review* 16, 298–319.

Yamanaka, K. and Piper, N. (2003), "An Introductory Overview," *Asian and Pacific Migration Journal* 12:1–2, 1–20.

Yeoh, B. and Huang, S. (1998), "Negotiating Public Spaces: Strategies and Styles of Migrant Female Domestic Workers in Singapore," *Urban Studies* 35:3, 583–602.

Yeoh, B. and Huang, S. (1999), "Singapore Women and Foreign Domestic Workers: Negotiating Domestic Work and Motherhood," in J. Henshall Momsen (ed.), *Gender, Migration and Domestic Service* (London and New York: Routledge), pp. 277–300.

Yeoh, B., Huang, S. and Devasahayam, T. (2004), "Diasporic Subjects in the Nation: Foreign Domestic Workers, the Reach of the Law and Civil Society in Singapore," *Asian Studies Review* 28:1, 7–23.

Yeoh, B., Huang, S. and Gonzalez, J.L. III (1999), "Migrant Domestic Female Workers: Debating the Economic, Social and Political Impacts in Singapore," *International Migration Review* 33:1, 114–36.

Zarembka, J.M. (2002), "America's Dirty Work: Migrant Maids and Modern-day Slavery," in B. Ehrenreich and A. Hochschild (eds), *Global Woman: Nannies, Maids, and Sex Worker in the New Economy* (New York: Henry Holt and Company), pp. 142–53.

Zelinsky, W. (1971), "The Hypothesis of the Mobility Transition," *Geographical Review* 42:2, 219–49.

Zlotnik, H. (1990), "International Migration Policies and the Status of Female Migrants," *International Migration Review* 24:2, 372–81.

Zlotnik, H. (1999), "Trends of International Migration since 1965: What Existing Data Reveal," *International Migration* 37:1, 21–62.

Index

Abdul Rahman, N. 10, 44, 57, 66–9, 71–2, 92, 108
agency 3–12, 18–19, 27, 51, 79, 177–229
  in migration theories 44–7, 51–8, 175–6, 60–9, 79–80, 108–11
  of FODW 8, 16, 18, 21–3, 25–27, 29, 44, 47, 51, 58, 72, 80–81, 85, 111, 116–61
see also capable agency; capable agency approach; Giddens; rights
Anderson, B. 5, 7, 9, 16, 18, 38, 40–43, 57, 59–60, 62–4, 105
Asia Pacific Mission for Migrants (APMM) 73, 78
Asian Migrant Centre (AMC) 37–8, 72–4, 76, 191
  reintegration program 12, 53
Asian Migrant Coordinating Body (AMCB) 73–5

Babaylan 22, 190

Canada 25–6, 55, 62, 64, 72, 78, 98
  migrant domestic worker policy 39, 43, 58–9, 76
  respondents' experience with 94,106, 155, 185, 187–8
capabilities 53, 86, 107–8, 110, 113, 116–17, 139, 144, 171, 173, 178
  as different from capability 16, 111, 166–70, 176
  Nussbaum's types of 14–5, 135, 145–6, 160
capability *see* capabilities
capability approach 14, 19, 26, 111, 167, 169, 177
capable agency 27, 72, 161, 165–6, 168, 170–71, 174, 229
capable agency approach 4, 71, 136, 165–6, 169
Comité Contre L'Esclavage Modern (CCEM) 22, 101, 156–7, 172, 179, 190

development 8, 10, 14–15, 18–9, 24, 27, 29–31, 47, 81, 111–12, 128, 134
  association with migration 12–3, 31, 33–4, 44, 47, 78, 175–6
  policies of 5, 13–14, 29–32, 34, 36–7, 53, 56–8, 77, 165, 172, 174–5
  see also underdevelopment

Emirbayer, M. 137–8, 141–2, 146–8, 150, 152
empowerment 4, 7, 9, 14–15, 26, 65, 67, 71, 79–80, 107, 109, 150, 165, 173, 179
European Union (EU) 7–8, 63, 190, 195
Euro-Pinoy Association 22, 106, 190

feminization of migration 5, 17, 34, 37–8, 40
Filipino Migrant Workers Union (FMWU) 76
Foucault, M. 10, 60, 69
  Foucaultian 9–10, 54, 60–61, 63, 72
France 3, 20, 22, 36, 38, 42–3, 59, 75, 89, 92, 97, 100, 105–6, 108, 127, 131, 174, 186–8, 190
  immigration policy 38–41, 94, 103, 179
  migrant domestic workers in 38, 41–2, 44, 172
  see also Paris
freedom 61, 64, 75, 106, 111–13, 116, 118, 120, 123, 166, 168–71, 178, 200
functioning 14, 79, 108, 115–17, 135, 141
  as different from functionings 168–9, 171

Gasper, D. 15, 112–14, 166, 176–7
Giddens, A. 4, 10–11, 18–9, 54, 62, 85–9, 92–3, 95, 98, 107–9, 111–12, 114–17, 137–40, 144, 146–7, 152, 166, 169
Goss, J. 11–12, 44–6, 51, 55, 65–6, 68, 71, 85, 89–90, 92, 95, 98–9, 107–9, 140

Hong Kong SAR 3–4, 11–12, 17–18, 21–4, 29, 33, 38, 42–4, 52–3, 59
immigration policy 20, 36, 39–40, 42–3
migrant domestic worker policy 38, 40, 42–3, 58, 60–61
NGOs in 72–9, 42, 53
human development 14, 26, 111, 114, 175–7
of FODWs 15, 29, 80, 174
see also human security
human rights 3, 5, 7, 9–10, 13–15, 27, 40, 43, 47, 74, 80, 109, 165, 177–9, 191, 203
-based NGOs 5, 42–3, 60, 73, 99, 191, 196
see also rights
human security 15, 176

illegal migration 35, 40–41, 78, 91, 94, 96, 102–3, 120, 155, 157, 176, 201
see also irregular migration; undocumented migration
International Monetary Fund (IMF) 5, 30–32, 36, 175
Indonesia 37–8, 74, 76, 187
migrant domestic workers from 10, 33, 38, 66–7, 73, 79, 92, 174
International Labor Organization (ILO) 3, 32, 34, 37, 43, 188
irregular migration 34–5, 39–40, 42–3
see also undocumented migration; illegal migration

Kalayaan 62–3

Lindquist, B. 11–12, 44–6, 51, 55, 65–6, 68, 71, 85, 89–90, 92, 95, 98–9, 107–9, 140
livelihood 3, 5–6, 8, 13–6, 26–7, 29, 44, 53, 63–4, 73, 78–80, 127–8, 135, 143, 165, 171, 175–9
see also mobile livelihoods

Massey, D. 31, 43–5, 66, 134
Middle East 41, 43, 55, 58, 105, 121, 172
migration theories 44–7, 51–2
Mische, A. 137–8, 141–2, 146–8, 150, 152
Mission for (Filipino) Migrant Workers in Hong Kong (MFMW) 22, 74, 102, 191
mobile livelihoods 13

New Condition of Stay 42, 73
see also Two Week Rule
non-governmental organizations (NGOs) 6, 42, 44, 53, 62, 69, 71–80, 91, 99, 155–6, 158–9, 173–4, 184–8, 190–91, 202
see also individual entries
Nussbaum, M. 14–15, 17, 26, 112–13, 116, 134–5, 141–2, 167, 178

Paris 3–4, 11–12, 17–8, 20–4, 29, 39, 44, 72
migrant domestic workers in 37–8, 54
respondents' experience in 91, 157, 94–107, 109, 118–23, 125–6, 128–33, 142–3, 150, 153–4, 156–8, 173, 178, 184–8, 190, 198
Parreñas, R.Z. 5, 9, 20, 29, 33, 37, 39, 57, 61–2, 79, 109, 131, 151
Philippines 6, 12, 23, 25–6, 37–8, 52–5, 57, 62, 64, 76–8, 80, 89, 52–6, 98, 131, 156, 174–5, 197, 198–200, 202–3
labor export 29, 36, 39, 56
respondents' experience of 3, 91, 94–5, 103–4, 107–9, 121, 123, 125–30, 132, 138, 143–4, 146, 150–51, 154, 158, 160, 184–8
Philippine Overseas Employment Administration (POEA) 36, 39, 77, 100, 129
Philippine Women Centre (PWC) 62, 64, 74, 78
Piper, N. 6–9, 17, 39, 42–4, 75–6, 94, 172–3, 175
postcolonial feminists 25, 176
power 6, 13, 18–19, 31, 33, 44, 51, 57, 60, 103, 108, 195
concept of 9–10, 18–19, 47, 53–4, 60, 65, 67–72, 78–80, 85–6, 109, 113–15, 143, 152, 159, 161, 170, 229
in structuration theory 10, 67, 71–2, 87, 89, 92, 98, 107, 139, 110, 113–15, 117, 139, 144

Pratt, G. 5, 17–18, 24–5, 40, 59, 63–5, 72, 78
prostitution 6, 8
  see also sex work
recruitment 8, 46, 60–61, 66, 77, 89–90, 97, 102–3, 107, 129, 131, 156, 184–8, 200
  illegal 33, 35, 42–3, 78, 100, 131
    abuse from 58–9, 108, 121–2, 127, 129–30, 133, 152
resistance 9, 25, 46, 61–3, 68, 71–2, 78–80, 92, 110, 166, 200, 229
  collective, 6, 9–10, 54, 69
  Foucaultian 10, 60–61
RESPECT Network 7, 38, 63, 72, 74, 173, 190, 195–6
rights of all migrant workers and members of their families 9, 74
rights 3–4, 7–9, 11, 20–21, 26, 29, 40, 42–3, 57–8, 63–5, 71, 75, 90, 121, 165, 172–3, 178, 179, 195–6
  association with agency 4, 8–9, 15–16
  specific to FODWs 80, 120, 123, 157
  see also human rights

Sen, A. 14, 111–17, 128, 135, 167–9, 171, 175, 177
Sewell, W. 137–41, 144, 146–7, 152, 160
sex work 7, 33, 135, 188
slavery 3–4, 6–7, 16, 23, 43, 62–3, 74, 118, 177, 179, 190, 201
  domestic 7, 53, 59–60
  respodents' experience of 22, 121–6, 128, 154

Overseas Workers Welfare Administration (OWWA) 77

smuggling 33, 35, 41–3, 103, 131, 184–5, 187–8, 200
  see also trafficking
structural adjustment programs 32, 37, 56
structuration theory 4, 10, 18, 51, 65, 68, 71–2, 87, 109, 111, 115–17, 135, 137–8, 148, 167, 169–70
  see also Abdul Rahman; Emirbayer; Giddens; Goss; Lindquist; Mische; Sewell

third world feminists
  see postcolonial feminists
trafficking 6–8, 33, 35, 41–3, 78, 122, 103, 131, 184–5, 187–8, 200
  see also smuggling
Two Week Rule 23
  see also New Condition of Stay

underdevelopment 8, 18, 26, 31, 111, 128, 134–5, 177
undocumented migration 3, 9, 12, 20–22, 33, 35, 37, 38, 41, 43–4, 52, 54, 59, 94, 96–100, 108, 120, 122, 127, 156, 172, 179, 188, 195
  see also irregular migration; illegal migration
United Filipinos in Hong Kong (UNIFIL) 75, 191
United Nations Convention on the Rights of All Migrants and their Families (ICMR) 9, 74,

World Trade Organization (WTO) 30–31, 175
World Bank 5, 30–32, 36, 64, 66, 175

Gender in a Global/Local World

Also published in the series

Women, Migration and Citizenship
Making Local, National and Transnational Connections
Edited by Evangelia Tatsoglou and Alexandra Dobrowolsky
ISBN 978-0-7546-4379-1

Transnational Ruptures
Gender and Forced Migration
Catherine Nolin
ISBN 978-0-7546-3805-6

'Innocent Women and Children'
Gender, Norms and the Protection of Civilians
R. Charli Carpenter
ISBN 978-0-7546-4745-4

The Gender Question in Globalization
Changing Perspectives and Practices
Edited by Tine Davids and Francien van Driel
ISBN 978-0-7546-3923-7 (Hbk)
ISBN 978-0-7546-7322-4 (Pbk)

Turkey's Engagement with Global Women's Human Rights
Nüket Kardam
ISBN 978-0-7546-4168-1

(Un)thinking Citizenship
Feminist Debates in Contemporary South Africa
Edited by Amanda Gouws
ISBN 978-0-7546-3878-0

Vulnerable Bodies
Gender, the UN and the Global Refugee Crisis
Erin K. Baines
ISBN 978-0-7546-3734-9

Fashioning Inequality
The Multinational Company and Gendered Employment in a Globalizing World
Juanita Elias
ISBN 978-0-7546-3698-4

www.ingramcontent.com/pod-product-compliance
Ingram Content Group UK Ltd.
Pitfield, Milton Keynes, MK11 3LW, UK
UKHW011002180926
475701UK00004B/521
9780367605612